In memory of Maurice Myers
and for Kirsty, Finbar, Orla and Elsa

Struggles for a past

*Irish and Afro-Caribbean histories in England,
1951–2000*

Kevin Myers

Manchester University Press

Published by Manchester University Press
Altrincham Street, Manchester M1 7JA

www.manchesteruniversitypress.co.uk

British Library Cataloguing-in-Publication Data
A catalogue record for this book is available from the British Library

Library of Congress Cataloging-in-Publication Data applied for

ISBN   978 0 7190 8480 5   hardback

First published 2015

Typeset
by Carnegie Book Production, Lancaster
Printed in Great Britain
by TJ International Ltd, Padstow

Contents

Preface and acknowledgements

Despite superficial signs to the contrary, academic research is always a collaborative exercise and I have accrued plenty of debts in preparing this book. A grant from the Nuffield Foundation (SGS/32251) facilitated research in various archives and libraries around England. At those libraries I found helpful and knowledgeable staff, but would like to record particular thanks to: Birmingham Heritage and Archive Services (Sian Roberts, Jim Ranahan, Fiona Tait and Rachel Macgregor); Liverpool Record Office (Ruth Hobbins); London Metropolitan Archive (Maureen Roberts); Working Class Movement Library, Manchester (Jane Taylor); Irish Studies Centre at London Metropolitan University (Tony Murray and Nicole McLennan); Black Cultural Archives, London (Jacine Cooper); George Padmore Institute (Sarah Garrod); Institute of Education Archives (Becky Webster and Kathryn Meldrum); National Archives, London; British Library, London.

Archival materials are, of course, a form of social knowledge. They only become significant with interpretation and analysis. I was helped in that task by those people who I interviewed, or conversed and corresponded with: Frank Anti; Mike Boyle; the late Dorothy Kuya; Ian Law; Michael Herbert; Bernadette Hyland; the late Ian McKeane; Izzy Mohammed; Garry Morris; Mike Phillips; Sian Roberts; Stephen Small; Chris Upton; Eileen Wilshaw.

Many colleagues, in a variety of disciplinary and institutional locations, gave me valuable advice and all sorts of generous help including Bob Carter, Malcolm Dick, Kathryn Ecclestone, Martin Lawn, Jane Martin, Gavin Schaffer, Magdalena Skrybant, Emma Smith, Ruth Watts, Christian Ydesen. Particular thanks to Ian Grosvenor, an inspiring mentor and optimistic friend. Despite all that help it took me a long time to write this book. I am especially grateful to Emma Brennan at Manchester University Press for her patience, her diplomacy in regard to deadlines and for organising the constructive comments of an astute and helpful anonymous reviewer; to Bryan Lewin for his fast and forensic reading of the draft manuscript; and, above all, to Kirsty, Finbar, Orla and Elsa.

Abbreviations

ACER	Afro-Caribbean Education Resource Centre
APHMF	African People's Historical Monument Foundation
BBPM	British Black Panther Movement
BEM	Black Education Movement
BHM	Black History Month
BPM	Black Parents' Movement
BSSM	Black Supplementary Schools Movement
CECWA	Caribbean Education and Community Workers Association
CRC/CRE	Community Relations Commission/Commission for Racial Equality
FIS	Federation of Irish Societies
GAA	Gaelic Athletic Association
GLC	Greater London Council
IBHG	Irish in Britain History Group
IBRG	Irish in Britain Representation Group
LICCE	London Irish Commission for Culture and Education
MCRC	Merseyside Community Relations Council
NLWIA	North London West Indian Association
RAT	Race Awareness Training
RURR	Research Unit on Race Relations
TAR	Teachers Against Racism
USBPP	United States Black Panther Party
WGEECP	Working Group on Education for the Eradication of Colour Prejudice

Introduction

I am a barbarian in this place because I am not understood.
(Brian Friel, *Translations*)

Because this is the thing about immigrants (fugees, émigrés, travellers): they cannot escape their history any more than you yourself can lose your shadow. (Zadie Smith, *White Teeth*)

Of all our studies, history is best qualified to reward our research. (Malcolm X, *Message to the Grassroots*)

This book is about cultures of history in post-war England. It explores the productions of segments of the past by people who were identified as, or came to understand themselves as, members of minority ethnic communities. These were first and second generation migrants with familial roots in parts of the former British Empire, specifically from the Caribbean, Africa and Ireland, who cumulatively produced a remarkable range of historical texts, performances, commemorations and representations. Recognising the social character of historical knowledge, this book aims to recover the labour of people such as Steve Brennan, Stella Dadzie, Bernadette Hyland, Valentine Jones, Dorothy Kuya, Ron Phillips, Pat Reynolds and hundreds of others.[1] Their work and that of so many others ranged across a number of institutional sites and disciplinary fields. It appeared in hundreds of published and unpublished studies, on television and in radio productions, in exhibitions and textbooks and in theatrical and musical productions. Out of all this activity slowly emerged new communities with a shared memory, vocabulary and strategy for political change.

What made these individuals and groups so extraordinarily productive? One short answer lies in their joint experience of prejudice, intolerance and racism. Their routine rejection as alien foreigners, as outsiders, deemed to threaten an exclusive national culture could not fail to prompt questions about identity and belonging. The past and history had a particular resonance in the search for answers. For whatever the particular circumstances of individuals or groups, one common strategy in the experience of becoming alien was a turn to the past, or as cultural historian Bill Schwarz puts it, 'an insistence on the effectivity of the temporal'.[2] This turn to history happened because that past had a new salience in the present; 'political realities in the present recomposed the shape of the past, and brought it into consciousness in the present'.[3] Yet this past does not simply arrive in the present through the objective work of scholars, or via the long reach of an individual memory. Instead, both personal and social identities are formed partly from the collective processes of memory and from the selections made and meaning imposed on the past by individuals and groups in contemporary societies. Moreover, selecting and inscribing memories and identities is an active process. As the philosopher Brian Fay argues, 'the identity of humans is in part what they have appropriated from their past. They are constituted out of the historical heritage they make their own, and they transform themselves in terms of the material provided to them from this heritage.'[4] This is an important reminder that notions of identity and the ways in which they have come to be expressed, in discourses of community, ethnicity, race or diaspora, are not naturally given or finite categories. Instead they are symbolic descriptions that people draw on or have imposed upon them.

However, it would be misleading and simplistic to assume a common immigrant experience of oppression that translated to a shared identity as the basis for collective resistance. This is what the sociologist Bob Carter has called an experiential empiricism and it assumes precisely that which requires explanation.[5] And what is required, as Schwarz has argued in the context of West Indians in Britain, is a 'detailed, situated and historical story' that helps to make clear how immigrants encountered and responded to the logics of racial thought.[6] This book makes a contribution to these stories. It is an exploration of how individuals and groups in the past experienced migration, racism and ethnicisation;[7] of how they came together in what Edward Said called communities of interpretation;[8] of how they used the past, as memories or as more formal history, as a way of creating social identities; and the legacies of that process for the cultural decolonisation of England.[9] Particular attention is reserved for the processes through which the past was recomposed, brought into consciousness and utilised as a tool for educational, cultural and political work. These are complex stories that require attention to politics, to the diversity of the communities in construction, cultural capital, language, state regulation and technology. But four key themes require early elucidation.

First, the nation state dominated identity constructions in the century between 1850 and 1950. Its myriad institutions, routines and symbols, simultaneously encouraged and suppressed particular social identities.[10] State-sponsored 'scientific history', for example, produced master narratives, or a single national past, that identified the time, space, actors and enemies of national history.[11] It also helped to champion the very idea of historical identities, that is of personal and social identities defined by a 'set of distinct characteristics which are developed over time and through interactions with a particular environment', which became so central to modernity.[12] A powerful component of scientific history and of the identities it helped to produce and legitimate, were race ideas. Although there were (and are) no discrete biological races, race ideas were a critical element of the ways in which the nation state established fundamental social classifications that became enshrined in law.[13] Those kinds of classifications, as subject and citizen for example, become embodied in politics and administrative procedures and symbolised in the rituals of state. Cumulatively all of this had important consequences for the manner in which people identify themselves and their place in the world.[14] Indeed, race concepts, ideas and propositions became so widespread and so powerful that it has proved difficult for historians and sociologists to resist the temptation to deploy them entirely descriptively.[15] In doing so, they have contributed to a commonsense understanding that races, and relations between them, exist as independent and objective realities. In this study, race is understood as one element, albeit a very powerful one, in a cultural system.[16] It was rejected or taken up by various social actors in pursuit of particular goals but its increasing significance, particularly in accounts of social change sponsored and promoted by state agencies, certainly conditioned the ways in which generations of post-war Britons thought about themselves and others.

The period between the middle of the 1940s and the mid 1960s witnessed a significant extension of the state. Conekin, Waters and Mort describe the quantitative expansion of experts and their forms of knowledge as 'on a scale quite as significant as earlier moments of professional growth' (1830s and 1840s, and years before the First World War) and that it was broader than before, extending beyond government, the state to areas of cultural taste … and the psychological well being of communities'.[17] Such experts were prominent in helping to develop a view of immigration, particularly but not exclusively from the New Commonwealth nations in the West Indies, Asia and Africa, as a 'colour problem' that permeated discussions in national and local government.[18] Immigration slowly became racialised and then ethnicised. Ideas about races and ethnicities, about skin colour, language and cultural traditions, became key markers for identifying those who belonged in Britain and those who did not. This racialised and ethnicised sense of belonging was central to an influential body of race relations research that developed alongside state administrative practices and fleshed out this sense of belonging in policy areas such as education, health and immigration.[19] The decades following the 1960s ensured that it was enshrined in law through successive Immigration Acts and the formal redefinition of British citizenship in 1971 and 1981. A body of recent work explains both these legislative changes, and other important cultural trends, by reference to debates around the meaning of Britishness prompted by the formal dissolution of the British Empire.[20] However, it would be more accurate to argue that the continued popularity of race ideas in the post-1945 period played a crucial role in the reassessment of what constituted national culture and, ultimately, had the cumulative effect of defining certain ways of being British in the post-war period.

A second key theme of this book is people. Quite how the racialised and ethnicised definitions of identity promoted by state activity were experienced, internalised and reworked is a topic that, despite the recent explosion of work on memory and history, has received rather scant attention.[21] Perhaps this rather surprising omission can be best explained by the origins of memory work in the cultural turn, and for an associated organising preference for discourse at the expense of agency in those control narratives identified by Billie Melman.[22] In contrast, this study retains a view of people as active agents with the capacity to experience, deliberate and rework those state-sponsored versions of the past that claimed to explain minority ethnic identities in post-war Britain. They were, in Wulf Kansteiner's phrase, 'memory makers'.[23] People could, and did, intervene in the process of making memories but did so as historical, not transcendental, subjects. They did so conditioned by historical circumstances and by their resulting assignment to different positions in society. Memory makers are always located in classes, part of distinct generations, assigned to genders and attributed the characteristics of races and ethnicities. Being differentially conditioned they experienced distinct opportunities and constraints in their attempts to think about, reflect on and fashion social identities. This will become clear by paying particular, if not exclusive attention, to young people.

Young people, those between the ages of approximately 5 and 21, are not well represented in the developing literature on history and memory. Indeed, and as far as migrant groups are concerned, there has been an understandable tendency to concentrate on those intellectuals and activists whose influence and legacy is clear and for whom archival sources are plentiful.[24] Yet young people were particularly subject to narratives of collective memory. Compulsory schooling was obviously an important site for the construction and distribution of collective memories, but so were various other formal and informal educational projects such as the development of supplementary or complementary schooling, community histories, record shops and autobiographical writing. In these and other spaces and sites, young people remembered, reflected and discussed the experiences that marked out their difference. Sometimes they emerged as fully historical subjects, simultaneously locating themselves in a wider socio-historical process and reflecting on and reworking constructions of that process.[25] In a period when theories of child development and learning stressed the importance of historical study and literary expression, and when radical theories of education were available for domestic struggles, young people had specific resources, opportunities and encouragement to consider themselves and their place in the world.[26] Quite how this reworking happened requires detailed historical attention and sensitivity to place.

Place is the third important theme in exploring how the past was recomposed and brought into the present. Although evidence is gathered from across England, three cities feature prominently; London, Birmingham and Liverpool. They do so because they have distinctive political and social histories and different patterns of migrant settlement. These differences themselves shape the activities of individuals and groups at the local level. So, instead of attributing a problematic unity to cultural, ethnic or diaspora groups, these studies have the potential to illuminate the localised aspects of historical identity formation. The focus here is on the agency of individuals and groups who uncover, represent and distribute stories and images whose purpose is to secure their historical identity. In struggling for a past, in writing community histories, migrants became more complex and more nuanced than the stereotypes of popular prejudice or the narrow confines allowed by race relations researchers. They became, in other words, historical subjects.[27]

A fourth and final theme is technology. Benedict Anderson's enormously influential *Imagined Communities* helped to demonstrate how technological developments could structure the processes of identification.[28] If, for Anderson, the emergence of the printing press facilitated the imagined community of the nation between the sixteenth and nineteenth centuries, so too did the accessibility of print, visual and audio technologies enable post-1945 migrants and their descendants to imagine, picture and write themselves into particular narratives of history. The artefacts that they helped to produce and make available form an important part of the sources used in this study. In newspapers, pamphlets and memoranda, calendars, posters and songs, in radio and television programmes and in oral testimonies, migrant scholar activists helped to shape and codify collective memories of distinctive historical experiences, ethnic pasts, that constituted an important site of difference. The significance of these memories lies in their use. Slowly, and not at all evenly, their struggles served to promote national narratives based on ideas of movement and migration; of faith and ethnic diversity and of race and racism. They gained a space in public discourse in the shape of various cultural, educational and political projects. And from these activities the idea of Britain as a post-imperial, multicultural nation was aired and debated.

It is worth stressing the significance of these activities and projects at the outset, not least because they do not fare well in the recent historiography of the period. Dominic Sandbrook's histories of the post-war period have little space for anti-racist campaigns and tend to dismiss or ignore their efforts to secure social and political change.[29] Mark Garnett's examination of the British experience since 1975 adopts a familiar historical perspective in reserving attention for minority communities when some of them are involved in rioting.[30]

Even for those historians interested in minority communities, the cultural and educational projects of minority groups have rarely been the subject of interest. Colin Holmes's important overview text, *John Bull's Island* (1988), notes, for example, the importance of schools and education for immigrant and ethnic minority groups, but discussion is limited to the observation that immigrant groups often established their own schools which, in the case of twentieth-century Jews at least, encouraged the enculturation of young people.[31] Similarly, Enda Delaney's recent account of the Irish in post-war Britain discusses the growth of Catholic schools in the 1960s and tentatively suggests, following sociologist Mary Hickman, that their focus on Catholicism mitigated against the development of distinctively Irish, and especially nationalist Irish, identities.[32] Yet the independent educational agency that was deployed in developing a new kind of Irish identity receives no sustained attention. And while historians of black immigration are more likely to note the existence of independent educational activity, actual empirical research that does not focus on important literary or political figures is rare. Indeed, whether one examines mainstream social histories, histories of education or political radicalism those projects and campaigns based on new understandings of the past are hard to find.[33]

Perhaps this should not come as a surprise. After all, and as Burrell and Panayi have argued in an important edited volume exploring the production of migrant histories and memories in Britain, research into minority ethnic communities continues to be 'a peripheral area of academic concern within the discipline of history'.[34] This diminished status is confirmed by the general failure on the part of historians of education to substantively engage with the educational experiences of ethnic minority communities, and related issues of race.[35] This is not a failure restricted to the discipline of history. Reay and Mirza have argued, for example, that the sociological literature on new social movements also routinely ignores educational projects.[36] As the educationalist Keri Facer has pointed out, this ignorance of the past is damaging because it supports a 'profoundly anti-progressive account of education history, one which does little justice to the dynamism of educators, educational activists and their capacity to act as a force for change in the world'.[37] This book attempts to recapture that dynamism and to critically explore it. It makes no claim to be comprehensive either in terms of source material (where the exclusion of visual and literary sources is a particular absence) or in terms of coverage (where a focus on different migrant groups may have produced a different study). The practicalities of research always entails difficult decisions but focusing on the largest migrant group, the Irish, and arguably the most influential, those from the Caribbean and from Africa, facilitates an analysis that goes beyond dichotomies of black and white immigration and which foregrounds the attempts of people to understand and refashion a world in pursuit of social justice.

The argument is developed in four chapters. The first examines the period between 1951 and 1968 when Britain's recovery from the Second World War was aided by the arrival of migrants whose reception and experiences ultimately resulted in the passing of the Race Relations Act in 1965. The chapter, beginning with the 1951 Festival of Britain, traces dominant perceptions of the national past in the period. It focuses particularly on how a contracting narrative of the nation located migrants as outsiders, a view that became evident in a burgeoning race relations literature. Examining local examples of this literature from London, Birmingham and Liverpool, the chapter traces the ways in which race relations developed as an empirical and applied science. It is argued that the empirical work of race relations scholars did open up a space where domestic traditions of intolerance were identified but, constrained by a racialised view of culture, these traditions were left either unexplored or turned into universal psychological processes that were susceptible to therapeutic and social interventions. Immigrant advisory councils, friendship committees and youth groups were a characteristic and practical expression of race relations analyses but their ignorance of history, and of migration to Britain in particular, made them seem hopelessly idealistic. They were the wrong solution to the wrong problem because there was no new 'race problem' in 1950s England. Such a view, it is argued, depended on a neglect of history and a tendency to employ concepts of community, citizenship and identity in a racialised manner. As the brief history of Irish and black migration then demonstrates, both groups had a long presence in England and, while they developed distinctive forms of historical education, neither constituted discrete ethnic communities separated from English residents.

The second and longest chapter explores a period of momentous change from 1968 to 1981. Amidst political crises in Northern Ireland, the formal dissolution of the remainder of the British Empire and the politicisation, and eventual severe restriction, of immigration from the New Commonwealth an unplanned and often incoherent multiculturalism emerged in Britain. This was partly the result of black cultural and educational projects that sought to unite those organised in opposition to racism.[38] The foundation and development of black publishing houses, the campaigns for Black Studies and the rise of a successful supplementary school movement were mechanisms that encouraged the production and distribution of new historical narratives in British society that made an equal claim to British citizenship. Initially at least, non-professional and grass-roots groups were responsible for the distribution and discussion of the nation's 'other histories'. As a result, this work rarely appeared in the form of polished monographs or learned journals, and it was only rarely articulated in certificated college courses. It was often verbal and registered only in the changing reading habits, leisure interests, political sympathies and outlook of individuals or groups. Alternatively, it is sometimes possible to trace fleeting glimpses of this work in those rare moments when it gained space on television and radio networks. Overall, however, and even if the evidence for this kind of activity can be difficult to gather, scattered documentary, aural and visual material does exist that attests to migrant struggles for a past.[39]

Yet these struggles for a past existed in, and were sometimes funded by, a political and social space dedicated to facilitating good race relations. In the work of the Community Relations Commission, later renamed the Commission for Racial Equality, historical perspectives were useful only in so far as they established ethnic difference or explained a supposedly universal cognitive tendency towards racial prejudice. The explanatory potential of long-term historical analyses did not disappear and, drawing on the energies of the post-1968 new social movements, local community centres, adult education classes, libraries and small publishing enterprises certainly helped to facilitate the emergence of new histories. Sometimes these histories were distinctly local. At other times they connected to wider civil rights, pan-African or Third World movements. But while they routinely sought to establish an identity as fully historical subjects outside the frame of crude racism, they remained constrained by the powerful assumptions of race relations work that assigned immigrants and their children to cultures in which they were supposed to find authentic identities.

The third chapter, spanning the period 1981–2000, traces the ways in which those new historical identities came to be applied in public spaces. Although 1981 is a somewhat arbitrary starting point for this chapter, it does represent an important moment in British culture and society. It was not only the year of rioting in almost all the major urban centres in England, it was also the year of the publication of the Rampton report and of Labour's victory in the London council elections. These seemingly disparate events are connected by the significant consequences they would have for cultural and educational activity in migrant groups. Even if Prime Minister Margaret Thatcher's public response to rioting was typically hard-line, Lord Scarman's investigation into the Brixton riots explicitly noted that any resolution to inner-city problems had to embrace a wide social context and the reality of racial disadvantage, racialism and discrimination against black people as a major source of social conflict and tension.[40] The Rampton report, interim findings from the Committee of Inquiry into the Education of Children from Ethnic Minority groups, made similar observations, arguing the need to eradicate unintentional racism in schools and to adopt a multicultural approach to education.[41] Such proposals were controversial and would become more so with the publication of the full Swann report in 1985.[42] But multiculturalism found a willing champion when Ken Livingstone emerged as leader of the Greater London Council in 1981 and helped to create a political environment in which progressive policies, designed to alleviate racial disadvantage, were taken seriously and, relatively speaking, generously funded. If one leading historian of London, Jerry White, remains unimpressed by this, noting some educational benefits but accusing Livingstone of 'spending endless time and bottomless resources in pursuit of ideological purity on gender, sexuality and race', it did mark a period in which the discrimination and prejudice experienced by ethnic minority communities was taken seriously and attempts at some kind of redress were developed.[43]

From the early 1980s onwards progressive municipal authorities facilitated, or at least tolerated, a series of educational and cultural policies that aimed at the development of more open, pluralistic and multi-ethnic cities. One part of this strategy was to recognise cultural difference, respect it and encourage a dialogue between communities in the hope of mutual understanding. History had a key role to play here. The Swann report, for example, spoke of the need for a pluralist approach to international and national history in which the patterns of migration which have created today's multiracial society would be prominent and which would help to combat the stereotyping of ethnic minorities. The findings of the Gifford Inquiry into Race Relations in Liverpool similarly began with a chapter exploring the 'Legacy of the past' and made recommendations about access to, and presentation of, Liverpool's history.[44] This kind of official recognition of what was coming to be called ethnic minority history was a clear sign that the struggles for a past had achieved some success. But this success was always ambiguous.[45]

The adoption of outsider history into official policies for a multicultural Britain removed that sense of the past from those scholar activists for whom it had a living and vital presence. The communities of interpretation that had developed, distributed and sustained these historical narratives were themselves beginning to fracture and disperse as wider political, economic and social changes took hold. Divorced from these critical voices, the meaning and purpose of their histories slowly became more exotic, more essential and more descriptive.[46] Political injunctions to recognise and celebrate difference became slogans, resented or championed according to political conviction, devoid of meaning. Where once these histories emphasised historical agency and informed a political strategy for the present, a softer version was enabled and co-opted by new pluralist politics predicated on the conditions of late capitalism.[47]

The concluding chapter summarises and reflects on this story. It is, in one sense at least, a straightforward social history that uncovers historical experiences previously hidden or marginalised. But, in seeking out some of those spaces and practices in which migrants researched and represented their past, a past that became understood and evoked as outside the national story, it also makes a contribution to a developing literature on cultures of history.[48] The scholar activists from ethnic minority communities clearly understood the power of the past, and were critical in the development and distribution of new historical narratives. In turn, these narratives provided the resources with which it became possible to imagine and discuss postcolonial Britain. Equally, however, any critical account of these activities must reckon with the profound transformations witnessed in British society, even since the early 1980s, and to question what kinds of histories will help us understand and live with those changes. In the age of super diversity it will be necessary to recapture an ethics of historical study that insists not on historical difference but on a shared humanity; not on the power of the past to determine identity but on the possibilities for transformation created by a properly historical consciousness.[49]

Notes

1 Raphael Samuel, *Theatres of Memory Volume I: Past and Present in Contemporary Society* (London: Verso, 1994), pp. 3–48. Popular Memory Group, 'Popular memory: theory, politics, practice', in Centre for Contemporary Cultural Studies, *Making Histories: Studies in History-writing and Politics* (London: Hutchinson, 1982), pp. 205–252.

2 Bill Schwarz, 'Not even past yet', *History Workshop Journal*, 57 (2004), 111.

3 *Ibid.*

4 Brian Fay, *Critical Social Science: Liberation and Its Limits* (Oxford: Polity, 1987), p. 164.

5 Bob Carter, *Realism and Racism: Concepts of Race in Sociological Research* (London: Routledge, 2002), p. 161.

6 Bill Schwarz, 'Afterword: the predicament of history', in Bill Schwarz (ed.), *West Indian Intellectuals in Britain* (Manchester: Manchester University Press, 2003), p. 251.

7 For the concept of ethnicisation, see Eva Morawska, 'Immigrants, transnationalism, and ethnicization: a comparison of this great wave and the last', in Gary Gerstle and John H. Mollenkopf (eds), *E Pluribus Unum? Contemporary and Historical Perspectives on Immigrant Political Incorporation* (New York: Russell Sage, 2001), pp. 175–212.

8 Edward Said, *Culture and Imperialism* (London: Vintage, 1994 [1993]), p. 406.

9 Jordanna Bailkin, *The Afterlife of Empire* (Berkeley, CA: University of California Press, 2012); Wendy Webster, *Englishness and Empire 1939–1965* (Oxford: Oxford University Press, 2005).

10 In the manner influentially set out by Phillip Corrigan and Derek Sayer, *The Great Arch: English State Formation as Cultural Revolution* (Oxford: Blackwell, 1985).

11 Stefan Berger (ed.), *Writing the Nation: A Global Perspective* (Palgrave Macmillan, 2007).

12 Chris Lorenz, 'Representations of identity: ethnicity, race, class, gender and religion. An introduction to conceptual history', in Stefan Berger and Chris Lorenz (eds), *The Contested Nation: Ethnicity, Class Religion and Gender in National Histories* (Basingstoke: Palgrave Macmillan, 2008), p. 27.

13 Catherine Hall, *Macaulay and Son: Architects of Imperial Britain*

(Yale, CT: Yale University Press, 2012), pp. 13–19 and ch. 6; Kenan Malik, *The Meaning of Race* (London: Palgrave Macmillan, 1996).

14 For one stimulating discussion on the emergence of modern historical consciousness, see Peter Fritzsche, *Stranded in the Present: Modern Time and the Melancholy of History* (Cambridge, MA: Harvard University Press, 2004).

15 Marci Green and Ian Grosvenor, 'Making subjects: history writing, education and race categories', *Paedagogica Historica: International Journal of the History of Education*, 33:3 (1997), 883–908.

16 Carter, *Realism and Racism*, p. 5.

17 Becky Conekin, Frank Mort and Chris Waters, 'Introduction', in Becky Conekin, Frank Mort and Chris Waters (eds), *Moments of Modernity: Reconstructing Britain 1945–1964* (London: Rivers Oram Press, 1999), pp. 14–15.

18 On the continuing significance of the science of race in post-1945 Britain, see Gavin Schaffer, *Racial Science and British Society, 1930–1962* (Basingstoke: Palgrave Macmillan, 2008).

19 Tony Kushner, *We Europeans? Mass Observation, 'Race' and British Identity in the Twentieth Century* (Aldershot: Ashgate, 2004); Kathleen Paul, *Whitewashing Britain: Race and Citizenship in the Postwar Era* (London: Cornell University Press, 1997); Ian Grosvenor, *Assimilating Identities: Racism and Educational Policy in Post 1945 Britain* (London: Lawrence & Wishart 1997).

20 Stuart Ward (ed.), *British Culture and the End of Empire* (Manchester: Manchester University Press, 2001); Wendy Webster, 'There'll always be an England: representations of colonial wars and immigration, 1948–1968', in Simon Faulkner and Anandi Ramamurphy (eds), *Visual Culture and Decolonisation in Britain* (Aldershot: Ashgate, 2006), pp. 189–214.

21 Peter Fritzsche, 'The case of modern memory', *Journal of Modern History*, 73:1 (2001), 87–117. Susannah Radstone and Bill Schwarz (eds), *Memory: Histories, Theories, Debates* (New York: Fordham University Press, 2010).

22 Billie Melman, *The Culture of History: English Uses of the Past, 1800–1953* (Oxford: Oxford University Press, 2006), p. 7.

23 Wulf Kansteiner, 'Finding meaning in memory: a methodological critique of collective memory studies', *History and Theory*, 41:2 (2002), 80.

24 Bill Schwarz (ed.), *West Indian Intellectuals in Britain* (Manchester: Manchester University Press, 2003).

25 Michel Rolph-Trouillot, *Silencing the Past: Production and the Power of History* (Boston, MA: Beacon, 1995), pp. 23–24, for the important distinctions between agents, actors and subjects.

26 A point made clear in the increasing interest in the concept of generation. See, for example, Stephen Lovell (ed.), *Generations in Twentieth-Century Europe* (Basingstoke: Palgrave Macmillan, 2007).

27 The term historical subjects is used advisedly here and consistent with the approach, best understood as a kind of weak constructionism, in Chris Lorenz, 'Representations of identity', in Berger and Lorenz, *Contested Nation*, pp. 24–59; Rolph-Trouillot, *Silencing the Past*, pp. 23–24.

28 Benedict Anderson, *Imagined Communities: Reflections on the Origin and Spread of Nationalism* (London: Verso, 1983).

29 Dominic Sandbrook, *White Heat: A History of Britain in the Swinging Sixties* (London: Little Brown, 2006) and *Never Had It So Good: A History of Britain from Suez to the Beatles* (London: Abacus, 2006).

30 Mark Garnett, *From Anger to Apathy: The British Experience since 1975* (London: Jonathan Cape, 2007).

31 Colin Holmes, *John Bull's Island: Immigration and British Society 1871–1971* (Basingstoke: Macmillan, 1988), pp. 35, 44, 49.

32 Enda Delaney, *The Irish in Post-War Britain* (Oxford: Oxford University Press, 2007), pp. 156–159.

33 A recent monumental study of British political radicalism found no room, for example, for modern pan-Africanism. See Edward Vallance, *A Radical History of Britain: Visionaries, Rebels and Revolutionaries – The Men and Women Who Fought for Our Freedoms* (London: Little Brown, 2009).

34 Kathy Burrell and Panikos Panayi, 'Introduction: immigration and British history', in Burrell and Panayi (eds), *Histories and Memories: Immigrants and their History in Britain since 1800* (London: I.B. Tauris, 2006), p. 16.

35 Kevin Myers, 'Immigrants and ethnic minorities in the history of education', *Paedagogica Historica*, 45:6 (2009), 801–816.

36 Diane Reay and Heidi Safia Mirza, 'Spaces and places of black educational desire: rethinking supplementary schools as a new social movement', *Sociology*, 34:3 (2000), 521–544.

37 Keri Facer, *Learning Futures: Education, Technology and Social Change* (London: Routledge, 2011), p. 3.

38 The term 'black' is used throughout the book to refer to people of Caribbean and African descent who experienced discrimination because of their skin colour and whose reclamation and use of the term was part of their struggle against racism.

39 Madge Dresser, 'Reaching out from the archive: minority history and academic method', paper presented to the History in British Education conference, Institute of Historical Research, February 2005. www.history.ac.uk/education/conference/index.html (last accessed 5/10/09).

40 Scarman Report, *The Brixton Disorders: Report of an Inquiry* (London: HMSO, 1981), paras. 6.1, 6.6, 6.35.

41 Rampton Report, *West Indian Children in Our Schools: Interim Report of the Committee of Inquiry into the Education of Children from Ethnic Minority Groups* (London: HMSO, 1981).

42 Swann Report, *Education for All: Report of the Committee of Inquiry into the Education of Children from Ethnic Minority Groups* (London: HMSO, 1985).

43 Jerry White, *London in the Twentieth Century: A City and Its People* (London: Viking, 2001), p. 397.

44 Antony Gifford, Wally Brown and Ruth Bundey, *Loosen the Shackles: First Report of the Liverpool 8 Inquiry into Race Relations in Liverpool* (Liverpool: Karia Press, 1989), p. 35.

45 Yasmin Alibhai-Brown, *After Multiculturalism* (London: Foreign Policy Centre, 2000).

46 Paul Gilroy, *There Ain't No Black in the Union Jack: The Cultural Politics of Race and Nation* (London: Routledge, 2002 edn).

47 For a summary of this argument, see Kevin Myers, 'Historical practice in an age of pluralism: educating and celebrating identities', in Burrell and Panayi, *Histories and Memories*, pp. 35–56.

48 Particularly pertinent here because of the way it investigates the erasure of refugee communities from the national story is Tony Kushner, *Remembering Refugees: Then and Now* (Manchester: Manchester University Press, 2006). See also Gemma Romain, *Connecting Histories: A Comparative Exploration of African-Caribbean and Jewish History and Memory in Modern Britain* (London: Kegan Paul, 2006).

49 On the age of super diversity and its implications, see Steven Vertovec, 'Super-diversity and its implications', *Ethnic and Racial Studies*, 30:6 (2007), 1024–1054. On historical practice, see B. Southgate, 'Memories into something new: histories for the future', *Rethinking History*, 11:2 (2007), 187–199.

1

The nation and its people
(1951–1968)

Introduction

The 1951 Festival of Britain was centred around twenty-two pavilions in London's South Bank but also, featuring a wide variety of travelling exhibitions and local events, was designed as an autobiography of the nation. Fun and enjoyment were certainly on the agenda: there were pleasure gardens, funfairs and great splashes of colour in the displays of domestic furniture. Yet, and as the *Picture Post* noted, the Festival also had a more serious, and educational, purpose. An act of 'national reassessment' following the difficulties and strains of war, the Festival would 'put on record the fact that we are a nation not only with a great past, but also a great future'.[1] In fact, and typically, the guarantee of the future was the past. As historian Becky Conekin has argued, 'the role of history in this project was to illustrate great universal truths about the British people'.[2] There is some evidence that it worked.

Visiting the pavilions in 1951 was diarist Vere Hodgson whose favourite exhibit was the Lion and the Unicorn. 'This is a must for everyone', she recorded in her diary, 'it is the British character. Obstinacy and imagination or whatever you like to call the two best characteristics of the British race. There was Magna Carta and Habeas Corpus. I was very pleased about this.'[3] Even if this rendition of national history and character was populist and pleasurable it was also, of course, quite particular. For histories, and their meaning, are always the result of selection, interpretation and argument. Even though Vere Hodgson might not have been aware of it, two important and quite novel interpretative themes emerged in the version of the past presented at the Festival of Britain.

The first was the idea that national history was domestic. The boundaries of the national community were drawn tightly around the island of Britain, whose soil and sea were the source of enduring national characteristics that made the British unique. In this process of making national identity more domestic, the British Empire, or what was usually called the Commonwealth by 1951, was the 'place that was almost absent'. This was not an 'international festival or even a Commonwealth festival', according to a satisfied Chair of the Council of the Festival of Britain, Lord Ismay, but was 'British in the purest sense of the word'. That purity was achieved by ignoring both Empire and the modern migration of people to Britain. As Conekin argues, 'the assumption that ran throughout the London-produced Festival guides and catalogues was that the British were a people who had been born and bred in the British Isles for generations and generations – more generations than anyone could count'.[4] This domesticated idea of British national identity was not, of course, entirely new. It was present, for example, in the inter-war period when it was taken up as an alternative to the militaristic discourse of imperial identity; it was appropriated by Baldwin's Conservatism and then, as Vere Hodgson's reaction to the Festival suggests, became important to popular patriotism during and after the Second World War.[5] This homely version of national history was arguably best expressed in George Orwell's *The Lion and the Unicorn*, where an essentially gentle, decent and domestic people, now divorced from the image of imperial greatness, were defined and united by their past. National characteristics were 'rooted deep in history', suggested Orwell in a famous passage, and 'English civilisation was continuous, it stretches into the future and the past, there is something in it that persists, as in a living creature'.[6] Yet if this domestic national history was not entirely new, it was increasingly evident as a specifically English past that defined an English character that had both persisted and developed through time.

The second notable theme at the Festival of Britain, implicit in the choice of Magna Carta and Habeas Corpus as moments of origin, was democracy. Consistent with the marginalisation of Empire, and the implicit elitism and masculinity of the Empire story, was the stress on a gentle people defined by their struggles for civil and religious freedoms, and for parliamentary democracy. Such people were the product of sea and soil. Remote from the passions of continental Europe and the politics of Empire, the English were rooted in the landscape and they were uniquely free and tolerant. These ideas, which gained popularity during the 'People's War', were central to post-war political and public discourse and they are evident in the popular histories of the period. 'The people', for example, is a central narrative device for both G.M. Trevelyan (whose *English Social History*, first published in 1942, had sold over 400,000 copies by 1949) and for Arthur Bryant, arguably the most popular of all historians in the early post-war period.[7] Similarly, a 'romanticised and pastoral celebration of the English character' constituted the wartime contribution of Cambridge historians D.W. Brogan and Herbert Butterfield and in 1965, A.J.P. Taylor's *English History, 1914–1945*, repeated a common trope of a decent and tolerant people who came of age during the Second World War.[8]

Yet the democratisation of national identity through history also had deeper roots. Both nineteenth- and early twentieth-century historians in Britain routinely allowed for the integration of class and nation, and cross-class consensus was a consistent theme of a 'reassuringly British' mode of national history writing.[9] Of course, British history writing ignored nationalist histories of Scotland, Wales and Ireland, and was heavily gendered but, in comparison to other European nations, where historical interpretations remained divided between republican and monarchic and revolutionary and conservative traditions, it was also relatively inclusive and integrative.[10] These comparatively deep roots help to explain why, in the post-war period, projects and policies that aimed to extend and embed the place of the people in national culture, could secure widespread political consent. They could be presented as the logical conclusion, the *telos*, to a history that stressed not only the gradual extension of political rights, but also the emergence of more educated, dignified and respected citizenry.

When Philip Leacock's public information film introducing the Festival of Britain advised that the British were 'a people who build with gladness on an old inheritance' it was pointing implicitly towards a range of social and educational projects in which the working class were encouraged to identify with a history of tolerance, courage, faith and freedom and to find refuge in that past.[11] This sentiment informed a wide range of social, cultural and educational projects in the post-war era. It was evident in adult education and community publishing, in the rapid extension of community theatre and, for a period, in the folk music revival. It was also, as Carolyn Steedman has convincingly argued, central for a progressive pedagogy in which creative or autobiographical writing gave dignity and voice to working-class children and their communities.[12] What these diverse practices had in common was a belief, retrospectively appearing almost metaphysical, in the restorative power of history. The central theme that ran through of all of these invocations of the working-class past was a radical romanticism that rescued ordinary workers from anonymity and identified a series of heroes and movements that could provide the basis of a historical identity. This was history viewed through the prism of the 'forward march of labour'. It bestowed on former struggles new meaning, and on their participants new wisdom. In the present, it provided a more democratic, and more authentic, national past and, in many ways, it was critical and politically progressive.[13]

Even though the concept of class and a methodological concern with working people were potentially universal, the study of what became social history remained firmly rooted within national boundaries. In Britain, early formulations of social history were typically concerned with 'tradition, habit and convention', and latterly, particularly concerned with the freedom and the agency of working-class communities.[14] It was also resolutely empirical, anti-theoretical and humanistic. Attempting to rescue the richness of working-class lives, and aggressively opposed to Marxist abstractions, social history ended up celebrating a desire for liberty and struggles for justice as specifically 'English peculiarities'.[15] Rooted in a domestic landscape, blessed with a thirst for justice and liberty, this historical vision of the English people was implicitly ethnic, and it was intensely parochial. The practice of English social history helped to create a code of difference. It identified 'differences that made a difference' by identifying specific common ancestry, particular shared historical memories, a common culture and a shared homeland. At the same time, popular democratic history in England largely ignored the presence of immigrant communities, and it denied the significance of colonial and imperial conquest in the formation of the 'English people'.[16]

If the narration and interpretation of national history was changing in 1951 it was at least partly because ideas about being British and English were also in flux. Being British was often conflated with a specifically English rendering of the national past that was about development of liberty, about a people pulling together, and about egalitarianism, or having the chance to share in the riches of the nation and the opportunities it offered. In this New Britain, rational planning, and the expertise of technocrats would deliver knowledge, culture and the benefits of science to the people. In these respects, the Festival of Britain represents an optimistic and modernising moment. It celebrated a national past and anticipated a prosperous and future for an honourable people. In reality, this confidence and optimism only masked deep anxieties at the decline of Empire and developments in the pace and scale of immigration. This chapter explores those anxieties and locates them, in part, in an imperial tradition that was suffused with ideas about race and which proved unable to comprehend the global impacts of British imperialism, or to identify and explain the historical processes it unleashed.[17] The applied science of race relations, it argues, exemplified those failures because it, too, tended to marginalise histories of immigration to England and to deny the distribution and transmission of race ideas that accompanied them. In turn, post-war immigrants routinely felt excluded from a national community and, slowly, some of them began to turn towards the past to interrogate those feelings and to explain their frequent experiences as the object of prejudice. They did so, of course, as historical subjects and using the language, images and resources that came to them from the past.

Englishness, the people and democracy

The marginalisation of Empire and immigration at the Festival of Britain was a response to both mounting difficulties in the Empire and growing apprehension at the arrival of immigrants to Britain, especially from the New Commonwealth. Wendy Webster has argued persuasively that by the middle of 1950s there was a clearly identi-fiable narrative of 'Britons under siege' in popular culture. In this narrative, Britain was pictured as a domestic sanctuary threatened by colonial violation. Feature films, newsreels, radio and television broadcasts all 'constructed Englishness against Empire and partic-ularly against immigrants'.[18] Even if the decolonisation of the British Empire was usually portrayed as orderly and peaceful, and offered another opportunity for a Whiggish vision of Empire, there were many moments when the British public were presented with more violent images by the media.[19] From the late 1940s onwards there was extensive reporting on the bloody partition of India, the emergence of independence movements in Malaya and, especially, the Mau Mau uprising in Kenya. Extraordinary images and stories, of refugee flight, armed conflict and gruesome atrocities, were presented to the public. These images were typically explained by references to oriental and African savagery and confirmed an idea of colonial natives as exotic and childlike.[20] With changes of emphasis and tone, these ideas continued to resonate as the dissolution of European empires proceeded during the 1950s and 1960s.

If a collective turn towards a specifically English domestic culture was prompted by the troubles of Empire and political decolonisation, it provided only temporary and partial respite. In domestic national life too, the legacies of Empire were becoming increasingly clear in the growing numbers of immigrants from both former and current members of the British Commonwealth. These immigrants were crucial in solving the post-war labour shortages and the largest numbers were Irish.

Irish immigrants had, of course, been a central feature of industrialising Britain. From the late eighteenth century onwards increased demand for labour, along with economic and political conditions in Ireland and, perhaps, the growing aspirations encouraged by migration networks, drew hundreds of thousands of workers to the growing towns and cities of Britain. The incorporation of Ireland into the United Kingdom by the Act of Union of 1800 made these Irish subjects part of the master narrative of the British people. Widespread and popular anti-Irish prejudice, not only as popish Catholics but also as Celts ascribed with racial characteristics of inferiority and backwardness, hardly declined, but inclusion in the national narrative, even if as a substandard and 'internal other', was possible.[21]

The Irish status as 'internal other' helps explain why, even after the declaration of the Irish Republic in 1948, Irish citizens retained the right to unrestricted entry into Great Britain and, indeed, to all the other benefits of British citizenship. In all, it is reasonable to estimate that, in the period after 1945 some 700,000 Irish migrated to Britain.[22] They came overwhelmingly from the province of Munster, were mostly Catholic, working class and, from the 1960s onwards, women outnumbered men. Among diverse responses to their arrival was a tendency to reproduce older stereotypes, 'thick Paddies', with a propensity for alcohol and violence, that, argued Liz Curtis some years ago, recalled older colonial relationships and provided evidence of the insecurities promoted by the scale of Irish migration and its effects in the towns and cities of Britain.[23] Indeed, the persistence of official and popular debates about the desirability of restricting immigration from Ireland, a matter that received serious discussion well into the 1960s, and whose children could be reported as causing 'even greater educational and social problems than Indian and West Indian immigrants', is suggestive of the 'long-standing reproduction of anti-Irish sentiment [that] was difficult to dislodge'.[24] In the end, however, this antipathy did not result in the restriction of Irish immigration because of continued political adherence to what Kathleen Paul has called 'different communities of Britishness'.[25] Paul's persuasive argument is that British national identity has always been fractured. So even while the 1948 British Nationality Act enshrined an open and generous definition of Britishness according to which all residents of the British Empire and Commonwealth were British subjects with equal rights, in practice policymakers worked with a differentiated notion of who could belong, and how, to the British nation. An inner core of Britishness consisted of a number of exclusive identities, defined by skin colour, specific ideas about gender and a racialised reading of history.[26]

The meaning and status of this singular and fixed Britishness became clear in the way in which policymakers responded to the major migrant groups of the post-war period. The Irish, for example, continued to be treated as de facto British subjects because, as one civil servant noted, there existed 'historical, racial and geographical links' or 'ties of kinship, ties of blood and intermingling of peoples which bound Eire to the older countries of the Commonwealth'.[27] Thus, the Irish inhabited their own distinct community of Britishness which managed to combine widespread prejudice with a sense that they somehow belonged to, or could be tolerated in, British society. The same was true for the continental refugees and aliens recruited to help solve the labour shortages of the post-war period. While these groups were certainly not always welcome, they could be at least tolerated on the basis that they were European and white.[28]

The same was not true for immigrants from the New Commonwealth, and the difference was fundamentally important. It points towards a different order of discrimination, sustained and systematic, that black immigrants from the Caribbean, Africa and South Asia faced in Britain. Against a tendency among some historians and commentators to naturalise this response, and see it as an inevitable reaction to the arrival of excessive numbers of immigrants, it bears repeating that the Irish were, by some considerable distance, the largest immigrant group in the immediate post-war period.[29] The figures for New Commonwealth, and non-white, immigrants were comparatively small with approximately 125,000 West Indians, 55,000 South Asians and fewer West Africans arriving in the period between 1945 and 1958.[30] In absolute terms these numbers may have been rather insignificant but it quickly became a commonplace theme of political and polite discussion that the immigrants from the New Commonwealth heralded the arrival of new and distinctive social problems that the state should manage.

Hostile responses to these immigrants cannot adequately be explained by their numbers. In any case, and as is made clear below, there is plenty of evidence that, in the mundane interactions of everyday life, immigrants from the Caribbean, from South Asia and Africa could all draw positive responses. They could be described as God-fearing, hard working and quiet, and were sometimes favourably compared to the 'fighting mad Irish'.[31] Reactions to immigrants were complex, they were shaped by both local and national contexts, and they defy easy conceptualisation. Overall, however, and as Kenneth Lunn has argued, 'it is clear that the dominant experience of opposition to immigrants and the construction of cultural and institutional racist ideologies are very significant dimensions of any British experience'.[32] Those ideologies were influenced by a long tradition of intolerance towards immigrants in Britain, they drew on race ideas and they were expressed in the Commonwealth Immigration Acts of 1962 and 1968 whose primary purpose was to curtail the numbers of immigrants arriving in Britain from the New Commonwealth.[33] Yet, as Gavin Schaffer has shown, in a nation whose self-image was underpinned by a Whiggish history of freedom and tolerance, explicit reference to race ideas were both rare and controversial.[34] Instead, and under the considerable influence of US social science, hostility to immigrants and prejudice against them became the science of race relations.

Race relations

One of the novel aspects about the post-war period was the emergence of a distinct area of scholarly activity that promoted research into the field of 'race relations' and championed self-proclaimed progressive and rational responses to it. Race relations scholars benefitted from a particular philosophy of social democracy in which the social sciences, and sociology and social psychology in particular, became important mechanisms in the description, analysis and amelioration of 'social problems'. As far as race ideas were concerned, the single biggest influence, not just for Britain but for other European nations, was provided by the United States of America (USA).[35]

Despite their 'rather inglorious scientific career', race ideas have been central to modern thinking about human difference.[36] Initially concerned largely with cultural–linguistic features, modern theories of race seemingly explained social, moral and physical differences in biological terms. These biological differences between so-called races were used to explain inequalities both within societies but also, and especially in the context of growing competition for global expansion, between nations.[37] In the USA, for example, race ideas were used to justify the emergence of a US Empire, to retrospectively explain the development of plantation slavery and they were central to the institutionalised and discriminatory system of separation between white and black people that was enacted after abolition. In fact, and although there is now widespread agreement that biological races do not exist, race relations were established social facts in early twentieth-century USA.[38]

Riots between imagined white and black races, and the prejudiced attitudes that gave rise to them, were the subject of important studies conducted by the Chicago School of Sociology. In an open and interdisciplinary milieu, which found room for women researchers and was devoted to the alleviation of social problems, Chicago scholars attempted to move beyond explanations of human difference rooted in biology.[39] In richly descriptive urban sociology and a distinctively social psychology, researchers investigated interactions between humans and their environments, probed the consequences of rapid industrialisation and analysed the impact of mass immigration. These consequences could be psychological, as in the identification of African-Americans and immigrants who were emotionally distressed and 'maladjusted' because they were caught between two different cultures, or sociological, as in the identification of a 'race relations cycle' in which immigrant groups moved from group conflict towards assimilation.[40] Whatever the particular findings of what was a large body of work, people were consistently understood as the products of cultural conventions, rather than biological races, and, partly because explanation tended towards a synchronic model, it was assumed that their attitudes and behaviours were also open to modification.[41]

In Britain, the Chicago model of race relations and prejudice studies had obvious attractions. For one thing, it was consistent with a political and cultural outlook that tended to associate explicit discussions of race with Nazism and to promote a liberal image that denied any deep-seated hostility to immigrants. The practical orientation of this work, helping individuals overcome their irrational prejudice for example, was also conducive in an environment where an expanding welfare state accepted increasing responsibility for the education and care of its population. Finally, race relations scholarship was influenced by, and drew on anthropology, and social anthropology; disciplines that may have lacked numbers, but not influence, on government and colonial administration in Britain.[42]

As a result, and by the early 1950s, the social science of race relations was expanding. It emerged as an interdisciplinary area of study, drawing on sociology, anthropology and social psychology, and in either provincial English universities (Liverpool, Birmingham, Bath) or those in Wales (Cardiff) and Scotland (Edinburgh). Its most famous practitioners were men such as Kenneth Little, Michael Banton and Anthony Richmond, but the disproportionately high number of women scholars (notably anthropologists Ruth Glass, Sheila Patterson and Ruth Landes) is also suggestive of a relatively open intellectual milieu. Located outside the disciplines and traditions of metropolitan and gentlemanly social science, race relations research was receptive to innovation. It mixed disciplines and crossed national boundaries and, despite modest beginnings, social scientists were beginning to challenge the predominance of historians as public intellectuals by the 1960s.[43] Landes, Glass and Patterson, Little, Banton and Richmond all published widely not only in academic journals on both sides of the Atlantic, but also in noticeably more populist outlets including Penguin paperback specials, in journalism and broadcasting. They also made rather more uneven, and gendered, contributions to public policy debate in conducting state-sponsored social research and providing expert advice to parliamentary investigations into race and immigration. As for the Chicago School in the USA, their works helped to rebut claims of biological difference between races, while simultaneously charting and systematising distinct immigrant and native cultures. Having helped to construct and legitimise cultural differences social scientists were empowered to improve communication between races, and to promote social harmony by sponsoring various educational projects.[44]

A dominant theme of social science was that social harmony would prove elusive, and 'coloured immigrants' would be unable to assimilate to British society, because of the existence of colour prejudice in the native population. Kenneth Little's *Negroes in Britain* (1947), based on research carried out in Cardiff's Tiger Bay, was a foundational text of this kind and it was followed by similar work by Banton and Patterson in London, by Richmond in Liverpool, and, in a distinctly less anthropological and more sociological mode, by Rex and Moore in Birmingham.[45] Despite changes of emphases resulting both from different disciplines, methodologies and geographical locations, all of these publications, and others like them, identified colour prejudice as a major stumbling block to the assimilation of immigrants. Even though white immigrants groups could appear more alien, as with the different language, religion and customs of Poles, and even though their behaviour could be judged more problematic, as with the consumption of alcohol and the supposed tendency to violence and criminality of the Irish, it was the visibility of black skin that was offered in explanation for the widespread prejudice against 'coloured immigrants'.

Crucially, however, social scientists rarely made any sustained attempt to explain the meanings attributed to black skin. Short narratives of slavery and eugenics sometimes appeared in their writing but, just as often, the inferiority and danger signalled by black skin were simply assumed. This meant that the distribution and transmission of race ideas in the past was rarely adequately addressed and, instead, the idea that prejudice was somehow an inherent and natural part of English culture or an abnormal individual response was promoted. In other words, a social science vocabulary ranging from racialised notions of cultural difference to individual psychological processes did not pursue the kind of historical research that might have been able to explain the development and application of race ideas by people in the past. Perhaps because early practitioners exhibited what one of their contemporaries, A.H. Halsey, called a 'provincial patriotism' which 'knew Britain as a relatively decent society', their research had the effect of naturalising hostile or ambivalent responses to immigrants.[46] As a result, their work played a crucial role in the racialisation of black immigration.

Anthony Richmond's work is a good example of how race relations scholarship simultaneously identified domestic traditions of intolerance but, conditioned by a liberal image of British society, failed to explain it. *The Colour Problem* (1955), a study of racial relations in Britain, Africa and the West Indies, attempts to bring social science knowledge to bear on the problems caused by the fact that 'throughout the world members of different racial and cultural groups are being brought into ever closer contact and communication with one another'. Even when disavowing biological theories of race, however, Richmond came close to making them reappear by employing the terms 'racial' and 'cultural' in tandem. Immigrant groups, it seemed, were distinguishable either by race or culture, or by both, and this made it inevitable that they conflicted. The inevitability of this conflict is then explained in two different kinds of ways.

Firstly, *The Colour Problem* includes a section of historical analysis that covers slavery, imperialism and migration, and which stresses an official imperial policy to emphasise the 'wide cultural differences' and 'a rigid social separation between European rulers and non-European ruled'.[47] Even if this exaggerates the actual degree of separation enforced, race ideas are accurately located in historical processes. These ideas were, in principle, open to critique and, as a result, to their dismantling. However, and as historian Chris Waters has argued, and as was clear from the celebration of an ethnic English past, there was a tendency in post-war society towards a kind of cultural determinism that interpreted history as decisively imposing fundamental and permanent differences on groups that were so reified they closely resembled races.[48]

A second interpretation of cultural conflict presented by Richmond argued that there was a psychological and universal tendency to ethnocentrism. Individuals organised themselves into exclusive groups on the basis of cultural traits and considered their own group characteristics as superior to that of others. A mild degree of prejudice was considered a normal and basic personality trait that functioned to resolve conflicts whose origins were hidden in the unconscious.[49] Such conflicts were understood psychoanalytically. They were the result of the authoritarian parenting that influential anthropologist Geoffrey Gorer saw as a key factor in the production of what was supposed to be a quintessential English characteristic: shyness.[50]

The Colour Problem thus pointed towards the ways in which slavery and imperialism had established differences between people of different skin colour that had become permanent and decisive. These differences had been consolidated by universal psychological processes through which individuals sought to achieve security by projecting repressed impulses onto identified strangers. All this is suggestive of the rather eclectic range of theoretical influences on early social scientists of race but, despite some of its evident naivety, this work can still be considered important and politically progressive. It helped shift attention from the problems caused by immigrants, and it at least began to recognise a domestic pattern of 'colour prejudice'.[51]

More specifically, *The Colour Problem* discussed the sea port attacks on black people by white working-class mobs in 1919 and explained them largely by reference to the insecurities that competition for scarce jobs in port cities brought. In Liverpool, Richmond explained, 'the climax was reached when a Negro was drowned in a scrimmage on the docks and the police had to make several baton charges on the crowd'.[52] This may have been a tentative recognition of domestic prejudice, and it would still be several decades before the murdered black civilian, Charles Wootton, was named and commemorated, it did begin to identify a domestic history of prejudice against black people in England.[53]

However, these historical cameos did not mean that race relations scholars managed to escape the assumptions of deep cultural difference that were embedded in their work. Indeed, after two decades of research, policy analysis and advice social scientists had established race relations as an applied field of study in which relationships between homogenous black and white populations, far from improving over time through everyday interaction, required permanent monitoring, intervention and education. Writing of the position of Liverpool's black population in 1969 and echoing US studies of marginal men, Patrick McNabb of Liverpool University considered what he called the 'Afro-English community' to present the most difficult problems for the future of race relations in Liverpool.[54] The children of mixed-race relationships, with almost always a father from Africa or the West Indies, and a white mother (whose origin was rarely given) were, 'unlike the immigrant', 'emotionally unstable', 'acutely conscious of their colour as a disability' and 'suffer a thorough-going ambiguity in their emotional life'. Going on to describe them in positively racialised terms, 'they are imaginative, they have a natural grace and very winning manners', McNabb saw them, nonetheless, as a group which has the 'potential for either good or evil'.[55] The reason for such foreboding was that mixed-race relationships and mixed-race children threatened the homogeneous groups that were central to the whole race relations imagination. Psychological health and good citizenship were thought to be unobtainable because, belonging to neither racialised culture, they had no secure identity and were vulnerable to the crude and fascistic appeal of Black Power.

As McNabb's work demonstrates, post-war social scientists were hardly without prejudice, but they still saw themselves in the vanguard of a movement that would study race relations objectively and promote mutual understanding on the basis of a shared project of education.[56] Indeed, the effort to transmit and evoke knowledge, skills, values and sensibilities became central to the ambitions of post-war social scientists.[57] This was an expansive notion of public education whose aim was for nothing less than a 'new set of values' and a 'new ideology' for populations facing what were frequently proclaimed as new times.[58]

Drawing on Kurt Lewin's internationally influential work on education for reconstruction, Richmond was typical in recommending a breaking down of the institutional barriers between groups and predicted that increased contact and collaboration, alongside educational campaigns, would result in experiences that would modify prejudices.[59] A study by social scientists based at Westhill Training College in Birmingham in 1961 clearly articulated the typically sunny optimism that underpinned these arguments for integration. In the 'new race relations problems' in Birmingham 'both sides had much to give – West Indians their gaiety and natural friendliness; English their patience, planning for children and technical training'.[60] All that was really required were more opportunities for face-to-face encounters and more opportunities for informal integration. The precise form of this education, and the institutions required to implement it, were rarely explicated in detail. Richmond recommended programmes of community development that would 'promote a sense of belonging' to nations, rather than to racial groups, and new social and political organisations that could facilitate the adjustment of both immigrants and natives towards new conditions. 'Tribal societies' should be valued, argued Richmond, because despite their tendencies towards nationalist politics and complaint against the host society, they helped immigrants maintain 'a measure of psychological security' and develop satisfying social relationships.[61] Similarly, Rex and Moore, who tried to retreat from what they saw as an excessive psychologism, saw the primary community, or 'colony' of immigrant groups, as a way of preventing a decline into a 'state of complete demoralisation and anomie'.[62] In other words, tribal societies, or immigrant social and political organisations, were valued, specifically and only, for educational and therapeutic reasons.

All this says much about the limitations of race relations work. It opened up a space where the existence of domestic traditions of intolerance were identified and at least tentatively discussed. Yet, race relations scholars were constrained by their racialised view of culture, by adherence to a view of English character as liberal and tolerant and by the fact that it had a tendency to reduce systemic discrimination which developed through history to the realm of psychology. As a result, the actual interventions designed to reduce prejudice can appear retrospectively trivial, mundane and completely unrealistic.

Take, for example, the emergence in the 1950s of friendship councils, immigrant liaison committees, good neighbour committees and consultative committees in towns and cities of immigrant settlement. These were often an explicit response to the challenges posed by immigration and they were promoted by race relations scholars for the role they could play in resolving cultural misunderstandings and smoothing the integration of immigrants into everyday life. The Willesden International Friendship Council (WIFC) was established in the immediate aftermath of the violent attacks on immigrants that occurred in Notting Hill in 1958. The WIFC was represented by all the usual civic dignitaries; the local mayor was the president and the executive committee included local MPs, borough councillors and other local voluntary associations. Constitutionally, the Council existed to 'to foster understanding and goodwill between immigrant citizens from the West Indies, Africa and other countries and the rest of the Willesden community' and 'to promote and assist the general good and well-being of such immigrant citizens in the Borough of Willesden'.[63] Practically, these aims were to be delivered by activities that promoted social contact and developed the knowledge and understanding that was presumed necessary for a fully integrated community. So, according to its publicity material at least, WIFC sponsored interracial clubs and activities; it published information and advisory pamphlets; promoted conferences and study groups; and provided a service of reconciliation for households affected by 'racial friction'.[64]

One attendant at an international friendship group in London was the self-declared black Englishman and race relations worker, Chris Mullard. 'Disappointingly dull' was his verdict on attending several meetings and socials in which 'overseas members', usually men 'dressed in blazers, sports coats and stiffly starched shirts', 'never seemed to have any views of their own' and 'spent most of their time laughing and joking as if they did not have a care in the world'. Mullard sensed a sexual attraction to these men by the white women who formed the majority of home members and who 'planned all the activities, made all the decisions and wrote all the newsletters'. Their talks and discussions on national cultures were carefully scripted with 'set questions and set answers' so that 'a liberal, understanding image of Britain was maintained by sweeping all serious matters under the carpet' and isolating those who did not regard the UK as 'the paragon of civilization'.[65] Mullard's frustration was that the distinctions between home and overseas members, or strangers and hosts, had no conceptual space for engaging with or listening to a young black Englishman with considerable personal knowledge of the ways in which racist discrimination operated in England. 'Unimaginative, paternalistic and tied to an image of Britain as tolerant and basically welcoming' was the retrospectively frank assessment of Communities Relations Commissioner Nadine Peppard.[66]

Nonetheless, and despite some evident weaknesses, the race relations agenda slowly gained in popularity as a policy response to post-war immigration. Its influence can be clearly seen in the Race Relations Acts of 1965 and 1968 whose combined effect was not only to make incitement to racial hatred and discrimination illegal but also to provide and promote the schemes of public education that were deemed necessary for a successful multicultural society. These schemes of education were to be promoted by the Community Relations Commission (CRC) that was established in 1968 and whose purpose was to promote racial harmony through 'integration work' which was initially defined as comprising the collation of information, the commissioning of research and the provision of advice to government. The legislation consolidated the gradual growth of post-war race relations and, in part, it also prompted a frustrated complaint from political scientist, philosopher of ethnic relations and future peer, Bikhu Parekh. Writing in 1974 Parekh articulated a deep frustration with the race relations obsession for the 'immigrant stranger' whose 'breeding habits are made a subject of careful statistical analysis, and the smell of his food, and the way he sleeps and relaxes are considered subjects worthy of national attention. It is almost as if the nation refused to accept him as a full human being, entitled to respect and dignity and to the ordinary civilities of a cultured society.'[67]

That feeling of inhumanity also surfaced in the important but strangely neglected 1964 film *The Colony* by radical documentary filmmaker Phillip Donnellan. Sociologist Sarita Malik regards the film as a landmark moment in British television history because it is a rare example of social issues being discussed from the perspective of immigrants and it features, on one of the first occasions on British television, Caribbeans talking directly and at length to camera.[68] Among those Caribbeans were Stan Crooke (railway signalman from St Kitts), Bernice Smith (Jamaican teacher), Victor Williams (bus conductor), Polly Perkins (Barbadian nurse) and preacher, Pastor Dunn. The film compares the expectations of the migrants of the mother country with the more disappointing reality: of gloomy weather, industrial smoke, the lack of space, the poor housing, and, a key theme of the film, prejudice against immigrants. The prejudice stimulates important observations on English culture and history and its consequences for the consciousness and identity of both the English and the immigrants, now increasingly identifying themselves as West Indians or blacks.[69] Two themes stand out; the exploration of national and local heritage and a critique of tradition.

The Colony presented viewers with a familiar narrative of local and national history. England and Britain, the terms are used interchangeably, is praised for its rich historical culture and its civilisation. There are long sections on the rise of steam power and the 'great men with open minds that revolutionised the world' and a section that introduces and explains the development of slavery and imperial relationships between Britain, Africa and Jamaica. Slavery's abolition is dated to 1838 and explained by reference to a decision by Queen Victoria that was encouraged by the work of abolitionist campaigners. London statues of Victoria and the most famous of the abolitionists, William Wilberforce, are shown in the film that ends with a long sequence in which a tour group are shown round a local stately home, Aston Hall, and introduced to its collection of arts and artefacts dating from around the seventeenth century. In one respect, therefore, Donnellan's *The Colony* presents a dominant version of the local and national past clearly reminiscent of the 1951 Festival of Britain. The English, and sometimes British, genius for invention and exploration are narrated and offered as causal explanations for industrialisation and the development of Empire. The British thirst for liberty, and a national culture of tolerance, explained the abolition of slavery. This was, in other words, another representation of the national master narrative in which the past became a story of English genius for trade and commerce, for political stability and for tolerating religious minorities and immigrants.

Yet *The Colony* was not just another paean to the glorious English past. In fact, the reason Donnellan sets out the dominant national narrative with such care is because his very purpose is a searching critique of it. A substantial section of the opening part of the film, for example, presents some reflections on Whig accounts of the past and an alternative historical narrative. The claim that imperialism spread false propaganda and created the myth of good and tolerant England is repeated more than once. A visit to the Science Museum prompts bus conductor Victor Williams to wonder what those Enlightenment figures would make of the contemporary city and its slum streets and racist graffiti. The ignorance of black history and culture suggested on the daubed walls prompts further historical reflection:

> It so happens that Africans were the great civilisations of the past ... If you were to turn around and tell a white man that up to about ad 333 that the man who ruled this country was a negro ... Septimus Severus was then the Emperor of Rome and he was a full blooded African negro. He died in this country in York organising the defences against the Scots when they used to break across and beat the hell out of you cats ... How on earth can you look at people with a background of this nature and cannot really recognise the fact that these people must have had a culture as well?[70]

That question, and the tension of living in a culture of rich history but one which remained ignorant about its past and its legacies, is a persistent presence in Donnellan's film. It is consistent with the New Left's anti-imperialist politics, its empathy for ordinary people and it is powerfully articulated in the sequences shot at Aston Hall that alternately concentrate on the national master narrative offered by the official tour guide and then on some local black children and adults whose history is erased by this rendering of the local and national past. The sequence ends with a voice-over from Mr Brown who says that:

> One doesn't want to put slavery on their mind, but if they read history it is something that they have got to look back onto. What I am proud about my forefathers is that although they have passed through such difficult times, they have not lost the value, the value of human living.[71]

Human beings, or the people, were a theme embodied in a kind of emotional withdrawal from Empire in England in the post-war period. The exigencies of war, the hardships of austerity and the troubled images of Empire in retreat encouraged a turn towards what appeared to be a more gentle, domestic and democratised history with a vision of the people at its heart. But even as this version of national history became more evident, the ghosts of Empire began to haunt. Arriving in the metropolitan centre, their cultures and characters scrutinised and categorised, immigrants had their own stories to tell, and their own studies to undertake.

The ascription of identities by race relations scholars, by the media and by state officials to immigrants became sites of struggle. If the meaning of 'Irish', 'coloured', 'West Indian' and 'black' were initially imposed they were also internalised and reworked in a broadly educational process that saw immigrant and minority groups produce significant numbers of what Stefan Collini's has called sociological and subjective intellectuals.[72] Either professionally (as teachers, writers, researchers, filmmakers or preachers), or as individuals and groups, these people demonstrated an interest in the ideas and the historical processes that explained their experiences of immigration and decolonisation. These ideas and processes were brought into consciousness, were produced, distributed and debated in a variety of mediums and at least some of them would form the basis of political, cultural and educational activity that would have important consequences for social change.

When migrant groups fashioned identities using the past they did so in a manner conditioned by the ways in which they were represented and treated as outsiders. The different communities of Britishness that Kathleen Paul has identified as operating in policymaking circles in the 1940s and 1950s were produced over preceding centuries in which Irish and black immigrants attempted to respond to the prejudice and denigration that accompanied their identification as national others. Their status as outsiders, based on a mixture of religion, skin colour and their assumed race characteristics, encouraged a range of social, cultural and educational activities that consolidated existing historical memories and produced new ones. These memories, the foundation of the ethnic communities constructed towards the end of the century, were, in turn conditioned by patterns of immigration and settlement that went back to the nineteenth century. It is those processes that attention now turns.

The Irish in Britain

Emigration to England during the nineteenth century was dominated by the Irish. In demand because of the Industrial Revolution, geographically close at hand and, after the Act of Union in 1800 formally British subjects, the Irish arrived in increasing numbers to build railways, spin cotton and work the docks. If the Irish are remembered in popular historical memory, it is as Catholic and in an overtly masculine fashion, as the brute strength on which British prosperity was made. The reality, of course, was somewhat more complex. Nineteenth-century migrants from Ireland could be Protestants from the north of Ireland, they could be skilled manual workers or middle class and, by the end of the century, a majority of them were women.[73] Yet, for most of the nineteenth century, the majority of Irish migrants to Britain came from the south and they were poor and Catholic.

The famines in Ireland of 1846 and 1847 fundamentally changed both the character of Irish migration to England and dominated subsequent perceptions and memories of the Irish in Britain.[74] In excess of half a million destitute Irish passed through Liverpool during the peak of famine migration, many en route for North America but large numbers of them remained in England. The 1841 census recorded 289,404 Irish in England, a figure that had increased to 566,540 by 1871 but which also excluded those people born in England to Irish parents who were likely to have regarded themselves as Irish.[75] Famine migrants were especially feared because of their numbers, their obvious poverty, the threat of disease that came from malnutrition and overcrowded housing, and because of their alien customs and religion.[76] National and local responses not only routinely ridiculed and scorned famine migrants for fraudulence, stupidity, heavy-drinking and fighting; they also sometimes drew explicitly on racial discourse and located the Irish within a hierarchy of distinct races.[77] In scholarly texts, official discourse and in popular publications, the Irish were identified as belonging to a Celtic race and were frequently and unfavourably compared to the Anglo-Saxon English.[78] In his influential text published in 1968 L.P. Curtis argued that race ideas were the primary influence on English perceptions of the Irish who were condemned as 'childish, emotionally unstable, ignorant, indolent, superstitious, primitive or semi-civilised, dirty, vengeful and violent'.[79] Moreover, and in an explicitly gendered discourse, the Irish were judged as effeminate, irrational and as having problematically long memories that made them excessively sensitive and given to smouldering over ancient or fancied wrongs.[80]

These race ideas became important to the writing of national history. Across nineteenth-century European societies a racialised concept of national character became a transcendental actor in human affairs. It could be called various things, national character, spirit or culture, but essentialist ideas of nationhood could be found across Europe. If these texts were important in the creation of national identities, they simultaneously helped to identify those who were outsiders, strangers and aliens. J.A. Froude's best-selling twelve-volume *History of England* (1856–1870) is a pertinent case in point.[81] 'An apologia for the developing nation state par excellence', Froude's history identified the Tudor age of discovery, and the Reformation, as the essential basis of the English national character.[82] From Protestantism developed the English genius for liberty, reason and democracy, a genius they were elected by God to impose on inferior and mystical societies. Froude was also an ardent supporter of imperial expansion. He justified English rule in Ireland by identifying the latter with irrationality and femininity, a view that, with some modification, was held by almost all of the first generation of professional historians in Britain.[83] It was the formation of Teutonic Englishness, of a national character determined by race, that was a central feature of national history, Whig or otherwise, and it was one that explained the project of Empire.

Quite how representative Froude's history was, and the extent to which the Irish became racialised, remains a matter of historical debate.[84] Historian Theodore Koditscheck is right to detect a hardening of attitudes on race and a declining belief that cultural difference could be transcended by the development of the British Empire.[85] There is certainly no shortage of evidence attesting to official and popular hostility directed at the Irish in England to confirm this. Yet he also rightly explores Froude's many critics, at least some of whom remained conscious of the legal status as subjects of the Union and whose views may have been affected by the increasing significance given to skin colour as a primary marker of assumed race differences. It may be that the phenotypical and linguistic similarity of the Irish, at least in comparison with other subjects of Empire, helped to prevent the development of more formal or institutionalised forms of discrimination.[86] Indeed, and although the condition and the cultural mores of Irish areas of settlement in England stimulated both concern and condemnation throughout the nineteenth century, environmental explanations for disease, destitution and violence were as common as, and sometimes combined with, racial ones.[87] Among the reasons for this were the complex and tangled relationships between ideas about British and Irish identities that prevented their simple opposition and, more practically, because the sheer scale of Irish migration to England in the nineteenth century, a range of political, cultural and educational activities developed that helped the Irish negotiate distinctive positions in English society that defy simple generalisations. The extent and significance of these activities varied according to local factors and, in particular, the size of towns and their economic and social structures, but they were arguably most significant in Liverpool.

By the middle of the nineteenth century, and in the immediate aftermath of the famine, a vast majority of the Irish in Liverpool were poor and working class, and existed in a geographically and culturally distinct space. The Irish poor were overwhelmingly found in slumdom, around the docks and increasingly in the north end, close to casual labour markets and where the disciplines of factory life were absent. These were vibrant streets, populated by street sellers, ragged children and dotted with 'Irish pubs' that seemed, to official observers at least, to be constantly busy.[88] Some of those observers formed part of a network of welfare and educational services established and delivered by middle-class Irish merchants and the Catholic Church. A similar pattern was apparent in both Birmingham and London.[89] High concentrations of Irish-born migrants and their children meant particular streets and wards would be identified as, and felt, Irish.[90] The residents of these streets helped to stimulate the nineteenth-century Catholic revival in England, providing new parishioners in need not just of spiritual salvation but a range of educational and welfare services. In Birmingham, for example, the arrival of the Irish held to justify the diocesan inauguration of 1850, the building of the first post-reformation Catholic Cathedral (St Chad's) in Britain and the foundation and expansion of a range of educational and welfare services. These services included an orphanage, unambiguously entitled the 'Children of St Patrick', and an impressive expansion of Sunday schools in the period before 1870 and Catholic elementary schools thereafter.

The Catholic Church has often been interpreted as a powerful tool of socialisation in Britain and a method through which an

English Catholic hierarchy imposed a version of faith divorced from
political nationalism.[91] Mary Hickman's has been the most detailed
and influential argument of this kind and it centres on the ways in
which Irish political and nationalist identities were systematically
dismantled by the implementation of Catholic elementary schooling
that had as its principal and deliberate objective the development of
an anglicised Catholicism that simultaneously and explicitly sought
to weaken Irish national identity.[92] Like Hickman, Alexander Peach
has argued that Catholic Sunday schools in Birmingham 'reinforced
identities, stereotypes, prejudices and sectarian schisms' and there
is evidence that they were 'very popular mixing entertainment and
outings, with instruction and invoking strong loyalties'.[93] In fact, the
evidence for schools as factories of identities is heavily dependent on
official records that easily lend themselves to accounts of regulation
and socialisation. In the absence of the voices and reflections of
pupils, that might have provided clues to the internal mental worlds
through which personal and social identities are formed, historians
have recently been investigating informal educational processes.

Two prominent historians of Liverpool have recently argued that,
rather than denying putative Irish identities, the Catholic Church
in Liverpool necessarily 'embraced Irish idioms and personnel in its
philanthropic, associational and pastoral provision'.[94] As evidence
of this, they offer the example of Father Nugent, a local Catholic
chaplain sympathetic to the environmental causes of migrant poverty,
who championed temperance movements, reformatories, industrial
schools and who, through the auspices of his League Hall and
Recreation Company, organised weekly concerts, seasonal galas
and special annual events all designed to appeal to Irish Catholic
tastes. Cultural historians now interpret these kinds of activities
not necessarily as moments of control, but negotiated practices
and performances central to the construction and maintenance of
what are usually identified as ethnic identities. Nugent's theatre
programmes are one good example of this. They combined priestly
exhortation and persuasion with a deliberately populist programme
of music, dance and performance. Attendees were encouraged to take
the temperance pledge but were also offered dancers performing Irish
jigs and musicians specialising in romantic ballads that sentimentally
recalled 'Old Ireland' or 'Poor Old Erin's Isle'.[95]

These ballads were part of a rich tradition of street entertainment
going back to at least the sixteenth century in which narrative

verses were set to music, sung and distributed in the form of printed broadsheets or chapbooks. They were sung in any public space, at markets and fairs, in squares and streets and in public houses and inns. Irish migrants were familiar with the genre. In Ireland, ballads were an important mechanism through which Irish Catholics evoked or constructed images of a happier past before the colonisers arrived. This tradition continued in England; ballads tended to explain the fact of migration, and indeed all of Irish history from the twelfth century onwards, as a direct consequence of the British conquest of Ireland, and of the land confiscations and penal legislation that followed.[96] Particularly in the period before the advent of mass literacy, these ballads were an important mechanism for the production and distribution of a shared historical narrative in which the British, and their Protestantism, appeared as oppressors, and the Irish, and their Catholicism, were downtrodden but heroic resisters who still looked forward to the freedom and independence of 'The Shamrock Green Island'.[97]

Yet the weekly concert programmes did not just look back across the sea to Ireland, or recall real or imagined memories of home. They were not simply about the maintenance of the kind of exclusive Irish identity celebrated in nationalist mythology. This much is clear from John Belchem's important discussion on the popularity of Negro minstrelsy imported from the USA and then adapted and developed to suit local tastes and circumstances. For the Irish, he argues, racist caricatures of black slaves offered in these shows not only established a white Irish ethnic identity, but they could also promote political messages by presenting pious and patriotic pictures, and the arts, pastimes and history of Irish nationality.[98] Similarly, the cultural and educational activities of the nationalist Gaelic League, which had sufficient appeal to have active branches in Liverpool, Birmingham and London throughout the first half of the twentieth century, provided a language of difference for the Irish in England. For the 'exiled kindred' who were 'obliged by stress of circumstances, and entirely against their will', to remain in England among those 'alien to them in race and creed, hostile to their national aspirations, and incapable of entering into their inner thoughts or of sharing their deeper emotions' the League branches organised Gaelic sports programmes, St Patrick's Day celebrations and classes in Irish language and history.[99] The League's attempts to create and sustain 'a link with an illustrious Irish past' have not been well examined.

Such attempts included the celebration of ancient Celtic festivals, the teaching of Celtic sagas and stories and lecture programmes (delivered in English and Irish) on Irish history all of which reflected, historian Tom Garvin has argued, an Irish obsession with the past.[100] It was an obsession not widely shared among the Irish in England and overall League membership remained small. Nonetheless, one attendee at League classes in London, Leytonstone-born John Stephenson, was later to achieve notoriety as the Provisional IRA's chief of staff. Stephenson, better known by his Gaelic name Seán MacStíofáin, remembered a teacher with a 'fondness for tables of grammar that made it all seem stale and dry instead of a living language' and explained his Irishness as a matter of 'blood, descent and deliberate choice'.[101]

Belchem's innovative study of Father Nugent and the activities of the Gaelic League are important because they offered the basic resources for the construction of distinct ethnic identities. As processes of dispersal took place, weakening the close proximity of people in Irish enclaves, these resources became more important, even if the weight of evidence is to suggest a process of 'ethnic fade' and the weakening of identification with Ireland.[102] Alan O'Day's recent work astutely concludes that what he terms mutative ethnicity could persist but that it depended not only on an ability to deliver material rewards (employment, housing and communal sociability) but also on the creation and sustenance of myths and histories about a collective past.[103] The repertoire of popular ballads and stories, the increasing availability of text in a print culture newly accessible to a literate population, and the organisation of formal and informal education all offered potential for constructing personal and social identities in which a sense of Irishness was prominent. Whether that potential was taken up depended on a number of contextual factors; it was certainly not the case that the Irish routinely belonged to a separate ethnic community.[104] However, in the associational cultures built around church, school and pub, and in the cultural and educational activities of the admittedly limited Gaelic revival in England, a pool of historical myths, stories and memories were created, sustained and available for the post-war generation of immigrants to England.

Post-war migration from Ireland brought something new: a generation of migrants who had grown up in the Irish Free State, subjected to nationalist ideology and schooled in a specifically anti-English, curriculum. The consequences of this schooling on the attitudes of the immigrants and their sense of self, and their new status as citizens of an independent Irish Republic after 1948, are difficult to summarise. But increased nationalist sentiment, allied to the geographical proximity of Ireland, and the frequent desire to return 'home' meant that assimilation or integration, the elusive goals of politicians, policymakers and social commentators, would always prove to be elusive for the Irish in Britain. Just as the meaning and significance attached to being Irish in Britain before 1945 had been a matter of reflection, negotiation and activity, so too did post-war migrants construct histories in the fashioning of group identity.[105]

A snapshot of these processes, albeit a highly masculine version, can be glimpsed in the recordings made for Philip Donnellan's 1965 film *The Irishmen*. Employing the same actuality methods as in *The Colony* and displaying the same interest in the lives of immigrants, Donnellan's film consisted of long sections of interview material with Irish labourers working in and around the English Midlands. The film was completed but never screened or made available for sale by the BBC because, argues film historian Lance Pettitt, of acute sensitivities about the direct identification of both class politics and anti-Irish racism in England.[106] But the voices that Donnellan recorded are of interest. These should not necessarily be presented as 'authentic' voices because, as the production notes make clear, Donnellan's interests were an important influence on both the interviews and the resulting film. This is clear from the actuality recordings in which interviewees are expressly asked to recall their knowledge of the English before arrival in Britain, and in the selection of both the accompanying music and the framing historical narrative that underpinned the film. The image of 'England as a place with guns pointing our way' was a recurrent theme among the interviewees, though some expressly denied any knowledge of the English at all prior to arrival, and Donnellan seemingly chose to accentuate an anti-Englishness that certainly existed in Ireland, particularly on the west coast and in the province of Munster.[107]

Anti-English sentiment was both confirmed and partly explained by the selection of music in the film. *Van Diemen's Land* juxtaposed nineteenth-century criminal transportation with a post-war migration motivated, so the song had it, solely by poverty. Ewan McColl's arrangement of the traditional song 'Farewell to Ireland' struck a similarly tragic note and there was no mistaking the cause of the sorrows of the migrants:

Young boys and old men and fathers of children,
In search of employment from Ireland must go;
Abandoned, disinherited, the landless of Ireland,
From Kerry, Cork and Leitrim and County Mayo.[108]

Again, Donnellan's anti-colonialism, as well as his own connections to Ireland through a paternal grandfather, seems to have attracted him to these emotive and ethnic nationalist renditions of migration. The historical notes prepared for the film were taken directly from the English Marxist and critic of imperialism T.A. Jackson's *Ireland Her Own: An Outline History of the Irish Struggle for National Freedom and Independence* (1949).[109] Wildly romantic and fiercely nationalist, extracts from the text were circulated among the production team and provided an explanation of the survival of a Gaelic culture that Donnellan idealised.

But they [hedge-schoolmasters] were sure of a warm welcome at any time in any thatched cabin because they were the last survivors of an integral feature of the old Gaelic social order. Many of them were the actual descendents of the hereditary chroniclers, pedigree keepers, brehons, bards and tellers of legendary tales of one or other of the clans; and it is due to them and those who sheltered them that the living stream of Gaelic culture never wholly failed. With the parish priests, who remained faithful to their vocation in circumstances which make the lot of a missionary to cannibals luxurious by comparison, the hedge-schoolmaster, and the wandering poet or musician kept glowing a spark of Gaelic fire among those humblest tillers of the soil who seemed in English eyes less to be regarded than the beasts of the field.

These tillers, the lowest strata of the conquered Irish – segregated by poverty, by language, by creed, by law and by the supercilious arrogance of the class which, in Grattan's phrase, 'knelt to England on the necks of their countrymen' – these people of the thatched cabins had one inestimably precious compensation. Around their turf fires they could hear retold again and again the legendary stories of the Gaels, and be solaced by poem, song and music preserved from days which far out-dated the oldest of their miseries – far-off days when the sun always shone and the blackbird's whistle never failed in the glen.

It was thus, and in these cabins, that the see was kept alive which in due time would burst forth in the rich profusion of a regenerated Irish Nationality.[110]

Of course, this kind of narrative was not simply a myth. There did remain a Gaelic culture that survived despite the imposition of English schools and the English language in Ireland. Its revival or, more accurately, its imagined reconstruction continued both in England and in Ireland during this period. It was the kind of memory central to de Valera's highly conservative image of Ireland. It was important too, to the rather austere cultural nationalism that continued to be championed in England by the music, language and dance championed by the Comhaltas founded in 1951. It was also central to the Marxist analysis of British imperialism in Ireland that was a defining feature of the Connolly Association whose education clause was committed to 'publishing, distributing or otherwise making known' the 'history of Ireland, the writings of Irish democrats and Republicans and a great storehouse of knowledge' that came from the European Enlightenment.[111] In England, this was a version of history tirelessly championed by Desmond Greaves and others, especially in the newspaper the *Irish Democrat*.[112]

These were historical memories that the left-leaning anti-colonial Phillip Donnellan was keen to read, hear and publicise. They were especially present in the extended testimony given by Jim McHugh in *The Irishmen* and which is used to make two important points. First, and as in *The Colony*, English prejudice against immigrants is explained as originating from a fundamental ignorance about the history and legacies of British imperialism. This was done in terms that were guaranteed to provoke controversy because, as McHugh related it, the average Englishman was 'that thick, which he thinks that he's not, thinks that he's educated, but in my mind he was definitely thick at that time'. Second, this ignorance is then contrasted with McHugh's wisdom, and implicitly that of at least some other migrants, in setting out some of the achievements of famine migrants from Ireland to the USA. 'Coffin ship migrants', McHugh says proudly, were not welcome in the USA but built the Union Pacific railroad. This historical knowledge was 'just what my father taught me, and I have it in a book myself' declares McHugh whose contribution ends with the declaratory and affirmative statement 'Yes, I have the history, and I experienced a good bit, and my father and everyone belongs to me.'[113]

This kind of historical affirmation was, as has already been argued, becoming increasingly common in the period in which 'the people' were to reclaim 'their history'. It marked what is often considered a democratising moment in the long process through which history became a source of authentic identity, individual or collective. If this has previously been a privilege of the European middle class and then colonial empires, history was now also a resource for newly independent nations and their citizens. Yet if this sounded progressive it also identified those who 'did not have the history' as targets for historical education. In a typically auto-didactic fashion McHugh does just this. He is critical of his fellow Irish migrants, who, he told Donnellan, lacked education, were intensely local in the loyalties and motivated, above all, by the attraction of 'big money'.[114]

There was some truth in these claims. Most of these Irish men had left formal education after primary school, usually earlier than girls and between the ages of 12 and 14.[115] Their attachments also certainly remained parochial, as the success of the county associations in the centres of Irish settlement make clear.[116] These associations were built on intensely local identities and acted, as *The Irishmen* shows, as informal employment and welfare agencies. There is also little doubt, and it should be no surprise, that these men were attracted by remuneration that brought them both new levels of wealth, and predictable clerical condemnation for being seduced by English materialism. These are, moreover, factors that certainly shaped how these men understood and articulated the significance of the past.

There is a highly revealing episode in the diary of the much cited auto-didact Donall MacAmhlaigh who recorded in his diaries an exasperation with those who were obsessed with 'Cromwell and history', thinking it 'a bit ridiculous to be putting the blame for the state of Ireland today on whatever happened over 300 years ago'.[117] The number of times that Cromwell, or the revolutionary nationalists, or the Civil War appears in the diary suggests a culture rich in historical analogy, discussion and celebration. Far from being ignorant of their history, the Irish in Britain could not avoid being reminded of it. Reports of prejudice, most frequently in the form of casual name calling and insults, are reported in MacAmhlaigh's diaries, in the actuality recorded for *The Irishmen* and, to a greater or lesser degree, the contemporary sociological and ethnographic studies of immigrants in Britain. These encounters encouraged many migrants, men and women, towards a limited and partial identification with English society. Yet it did not follow that the migrants adopted the kinds of histories and heritage promoted by the Irish state, by various kinds of cultural nationalists or by socialists. Instead, MacAmhlaigh's diary, and other sources of the period, reveals a historical pragmatism, heavily inflected by the continuing significance of the Catholic Church that could simultaneously draw on, remember and enact highly politicised episodes from the past but also refuse their contemporary significance and any political activity that might follow from it.

In October 1965 the *Birmingham Mail* conducted a special investigation into the Irish in the city. In it journalist Martin Davies reported that even if the numbers of Irish migrants were declining from a mid-1950s peak, the Catholic Information Centre in Moat Street still provided an important service for new arrivals. Its housing and welfare work was, the report noted, funded partly by a shop in whose window could be found 'crucifixes and religious statues; songbooks called *The Irish Troubador* and *Erin's Own Songs*; plates bearing pictures of the Kennedys; books about Michael Collins, Roger Casement and *With the IRA in the Fight for Freedom*'.[118]

In some ways the shop told both an old story and a new one. Religious statues and sentimental songs that recalled Old Ireland retained their appeal. Nationalist sentiments now had modern heroes to celebrate, however, and the commemorative Kennedy plates hinted at the importance of a developing sense of an Irish diaspora scattered around the globe. No doubt the Kennedys' dazzling celebrity status partly accounted for this, but it was also an indication of the ways in which migrant populations across the globe were increasingly connected through texts and images that promoted memories of shared origins.[119]

For contemporary policymakers and activists interested in community relations these memories could be a source of some frustration. Molly Barrow's welfare and community-building projects in Birmingham, for example, were clear about the ways in which Catholic schools frustrated the institutional dispersal that, they felt, would have aided assimilation. Their specific concern in the autumn of 1962 was the behaviour of Irish 'tinker children' who migrated and settled in their primary group and, if they went to school at all, attended local Catholic schools and so tended to remain in contact with a selection of children with the same attitudes. According to their discussion group 'This attitude was one of exploitative hostility to England, English people being perceived as here and now directly responsible for the ills that had befallen the Irish for three hundred years. This attitude was strengthened by strong anti-Protestant feelings, which caused them to see the English with whom they came in contact as in any case culpable and inferior.'[120]

In fact, and despite the escalating demand for denominational Catholic schools caused by Irish migration, Catholic schools probably did not contribute significantly to these attitudes. Delaney is broadly accurate when he observes that in these schools teaching about 'faith rather than fatherland predominated, and that communicating the distinctive features of Catholicism was the overriding objective'.[121] 'On the face of it', he summarises, 'English Catholic schools certainly did nothing to encourage the articulation of Irish identities', a role that remained to a considerable degree in the private sphere.[122] Nonetheless, and regardless of the intentions of Catholic schools, the weight of evidence clearly suggests that first, second and even third generation Irish children had no difficulty in combining strong religious and nationalist sentiment.

Allegiance to a specifically Catholic Ireland developed partly out of the experience of migration but was one that was supported by an infrastructure of parishes, social clubs, county associations and cultural organisations that often stretched back to the middle of the nineteenth century. In some of these places historical memories, of the English invasion of Ireland and of cultural domination and resistance, were made, solidified and shared. It was precisely this background, argued John Archer Jackson in a perceptive study of 1963, that made 'the Irish a distinctive population in British society and it remains to dominate their memory and imagination, as well as to leave them and often their children disorientated and uncertain in their relationship to the society in which they live – in it but not of it'.[123] Similar judgements were made, of course, about West Indian migrants and, argue Dabydeen and Wilson-Tagoe, these feelings served to shatter the 'illusion of belonging' to England, of being able to participate in its 'romantic and fabulous history' and they prompted a re-examination of the past.[124] Yet, and as for the Irish, reviewing the past to make sense of the present was a tentative activity and one often undertaken within a framework of religious faith.

The emergence of black community

It was commonplace in England in the 1950s and 1960s to assume that 'coloured immigration' was a new and disturbing phenomenon. A trickle of immigrants, a term increasingly reserved for migrants of colour, had turned into a flood, threatening the character of England and placing a strain on the national tradition of tolerance.[125] If such claims were born of ignorance, they were widely shared. Even race relations scholars tended to date the arrival of black people in Britain to the sixteenth and seventeenth centuries and to the growth and development of transatlantic slavery. In fact and as the struggles of black migrants for a past would show, there had been a black presence in Britain since Roman times. Numerically small, and overwhelmingly located in seaport cities, in Liverpool, Bristol, Cardiff and London, black people were often sojourners rather than permanent settlers. Although the experiences of black people in England were varied, all were affected by the rise of the transatlantic trade in enslaved Africans.[126] For while transatlantic slavery was not accompanied by a widely shared and systematic racist ideology, ideas about the biological inferiority of black people were widespread and, as historian David Eltis has influentially argued, 'enslavement remained a fate for which only non-Europeans were qualified'.[127]

Transatlantic slavery may not have produced a single or coherent racist ideology or discourse but, especially by the end of the nineteenth century, race ideas saturated both elite and popular culture in England. Their very inconsistency and imprecision made them more useful in populist explanations of the rise of the British Empire. Froude's national history writing was not alone in allocating race a central role for British (or Anglo-Saxon) global dominance but scholars continue to debate what the sometimes vicious references to race actually meant. What can be said with some certainty is that visions of a race hierarchy frequently condemned black people in the West Indies for their supposed indolence, stupidity and childishness. These kinds of ideas were central to an increasingly centralised vision of a national people, united by their race characteristics and their historical experiences, and so part of the repertoire of cultural resources that were available to discuss and understand the presence and position of black people in England.[128]

All this helps to explain how, despite relatively small numbers and probably not exceeding 20,000 in total, black people living in Britain in the inter-war period stimulated such hostility, both popular and official, to their presence.[129] Reactions to black seamen, usually British subjects but routinely labelled 'alien', provide evidence of some of the most virulent responses. The seamen, who made up the majority of Britain's black working class before the Second World War, worked long hours in difficult and dangerous conditions. They were popular because they were cheap and had a reputation for political docility brought about by their exclusion from formal trade union representation.[130]

Despite the racism evident in such responses, the employment prospects of black seamen and dock workers improved during the First World War. With white British workers conscripted or involved in essential war work, a shortage of labour was created and was filled with the further immigration of black workers. Some black seamen left work on ships to settle on land not only around the docks, but in munitions factories in the North and in the Midlands. In doing so they often worked alongside women and, in some cases, developed relationships that, although the catalyst for sporadic violence, brought a sense of permanence to their presence.[131] Increased numbers of black subjects in Britain may have been tolerated because of war conditions, but peace brought economic downturn and growing resentment at the presence of aliens who, it was protested, took both local jobs and local women. Yet, while there were specific local circumstances to these protests, there was a common pattern across ports around Britain and, to some extent at least, across the British Empire.[132] In each case white crowds, usually numbering hundreds but sometimes counted in thousands, in which unskilled men were predominant, attacked black workers, their families and their homes. Houses and businesses were destroyed, physical assault was commonplace and there were murders. Moreover, recent research has made clear the extent of discrimination against the black victims of the violence. They formed a disproportionate number of those arrested in the violence and even if only half of those charged with offences were convicted, both the police and the courts clearly discriminated against black people.

Official responses to the violence and to the alien question in inter-war Britain more generally, attest to the beginning of a profound and important shift in the idea of Britain. Even though racialised thought became increasingly important to ideas of Britishness at the 1914 height of imperial power, it was also the subject of important claims from imperial dominions. The idea of Great Britain as a global community, of people united by a set of political values and bound together by settler and imperial networks, had considerable political and emotional currency.[133] But the seaport riots of 1919 symbolised the decline and dismantling of the idea of Great Britain as a global community of English-speaking peoples committed to equality. Indeed the inter-war period witnessed a programme of

Empire strengthening encompassing both political lobbying and cultural and educational projects; in the work of the Round Table Group, the Rhodes Trust, in school curricula, Imperial Exhibitions and a whole range of images promoted through film and radio.[134] Despite the liberal rhetoric of inter-war imperialism, of 'trusteeship', 'Commonwealth' and 'self-determination' for the colonies, these projects were underpinned by ideas of racial inequality, by a view of black people as 'primitive' and 'backward' in comparison with a cultured and civilised Anglo-Saxonism whose responsibility it was to educate and uplift the colonies.

The growing number of black migrants in Britain, and the intensification of both official and popular racism in the aftermath of the First World War and the 1919 riots, proved an important stimulus in the formation of local black communities in Britain. Until that point the relatively small, geographically and culturally disparate black presence could not be considered a distinctive or cohesive community. Localised community organisations did, of course, develop. Most towns and cities with a sizeable black presence had developed some organisations but their philosophy and purposes differed widely.[135] A black intelligentsia, for example, comprising mostly students studying in the imperial centre, were beginning to establish and promote pan-Africanism. Barbadian teacher, lawyer and political activist Henry Sylvester Williams's *African Association* (1897) sought to 'promote and protect the interests of all subjects claiming African descent, wholly or in part, in British colonies'. Williams, and this diasporic vision of a global people united by a point of origin, organised the first Pan-African Conference which was held in London in 1900. A diverse and international range of speakers explored various aspects of race ideas and practice in the modern world and there was a noticeable historical flavour to the proceedings which discussed, among other matters, the legacies of slavery, European imperialism and the role of Africa in world history.[136] Similarly, the tentative emergence of a critical black press of more than a dozen publications in the first decade of the twentieth century was, despite tiny circulations, critical in the construction and distribution of a shared black history. Marcus Garvey's 1913 historical essay, 'The British West Indies in the Mirror of Civilisation', might have been optimistic in predicting that the 'people of the West Indies will be the instruments of uniting a scattered race', but favourable transatlantic responses suggested that the attempt to imagine diaspora in a historical perspective was a reading of history with at least some appeal.[137]

Nonetheless, that appeal remained rather minimal. Black organisations were limited in number and, for the most part, divisions of class, gender and geography were far more significant than shared origins in Africa.[138] The 1919 riots signalled an early turning point. In confirming that black people in the United Kingdom were legitimate targets for popular violence and state discrimination, they provided a further stimulus in the development of political, welfare, cultural and educational organisations specifically for black people. These organisations were often founded by black students or professionals, were small and were often short lived. Examples of these groups are the London based African Progress Union, established by Liverpool-born John Archer who became England's first black mayor, the largely student Society of Peoples of African Origin who also produced a newspaper entitled the *African Telegraph*; the International African Service Bureau (IASB) founded by George Padmore and responsible for several publications; and, in Liverpool, an African Churches Mission.[139] Obviously these organisations were diverse. Some provided welfare services only, while others were bodies with political aims. Some focused on the fight against imperialism in international politics. Others campaigned against domestic prejudice and segregation based on race ideas, the so-called colour bar. Some were secular, others were religious. Some were explicitly black organisations but a number of others welcomed mixed black and white membership. Yet, whatever the differences in their establishment, aims and functions, all of them signalled the emergence of a black community that was constituted by something other than proximity and a shared experience of racism and discrimination. A crucial part of that 'something other' was the exploration of history and a reimagining of the past. It involved a new appropriation of the past and new claims on historical heritage. Eventually it would facilitate the ability to imagine others, not directly known and geographically distant, as belonging to a group who were united by a particular relationship to slavery and colonialism. But that history was not yet constructed and not yet widely known or discussed. It certainly was not regarded as the foundational historical experience for black people in Britain.

David Killingray's important study of Harold Moody, founder of the liberal, Christian and mixed membership League of Coloured

Peoples (LCP) in 1931, provides an instructive example of what happened in this turn to the past. Moody's schooling in Jamaica was typical of an imperial education which encouraged identification with the mother country. On his arrival in England in 1904, as a medical student, he sought to assimilate, to become English by denying and discarding everything Jamaican. Killingray quotes from a reflection written towards the end of his life:

> I had been educated away from my heritage and towards the country which I had learnt to call home. My desire then was to have as little as possible to do with my own people and upon Africans I looked down as a species too low in the rank of human development for me in away to associate with. I was black indeed but I was not African, nor was I in any way related to Africa. To what family of man I belonged I really did not know. At heart I really believed I was English.[140]

As for so many others, and especially from the Caribbean, that belief did not survive Moody's experience of British racism. Moody read widely, 'on theology, history, contemporary politics and economics' and, says Killingray, his 'intellectual capacities enabled him to set the racial problems he encountered in their historical context'. It is no surprise then, that *The Keys*, the LCP journal founded in 1933, regularly published articles on African and British imperial history that simultaneously encourage readers to embrace a shared point of origin and to emancipate themselves from the slave mentality that was a result of imperialism.[141]

If the LCP was a liberal grouping with a gradualist philosophy, there also existed a much more radical, somewhat looser, but also celebrated group of Pan-Africanists. The group was small in number, dominated by the Trinidadians George Padmore and C.L.R. James, and based in London during its golden period of publication in the years 1936–1938. In their journalism and pamphleteering, in global correspondence with Pan-African activists, as well as in their public speaking, these black radical writers, and the group that gathered around them, challenged a dominant view of a benevolent British imperialism. Carol Polsgrove's careful and incisive study *Writers in a Common Cause* persuasively argues that 'in the communal act of writing and publishing, they created an "imagined community" – an Africa free of imperial rule'.[142] More or less implicit in this argument is that it was history, and historical research, that would provide much of the material for this new community.

This history could be produced as formal historical study, as with James's *Black Jacobins*, a text that clearly articulated a changing relationship to the past. A history of the Haitian revolution in the 1790s, it set out, with all the 'fever and fret' of the period, 'the transformation of slaves, trembling in hundreds before a single white man, into a people able to organise themselves and defeat the most powerful European nations of their day'.[143] The originality of the argument was precisely in seeing the agency of slaves. It was, for the political activist, also an argument with an irresistible contemporary relevance. Written against the background of the Italian invasion of Abyssinia, James wrote that those who struggled against imperialism in Africa were 'more advanced, nearer ready than were the slaves of San Domingo ... The African faces a long and difficult road and he will need guidance. But he will tread it fast because he will walk upright.'[144] Its purpose, James later reflected, was to demonstrate that 'we had a history and in that history there were men who were fully able to stand comparison with great men of that period ... I was trying to make clear that black people had a certain historical past'.[145] This was, in other words, a history of heroes 'sweeping, impassioned and powerful' designed to guide and inspire contemporary actions.[146] Its power derived from a narrative that, as historian and philosopher Jörn Rusen has argued, functions to transform an inert past into an active history, part of the internalised mental furniture of individuals, by combining experience and expectation.[147] James's history was Marxist and heavily didactic but its appeal lay in its identification of a diasporic consciousness that centred on dispersal from an African homeland, violent oppression and resistance to continued marginalisation.[148]

Despite these important developments, the relatively limited appeal of Pan-Africanism, and the absence of successful cross-class black community organisations until the post-war period more generally, demonstrates just how far there was to travel in the creation of a black community with shared values and a distinctive identity. Even in the geographically distinct area of Bute Town in Cardiff, the resident black community shared no distinctive sense of black consciousness, leading Moody to complain about a lack of 'pride in race' and the contentment with being considered English.[149] Similarly, Michael Banton's research into race relations in Stepney in the early 1950s found 'tribal associations' of Kru, Mende and Yoruba but none for West Indians.[150] In fact, the absence of formal and sustained community organisations is suggestive both of the continued appeal of an inclusive notion of Britishness that was not defined by skin colour and the related absence of a shared black migrant consciousness before the post-1945 period. The notable exceptions that have already been discussed were important precisely because they were often the forum in which the imaginative acts necessary to create and sustain a sense of shared identity among a diverse black presence in Britain began to happen. It is in this work that scholar activists began to research, write and publicise a shared historical narrative, a black history, initially focused largely on Africa, which was slowly to become more widely available and more meaningful over the next four decades.[151]

But this is to anticipate. In the 1940s the participation of black men and women in the Second World War clearly demonstrated the continuing attachments to British citizenship and identity among people of colour.[152] Volunteers demonstrated their patriotism by sailing to Britain to work in the armed forces or as civilians in the workforce. Yet, and just as happened in the First World War, their experiences served to correct any naive ideas about a mother country of milk and honey and revealed complex experiences shaped by prejudice and discrimination.[153] Despite an official welcoming of the volunteers, and rhetoric of tolerance and equality, the British state continued to be guided by a belief in race ideas in which black was equated with dangerous difference. They sought to limit the arrival of black workers and military volunteers and seriously considered an anti-'miscegenation' law that would have outlawed sexual relationships between black men and white women.[154] Despite an insistence to the contrary, it was also clear that an informal colour bar was widely in place for black British citizens. Encouraged by the presence of a segregationist US army, race bans from dance halls, cinemas and hotels were commonplace.

The LCP continued to campaign against this discrimination but, by 1945 and the fifth Pan-African Congress held in Manchester, a new politics, based on different mobilisations of the past was emerging. Although attended by fewer than 200 delegates it was both practically and symbolically important. Practically, it brought together working-class and bourgeois intellectual blacks from around Britain; US pan-Africanists (like W.E.B. Du Bois), trade unionists and an assortment of various other political activists. In doing so it aided the development of information, networks and political strategies in Britain, the USA, and in parts of Africa and the Caribbean. Symbolically, the Congress seems to indicate the growing appeal of a black political consciousness that demanded both independence in the colonies and recognition of, and redress for, colour prejudice in Britain.

Part of the reason for the growing appeal of a distinctively black consciousness was the changing scale and pace of black immigration to Britain. Whereas West Indian migration to Britain in the period 1800–1945 probably totalled around 10,000, the docking of SS *Windrush* in Tilbury, Essex in June 1948 symbolised the start of a process in which approximately 400,000 West Indians would eventually arrive in Britain.[155] Responses to West Indian and African arrivals stimulated, at both official and popular levels, a re-examination of the migrants' loyalty to Britain and the imagined past on which it was based. Wallace Collins was probably typical in this respect. Though for the first time he felt 'a part of history' in Britain, with all of the images of his colonial education now before him, the feeling did not persist. Instead, and finding it necessary to work within the confines of popular stereotypes, he performed as a 'black senseless robot, an illiterate migrant from the land of banana and sugar cane'.[156] But such denial demanded resolute personal discipline and it extracted a heavy psychological price. Once the racism of British society was more widely experienced, then alternative strategies for countering racism and becoming black became more evident.

The year 1958 may have been something of a turning point for post-war migrants in this respect. Attacks on black people in Wolverhampton, Nottingham but, especially during the sustained violence perpetrated against West Indians in Notting Hill in London in August and September, made the idea of Mother Britain seem like 'a cruel joke'. Mobs, armed variously with sticks, stones, milk bottles, iron railings and knives, attacked black people and their property and Oswald Moseley's Union of Fascists attempted to harness the racist energies that motivated what were frankly expressed as 'nigger hunts'.[157] While there was no shortage of condemnation of the nine white youths jailed for leading the violence, neither was there much attempt to deviate from the popular idea that the riots had somehow been caused by the presence of excessive numbers of West Indian immigrants in Britain. Justice Salmon could condemn the 'dark thoughts' and brutal feelings' that led to savage acts, but, as Edward

Pilkington has argued, the only substantive official response was to intensify efforts to restrict black immigration to Britain which led to the 1962 Commonwealth Immigration Act.[158] Writing thirteen years after the riots, the journalist Dilip Hiro, like many commentators both at the time and later, saw 'an age of innocence' coming to a 'dramatic end'. 'West Indians were made to realise', he wrote, 'that they were not "overseas British" now living in Britain, but were black men and women living in a white society'.[159]

The realisation prompted the foundation of several important nascent black community political and cultural organisations. All reflected an immediate desire for self-defence but the United Africa–Asia League, the Coloured People's Progressive Association and the Association for the Advancement of Coloured People also expressed a growing philosophy of self-help informed by particular historical memories. Practical services, providing accommodation and employment information for example, were prominent in these organisations but so too was the desire to assert the presence and the identity of migrant communities. Perhaps this was best expressed by the foundation in March 1958 of the *West Indian Gazette and Afro-Asian Caribbean News* by the Trinidadian communist Claudia Jones.

In Benedict Anderson's influential formulation, newspapers, and print culture more generally, were crucial elements in the acts of imagination that made national communities possible. Newspapers helped geographically distant individuals imagine themselves a part of a community, sharing the same experiences and the same information and existing in, and through, simultaneous time. In their reporting and commentary newspapers selected and inscribed events, locations and people as having significance for the imagined nation. An analogous argument can be made for the building of diasporic consciousness. The *Gazette* may have been a radical political intervention but in its detailed coverage from Jamaica (especially the Jamaican independence movement), from the wider West Indies (especially sportsmen), from Britain (particularly against the passage of the Commonwealth Immigration Bill) and, lastly, from the USA (protests against Jim Crow), it began to flesh out a diaspora space. What united these spaces was, of course, their population by people with shared origins in Africa.

Readers of the *Gazette* were regularly reminded of a heritage of forced removal from Africa, enslavement and subsequent freedom struggles. It was this history that was the basis of their common identity and it informed both the routine reporting of contemporary events and the particular sections of the paper dedicated to history. Thus, when in 1961 Sir Grantly Adams, Prime Minister of the West Indies Federation, offered the discovery of the West Indies by Columbus, the abolition of slavery and the visit of Harold Macmillan as the three most important events in the history of the islands, it brought an extended rebuke in an editorial that offered a revolutionary narrative including the heroic Maroons, the Caribs and the upsurge of the 1930s. The *Gazette's* 'Know Your History' column repeatedly offered episodes from this revolutionary narrative as the basis of a critical historical consciousness and its output was characterized by the space it gave to historical study. Projects and institutes for historical research in Africa, established by the Soviet Union and the United Nations, were greeted with enthusiasm; Peter Blackman's articles on African Links were necessary because of the 'myths which have gone to shape the minds of men and women of this generation'; and developments in history teaching at the University of West Indies were an opportunity to remind readers that 'a man who does not know his origins or his background and who does not recognise his loyalties wonders secretly who he is and is constantly anxious about his associations until he feels to his cost that a part of his unique identity is missing'.[160] This was an attempt to restore immigrants from the Caribbean to history, to claim ownership of a history that was hidden and occluded but also open for reclamation and recovery. This is why, as Bill Schwarz has argued, that the *Gazette* represented not only a new kind of politics in Britain based on the recognition of oppression on the grounds of race ideas, it also marked a moment 'in which the diasporic or black Atlantic dimensions of being a West Indian registered as a critical resource from which Britain and its civilisation might be understood'.[161]

The year 1958 was also significant thousands of miles away in Accra, in newly independent Ghana. There, Prime Minister Kwame Nkrumah called an All-African People's Congress, inviting an assortment of political parties, trade unions and student groups, to discuss methods for achieving the African non-violent revolution. One delegate, Frantz Fanon, urged the conference to dispose of a non-violent stance but at the same time was already beginning to argue against notions of negritude and against a metaphysical blackness supported by myths of a pre-colonial African idyll unspoilt by colonialism. However, cultural nationalism, with ethnicised histories, songs and symbols, would prove difficult to resist, with devastating consequences in Africa.[162] For black immigrants in England, the sense of historical identity that Ghanaian independence seemed to offer, divorced from colonialism, stressing African agency and consisting of an open acknowledgment of slavery, was understandably powerful. Ending the conference proceedings, the Kenyan trade unionist and conference chair Tom Mboya spoke to this sense of a new historical epoch dawning when he declared that the colonial scramble for Africa had to reverse; 'your time is past' he told them.[163]

Time was also on the mind of a young Walter Rodney in 1958. The winner of a secondary school scholarship offered to celebrate the coronation of Queen Elizabeth II five years earlier, Rodney was coming towards the end of his time at the elite Queen's College in Georgetown, Guyana. This was evidently still a distinctively colonial education because his ten passes in the general certificate of education were in subjects and papers set in London. Yet, just as in London and in Accra, the sense of a new historical epoch was already taking shape in Rodney's mind. Introduced to a new generation of West Indian historians, Eric Williams and Elsa Goveia among them, Rodney excelled in his historical studies and, by the time he graduated from the newly established University of West Indies in 1963, he had already started to study contemporary economic and political difficulties in a distinctively historical fashion. Rodney felt, but in the mid 1960s could not yet articulate, the significance of Africa for understanding the Caribbean. This accurately mirrored the situation in the Caribbean where Africa was known as an ancestral home for large sections of the population but which escaped any factual attention in the educational system and, says historian Rupert Charles Lewis, was defined by images of barbarity. It was precisely because of this ignorance, and the images of inferiority and shame associated with Africa, that the West Indies needed a new history. A 'presentation of new heroes with whom the West Indian people would identify themselves' was, argued Rodney, 'an important psychological necessity'.[164]

That necessity would bring Rodney to the University of London and the School of Oriental and African Studies in 1963 where he was an important early influence on the emergence of post-colonial African history. This was, however, a transatlantic crossing significant beyond academic historiography. Rodney was certainly an intellectual and a scholar, but he was also a political activist committed to the elaboration and popularisation of the historical narratives he thought central to the future development of the West Indies. The elaboration came from his academic studies but also, and crucially, from his participation in a study group organised in London by Richard Small and Norman Girvan and in which C.L.R. James was a vital influence. These study groups were well established in transatlantic Marxist and Pan-African circles.[165] They typically consisted of a group reading of some selected, and usually, established texts deemed important for the purposes of contemporary consciousness and activism. The more sterile versions of these groups might only confirm the existence of some prescribed theory or narrative, as in the determination to find in pre-colonial Africa those standards of Marxist analysis, feudalism or primitive communism. Sometimes, however, they could produce important new work. In their reading and their discussion, they identified gaps in their knowledge and, in so far as they could do so, began research to address those gaps and to produce papers, often handwritten but also mimeographed, for debate. There was a distinctive pedagogical approach that owed much to the idea of the 'present as history'.[166] In the middle of the 1960s, working on his Ph.D., Rodney was also speaking at Hyde Park corner where he found 'quite a number of West Indians ... who were under pressure and they wanted to find ways of talking and dealing with their exploitation and with racism'.[167]

Rodney's brand of secular history, heavily inflected by Marxism, offered one method of dealing with the challenges of migration and racism. But, in the mid 1960s at least, it was certainly not the only method and certainly not the most popular. Despite the marked decline in church allegiance and participation that accompanied arrival in Britain, for roughly one in five of those who attended church regularly, religious belief and communal prayer initially offered the most meaningful response to experiences in England. Yet it was a distinctive form of syncretised Christianity, a set of beliefs and practices that synthesised European and African traditions, that attracted Caribbean migrants and which lay behind the 'foundation, growth and development of Black-led Churches' a phenomenon historian Gerald Parsons is surely right to regard as 'one of the most striking developments in the religious life of post-war Britain'.[168]

The success of black-led churches has been partly explained in terms of their distinctive, expressive and communal form of worship, and in terms of its attraction as a space free from racism.[169] Yet it is also significant that syncretic Christianity had a historical component that had helped to construct a memory or image of Africa.[170] In the writings of theologians Edward Wilmot Blyde and Alexander Crummell, as well as in the influential synthesis offered by Marcus Garvey, syncretic Christianity drew on and reflected various romantic constructions of black and African history.[171] Moreover, Pentecostal Churches routinely combined a belief in the Second Coming with what the theologian Robert Beckford calls a subliminal affirmation of black history.[172] The recounting of the congregational story, of the establishing and development of church, was itself an important part of the development of black history in Britain. It located the congregation within a local landscape, explained their arrival and affirmed the agency of black immigrants in Britain. As churches were built and congregations developed it became possible to represent a black history of achievement by both men and women; of monies raised, missions carried out and Sunday schools staffed.

Early ethnographic studies of black Pentecostal churches tended to portray them in both exotic and problematic terms. Malcolm Calley's 1965 book argued that Pentecostals were 'a stumbling block to the assimilation of Britain's West Indian minority, providing as they do a magico-religious refuge from the stresses and strains of settling down in a new country'.[173] This refuge was presented as a problem precisely because, convinced of the Second Coming, members showed no interest in the past or the present; they lived only for today. Calley repeatedly refers to members who 'are totally lacking in historical time-sense', 'lack appreciation of historical time-depth' and whose 'belief in the imminent dissolution of the world is also a specific sanction for lack of interest in the past and the future'.[174] It is true, of course, that worshippers tended to relate their histories to a divine purpose; to God's plan for his people on earth that was set out in the Bible. While it may not be possible to identify this kind of ordained agency as historical consciousness, its reading of scripture still worked against prevailing historical narratives.

Through both prayer and Bible study worshippers sought new understandings of Scripture based on Afro-Caribbean history and experience. As has already been argued, key features of those experiences were prejudice, intolerance and racism in the streets of metropolitan England. Despite their formal status as British subjects and their emotional allegiance to an inclusive British identity, black immigrants were widely rejected as alien foreigners, as outsiders who threatened an exclusive national culture. This could not fail to prompt questions about identity and belonging. The past and history had particular resonance in the search for answers and it informed every aspect of the Caribbean imagination.[175]

Conclusion

In April 1968 Enoch Powell delivered his infamous 'Rivers of Blood' speech in Birmingham. In it, and in later similar arguments, Powell set out a history whose purpose was to present a coherent British identity in a period of profound transformation. The speech spoke powerfully to a feeling of national decline prompted by the end of Empire, the loss of political influence, the emergence of newly assertive youth culture and what, in hindsight, appear to be the early signs that the 'Golden Age' of full employment and rising incomes was coming to an end.[176] What remained was the past. Among all the contemporary angst and anxiety, history was increasingly valorised in popular patriotism because it, rather imperial possession or global influence, explained the uniqueness of being British. The thousand years of British history invoked by Powell was a precious possession of white England.[177] It was the basis of nationhood, the source of British identity and only those who viscerally felt this history, who shared its experiences, lived its culture, spoke its language and practised its religion, could really belong to Britain.[178] It was this past and this historical identity that Powell wanted to protect. It is also clear that significant sections of the population agreed with him; his elaboration of national identity felt right because it drew on a series of myths, feelings and attitudes that had been pervasive in national culture for decades. After all, stories of British exceptionalism that drew on the ideas of race, nation and empire had been central to school history (and other subjects), had been endlessly championed in the fight against Nazism, and had remained present in a post-war settlement committed to the promotion of a common historical imagination.[179]

In Liverpool there was a very specific and local rendition of the national master narrative. As a maritime and trading city, Liverpool had a long history of migration and it had intimate connections with the two historical episodes that were to become so important to modern migration memory: the Great Famine in Ireland and both plantation and domestic slavery. The growth of Liverpool's nineteenth-century Irish community, and its impressive array of religious, cultural and educational facilities, left an important legacy, even as the scale and pace of migration slowed from the inter-war years and slum clearances ended the residential segregation of city's 'green half'. As John Belchem has shown, the emergence of the hyphenated Liverpool-Irish identity that was increasingly articulated and celebrated in local heritage made the Irish an important element in the city's official history and its popular memory.[180] The same was not true for Liverpool's black community. Unlike both Birmingham and London, the majority of the city's black community were long-time resident, especially in Liverpool's notorious Toxteth area, where pockets of severe deprivation tended to be overlooked by official concentration on the problems allegedly posed by the psychology and behaviour of mixed-race Liverpudlians. Yet these connections, and their legacies, were widely denied in Liverpool. Indeed, an official history of the city published in 1957 could speak on the civilising benefits of slavery on those who were owned and disciplined by slave masters.[181] It was said repeatedly that Liverpool had a proud history of welcoming strangers and that, even if there were sometimes problems, these were always temporary.

The same boast, and its echoes of the dominant national narrative, could be heard in both Birmingham and London in the 1950s and 1960s. But even though responses to immigrants were mixed and defy easy generalisation, and included positive and indifferent reactions, in both those cities both Irish and New Commonwealth immigrants and their children experienced prejudice and discrimination. Ignoring earlier histories of settlement, and of the global attachments to the British Empire, these migrant groups were understood as a threat to the imagined unity of an England that, in the slow withdrawal from Empire, was beginning to articulate its own, specifically domestic, identity.

This imagined past of the nation presented both a challenge and an opportunity to migrant groups in England. Located outside of English history and misrecognised as alien, among the many challenges facing migrants was how to settle down and adapt to life in Britain. One common strategy in coping with the sense of physical and cultural dislocation from home was to turn to the past and to embrace what was increasingly described as 'their own culture, community, [and] a sense of belonging'.[182] The strategy was not new, of course. Generations of Irish and black migrants had engaged in similar processes in the nineteenth century and their legacy was a set of fragile resources, of institutions, movements, newspapers and oral traditions, that provided the basis of new social identities. For migrants, and especially their children, these resources were especially precious. The act of migration necessarily weakened the power of social continuity and conformity because migrants were confronted with new customs, strange traditions and unsettling experiences. This chapter has shown how some immigrants were already used to thinking about themselves, their place in England and their relationship to histories of empire, migration and diaspora. Yet, and as the next chapter demonstrates, as decolonisation progressed, as immigration became increasingly politicised and as the children of migrants became increasingly confident and assertive, new social movements were enabled to think globally by technological advances, the depth and significance of those historical reflections intensified.

Notes

1 Cited in David Kynaston, *Family Britain, 1951–57* (London: Bloomsbury, 2010), p. 8.
2 Becky E. Conekin, *The Autobiography of a Nation: The 1951 Festival of Britain* (Manchester: Manchester University Press, 2003), p. 193.
3 Cited in Kynaston, *Family Britain*, p. 7.
4 Conekin, *Autobiography of a Nation*, p. 193.
5 The historian Kenneth O. Morgan, a youthful visitor, confirms this impression in K.O. Morgan, 'The British Identity, 1851–2008', *British Scholar*, 1:1 (2008), 5–6; Jed Esty, *A Shrinking Island: Modernism and National Culture in England* (Princeton, NJ: Princeton University Press, 2003).
6 George Orwell, 'The Lion and the Unicorn: Socialism and the English Genius', in Sonia Orwell and Ian Angus (eds), *The Collected Essays, Journalism and Letters of George Orwell Volume II* (Harmondsworth: Penguin, 1970), p. 76.
7 John Kenyon, *The History Men: The Historical Profession in England Since the Renaissance* (London: Weidenfeld & Nicolson, 1983), p. 234.
8 Miles Taylor, 'The Beginnings of Modern British Social History?', *History Workshop Journal*, 43 (1997), 159; A.J.P. Taylor, *English History 1914–1945* (Oxford: Oxford University Press, 1965); Stefan Collini, *Absent Minds: Intellectuals in Britain* (Oxford: Oxford University Press, 2006), pp. 383–384. For the continuing influence of 'whiggism', see Michael Bentley, *Modernising England's Past: English*

Historiography in the Age of Modernism, 1870–1970 (Cambridge: Cambridge University Press, 2005).

9 Jim Obelkevich, 'New developments in history in the 1950s and 1960s', *Contemporary British History*, 14:4 (2000), 137.

10 Gita Deneckere and Thomas Welskopp, 'The "nation" and "class": European national master-narratives and their social "other"', in Berger and Lorenz (eds), *Contested Nation*, pp. 141–142; John Burrow, *A Liberal Descent: Victorian Historians and the English Past* (Cambridge: Cambridge University Press, 1983).

11 Phillip Leacock, *Festival in London* (1951); Humphrey Jennings, *Family Portrait* (1950). For analysis, see Conekin, *Autobiography of a Nation*, ch. 5; and Phillip C. Logan, *Humphrey Jennings and British Documentary Film: A Re-Assessment* (Farnham: Ashgate, 2011), pp. 321–335.

12 Carolyn Steedman, 'State sponsored autobiography', in Conekin, Mort and Waters (eds), *Moments of Modernity*; Paul Long, *The Aesthetics of Class in Postwar Britain* (Newcastle: Cambridge Scholars Publishing, 2008).

13 Deneckere and Welskopp, 'The "nation" and "class"', pp. 163–164; Collini, *Absent Minds*, p. 181.

14 Taylor, 'Beginnings of modern British social history', p. 169.

15 E.P. Thompson, 'The Peculiarities of the English', in E.P. Thompson, *The Poverty of Theory and Other Essays* (London: Merlin Press, 1978); Patrick Joyce, 'More secondary modern than postmodern', *Rethinking History*, 5:3 (2001), 367–382.

16 Bill Schwarz, 'Introduction: the expansion and contraction of England', in Bill Schwarz (ed.), *The Expansion of England: Race, Ethnicity and Cultural History* (London: Routledge, 1996), pp. 44–46.

17 Paul B. Rich, *Race and Empire in British Politics* (Cambridge: Cambridge University Press, 1986), p. 1.

18 Webster, *Englishness and Empire*, p. 8.

19 Faulkner and Ramamurthy, *Visual Culture and Decolonisation*; Emily Lowrance-Floyd, 'Losing an empire, losing a role? The Commonwealth vision, British identity and African decolonization, 1959–1963' (Ph.D. dissertation, University of Kansas, 2012), ch. 2.

20 Phillip Woods, 'Newsreel coverage of Indian independence and partition', in Chandrika Kaul (ed.), *Media and the British Empire* (Basingstoke: Palgrave, 2006); Catherine Hall and Sonya O. Rose, 'Introduction: being at home with the empire', in Catherine. Hall and Sonya O. Rose (eds), *At Home with the Empire: Metropolitan Culture and the Imperial World* (Cambridge: Cambridge University Press, 2006); Caroline Elkins, *Britain's Gulag: The Brutal End of Empire in Kenya* (London: Jonathan Cape, 2005), pp. 307–309.

21 For an overview of these issues and a discussion of associated controversies, see Donald M. MacRaild (ed.), *The Great Famine and Beyond: Irish Migrants in Britain in the Nineteenth and Twentieth Centuries* (Dublin: Irish Academic Press, 2000); Roger Swift, 'Identifying the Irish in Victorian Britain: recent trends in historiography', *Immigrants and Minorities*, 27:2–3 (2009), 134–151. On the Irish as internal others, see Laura Tabili, 'A homogeneous society? Britain's internal "others": 1800–present', in Hall and Rose (eds), *At Home with the Empire*. See also Keith Robbins 'Ethnicity, religion, class and gender and the 'Island story/ies: Great Britain and Ireland', in Berger and Lorenz (eds), *The Contested Nation*; Duncan Bell, *The Idea of Greater Britain: Empire and the Future of World Order, 1860–1900* (Princeton, NJ: Princeton University Press, 2007), chs 4 and 7.

22 Delaney, *Irish in Post-War Britain*, p. 4. Also see estimates in Panikos Panayi, *An Immigration History of Modern Britain: Multicultural Racism Since 1800* (Harlow: Pearson, 2010), p. 44.

23 Liz Curtis, *Nothing But the Same Old Story: The Roots of Anti-Racism* (London: Information on Ireland, 1984).

24 Holmes, *John Bull's Island*, p. 252. Birmingham Heritage and Archive Services, Birmingham Newspaper Cuttings, Ethnic Communities File, 1954–1968, I. Hamilton Fazey, 'Children from Eire are immigrants', *Birmingham Post* (18 March 1966); Delaney, *Irish in Post-War Britain*, pp. 76–82; John Corbally, 'The Jarring Irish: Postwar Immigration to the Heart of Empire', *Radical History Review*, 104 (2009), 114–116.

25 Paul, *Whitewashing Britain*, pp. 9, 13–14, 98–99; Kathleen Paul, 'Communities of Britishness: migration in the last gasp of empire', in Stuart Ward (ed.), *British Culture and the End of Empire* (Manchester: Manchester University Press, 2001).

26 Paul, *Whitewashing Britain*, pp. 105–106; Kathleen Paul, 'From subjects to immigrants: black Britons and national identity, 1948–1962', in Richard Weight and Abigail Beach (eds), *The Right to Belong: Citizenship and National Identity in Britain, 1930–1960* (London: I.B. Tauris, 1998), p. 228.

27 Paul, *Whitewashing Britain*, p. 105.

28 David Cesarani, *Justice Delayed: How Britain Became a Refuge for Nazi War Criminals* (London: Heinemann, 1992) especially ch. 4; Paul, *Whitewashing Britain*, pp. 85–88; Tony Kushner, *Remembering Refugees*, p. 210.

29 David Goodhart, *The British Dream: Successes and Failures of Post-War Immigration* (London: Atlantic, 2013), ch. 2.

30 Peter Fryer, *Staying Power: The History of Black People in Britain* (London: Pluto, 1984), p. 372; Panayi, *An Immigration History of Modern Britain*, p. 44.

31 On the 'fighting mad Irish', see John Rex and Robert Moore, *Race, Community and Conflict: A Study of Sparkbrook* (Oxford: Oxford University Press/Institute of Race Relations, 1967), p. 70. For analyses that stress the complexity of responses, see Holmes, *John Bull's Island,* pp. 255–270; Mica Nava, 'Sometimes antagonistic, sometimes ardently sympathetic: contradictory responses to migrants in postwar Britain', *Ethnicities,* 14:3 (2014).

32 Kenneth Lunn, 'Immigration and reaction in Britain, 1880–1950: rethinking the "legacy of empire"', in Jan Lucassen and Leo Lucassen (eds), *Migration, Migration History, History: Old Paradigms and New Perspectives* (New York: Peter Lang, 1999), p. 349.

33 On traditions of intolerance see, for example, Tony Kushner and Kenneth Lunn (eds), *Traditions of Intolerance: Historical Perspectives on Fascism and Race Discourse in Britain* (Manchester: Manchester University Press, 1989).

34 Schaffer, *Racial Science and British Society,* pp. 148–165.

35 On the ambitions and significance of American psychology, see Ellen Herman, *The Romance of American Psychology: Political Culture in the Age of Experts* (Berkeley, CA: University of California Press, 1995); Mark Clapson, 'The American contribution to the urban sociology of race relations in Britain from the 1940s to the early 1970s', *Urban History,* 33:2 (2006); Peter Mandler, 'Margaret Mead amongst the natives of Great Britain', *Past & Present* 204:1 (2009), 195–233; and overview by Stephen Small and John Solomos, 'Race, immigration and politics in Britain: changing policy agendas and conceptual paradigms 1940s–2000s', *International Journal of Comparative Sociology,* 47:3–4 (2006), 235–257.

36 Carter, *Realism and Racism,* p. 2.

37 Elazar Barkan, *The Retreat of Scientific Racism: Changing Concepts of Race in Britain and the United States between the World Wars* (Cambridge: Cambridge University Press, 1992); Kenan Malik, *The Meaning of Race* (London: Palgrave Macmillan, 1996), pp. 71–177.

38 Karen E. Fields and Barbara J. Fields, *Racecraft: The Soul of Inequality in American Life* (London: Verso, 2012), pp. 39–40; Paul Kramer, 'Empires, exceptions and Anglo-Saxons: race and rule between the British and the United States empires, 1880–1910', *Journal of American History,* 88:4 (2008).

39 Martin Bulmer, *The Chicago School of Sociology* (Chicago, IL: University of Chicago Press, 1984), pp. 36–37, 89–94; Ellen Fitzpatrick, *Endless Crusade: Women Social Scientists and Progressive Reform* (Oxford: Oxford University Press, 1990).

40 Chad Alan Goldberg, 'Robert Park's marginal man: the career of a concept in American sociology', *Laboratorium,* 4:2 (2012).

41 Bulmer, *Chicago School of Sociology*, pp. 68, 74–80. Dorothy Ross, 'Changing contours of the social science disciplines', in Theodore M. Porter and Dorothy Ross (eds), *The Cambridge History of Science Volume VII: The Modern Social Sciences* (Cambridge: Cambridge University Press, 2003), p. 219.

42 Frank Furedi, *The Silent War: Imperialism and the Changing Perception of Race* (London: Pluto, 1998), ch. 5 for discussion of how inter-war colonial politics informed the emerging sociological and policy literature on race relations. Henrika Kuklik, *The Savage Within: The Social History of British Anthropology, 1885–1945* (Cambridge: Cambridge University Press, 1991).

43 On race relations, see Chris Waters, '"Dark strangers" in our midst: discourses of race and nation in Britain, 1947–1963', *Journal of British Studies*, 36:2 (1997), 217–221; Bailkin, *Afterlife of Empire*, ch. 1; Mike Savage, *Identities and Social Change in Britain Since 1940* (Oxford: Oxford University Press, 2010). Mica Nava, *Visceral Cosmopolitanism: Gender, Culture and the Normalisation of Difference* (Oxford: Berg, 2007), ch. 6. On the decline of historians as public intellectuals, see Savage, *Identities and Social Change*, pp. 118–119.

44 Waters, '"Dark strangers"', 219–220; David Mills, *Difficult Folk? A Political History of Social Anthropology* (Oxford: Berghahn, 2008), ch. 8.

45 The significance of disciplinary differences in studying race relations warrants further attention. The interpretation offered here sees race relations as typically eclectic and interdisciplinary but alternative arguments can be found in Bailkin, *Afterlife of Empire*, pp. 24–34; Rex and Moore, *Race, Community and Conflict*, pp. 11–18.

46 A.H. Halsey, *A History of Sociology in Britain* (Oxford: Oxford University Press, 2004), pp. 73, 84, 88; Bailkin, *Afterlife of Empire*, p. 31; Waters, '"Dark strangers"', 233–238.

47 Anthony Richmond, *The Colour Problem: A Study of Racial Relations* (Harmondsworth: Penguin, 1955), p. 12.

48 Waters, '"Dark strangers"', 219–220. The tendency is consistent with what Chris Lorenz calls the paradoxical quality of a historical identity based on change through time. See Lorenz, 'Representations of identity', p. 28.

49 Richmond, *Colour Problem*, pp. 19–20.

50 *Ibid.*, p. 240; see also A.H. Richmond, 'Theoretical orientations in studies of ethnic group relations in Britain', *Man*, 57 (1957), 121–123; A.H. Richmond, 'Applied social and public policy concerning racial relations in Britain', *Race*, 1:2 (1959), 18. A.H. Richmond, 'Social and psychological explanations of racial prejudice: some light on the controversy from recent researches in Britain', *Pacific Sociological*

Review, 4:2 (1961), 63–68. For influence of this work, see G. Richards, '*Race*', *Racism and Psychology: Towards a Reflexive History* (London: Routledge, 1997), pp. 227–237.

51 Nava, *Visceral Cosmopolitanism*, p. 112.

52 Richmond, *Colour Problem*, p. 235.

53 Jacqueline Jenkinson, *Black 1919: Riots, Racism and Resistance in Imperial Britain* (Liverpool: Liverpool University Press, 2008). For cautionary comment on the supposedly causal role of race in explanation, see M. Rowe, 'Sex, "race" and riot in Liverpool, 1919', *Immigrants and Minorities*, 19:2 (2000), 53–70.

54 On the explicitly racist background to this concern, see Richmond, *Colour Problem*, pp. 236–237; Schaffer, *Racial Science and British Society*, pp. 23–25, 51.

55 Select Committee on Race Relations and Immigration, *The Problems of Coloured School-Leavers* (HC 1968–69, 58–xvii and 58–xviii), 26 March 1969, pp. 823–824; John Belchem, *Before the Windrush: Race Relations in 20th century Liverpool* (Liverpool: Liverpool University Press, 2014), pp. 209–211.

56 See Nava, *Visceral Cosmopolitanism*, pp. 114–115; Liverpool Youth Organisations Committee, *Special But Not Separate: A Report on the Situation of Young Coloured People in Liverpool* (Liverpool, n.p., 1968), pp. 17–18.

57 Lawrence Cremin, *Traditions of American Education* (New York: Basic Books, 1977), p. 134.

58 Richmond, *Colour Problem*, p. 300.

59 Mandler, 'Margaret Mead', 195–233.

60 Birmingham Heritage and Archives Services, MS 2141/A/7/1. F. Milsom *et al.*, 'Operation integration: an enquiry into the experience of West Indians living in Birmingham, with particular reference to children and young people', unpublished paper, June/July 1961, p. 6; Handsworth Good Neighbours Committee, 'Your white neighbour', undated pamphlet.

61 Richmond, *Colour Problem*, pp. 313–314, 275–276.

62 Rex and Moore, *Race, Community and Conflict*, p. 15.

63 London Metropolitan Archive ACC 1888/112. London Council of Social Service: Race Relations. Constitution of the Willesden International Friendship Council (undated, *c*.1963); Birmingham Heritage and Archive Services, MS 2141/A/7/1 Handsworth Good Neighbours Committee, 'Your white neighbour', undated pamphlet.

64 London Metropolitan Archive ACC 1888/112. London Council of Social Service: Race Relations. Constitution of the Willesden International Friendship Council (undated, *c*.1963); similarly, see Birmingham Heritage and Archive Services MS 2141/A/7/1 Handsworth

Good Neighbours Committee, 'Your white neighbour', undated pamphlet.

65 C. Mullard, *Black Britain* (London: George Allen & Unwin, 1973), pp. 26–29.

66 Nadine Peppard, 'Into the third decade', *New Community*, 2 (1972), 93–94.

67 Bhikhu Parekh (ed.), *Colour, Culture and Consciousness: Immigrant Intellectuals in Britain* (London: George Allen & Unwin, 1974), p. 233.

68 Malik, *Representing Black Britain*, p. 39; Webster, *Englishness and Empire*, pp. 163–164.

69 Paul Long, 'Representing race and place: black Midlanders on television in the 1960s and 1970s', *Midland History* 36:2 (2011), pp. 265–269.

70 Birmingham Heritage and Archive Services, MS 4000/2/101, 'The Colony' shooting script, p. 6.

71 *Ibid.*, 'The Colony' actuality transcripts, p. 163.

72 Stefan Collini, *Absent Minds*, pp. 45–48.

73 Roger Swift and Sheridan Gilley (eds), *The Irish in Victorian Britain: The Local Dimension* (Dublin, Four Courts Press, 1999); Bronwen Walter, 'Strangers on the inside: Irish women servants in England, 1881', *Immigrants and Minorities*, 27:2–3 (2009), 279–299.

74 For an overview of the historiography of the Great Famine, see Cormac Ó Gráda, 'Making Irish Famine history in 1995', *History Workshop Journal*, 42 (1996), 87–104.

75 Holmes, *John Bull's Island*, pp. 20–21.

76 Colin Pooley 'Living in Liverpool: the modern city', in John Belchem (ed.), *Liverpool 800: Culture, Character and History* (Liverpool: Liverpool University Press, 2006), p. 187.

77 Howe, *Ireland and Empire: Colonial Legacies in Irish History and Culture* (Oxford: Oxford University Press, 2000), pp. 51–52.

78 L.P. Curtis, *Anglo-Saxons and Celts* (Cambridge: University of Bridgeport, 1968); R.N. Lebow, *White Britain and Black Ireland: The Influence of Stereotypes on Colonial Policy* (Philadelphia, PA: Institute for the Study of Human Issues, 1976).

79 Curtis, *Anglo-Saxons and Celts*, p. 53.

80 *Ibid.* See also Mary Poovey, 'Curing the "social body": James Kay and the Irish in Manchester', *Gender and History*, 5:2 (1993), 196–211; Donald M. MacRaild, 'Irish immigration and the "condition of England question": the roots of an historiographical tradition', *Immigrants and Minorities*, 14:1 (1995), 67–85.

81 Richard A. Cosgrave, 'A usable past: history and the politics of the national past in late Victorian England', *Parliamentary History*, 27:1 (2008): 30–42.

82 Benedikt Stuchtey, 'Literature, liberty and the life of the nation: British

historiography from Macaulay to Trevelyan', in Stefan Berger, Mark Donovan and Kevin Passmore, *Writing National Histories: Western Europe Since 1800* (London: Routledge, 1999), p. 36.

83 Burrow, *A Liberal Descent*; Hall, *Civilising Subjects*; Theodore Koditschek, *Liberalism, Imperialism and the Historical Imagination: Nineteenth Century Visions of a Greater Britain* (Cambridge: Cambridge University Press, 2011). In terms of historical education in Victorian Ireland, see the short but suggestive Patrick Walsh, '"Paltry abridgements": school texts and teaching history in nineteenth century India and Ireland', in David Dickson, Justyna Pyz and Christopher Shepard (eds), *Irish Classrooms and British Empire: Imperial Contexts in the Origins of Modern Education* (Dublin: Four Courts Press, 2012), pp. 53–61.

84 For contrasting views see, for example, the foundational text on the racialisation of the Irish by Lewis Perry Curtis, *Apes and Angels: The Irishman in Victorian Caricature* (Washington, DC: Smithsonian Institute Press, 1971); and, more recently, Luke Gibbons, 'Race against time: racial discourse and Irish history', in Catherine Hall (ed.), *Cultures of Empire: A Reader: Colonizers in Britain and the Empire in the Nineteenth and Twentieth Centuries* (Manchester: Manchester University Press, 2000), pp. 207–223. The opposing view, placing clear limits on racialisation, is best summarised in Howe, *Ireland and Empire*.

85 Koditschek, *Liberalism, Imperialism and the Historical Imagination*, chs 4 and 5.

86 On the growing significance of colour see Malik, *Meaning of Race*, p. 177.

87 A. Peach, 'The Irish in Birmingham during the nineteenth century' (Ph.D. dissertation, De Montford University, 2000), pp. 109–119 on the Irish as a source of contagion and criminality.

88 John Belchem, 'Priests, publicans and the poor: ethnic enterprise and migrant networks in mid-nineteenth century Liverpool', *Immigrants and Minorities*, 23:2–3 (2005), 207–232.

89 C. Chinn, 'The Irish in early Victorian Birmingham', in R. Swift and S. Gilley (eds), *The Irish in Victorian Britain: The Local Dimension* (Dublin: Four Courts Press, 1999), p. 57; Hollen Lees, *Exiles of Erin*, p. 46.

90 Patsy Davis, 'Birmingham's Irish community and the Murphy riots of 1867', *Midland History,* 31 (2006), 37–66; Kaja Ziesler, 'The Irish in Birmingham, 1830–1970' (Ph.D. thesis, University of Birmingham, 1989), pp. 322–328.

91 Raphael Samuel, 'An Irish religion', in Raphael Samuel (ed.), *Patriotism: The Making and Unmaking of British National Identity Volume II: Minorities and Outsiders* (London: Routledge, 1989), p. 94.

92 Mary J. Hickman, *Religion, Class and Identity: The State, the Catholic Church and the Education of the Irish in Britain* (Aldershot: Avebury, 1995) and 'Alternative historiographies of the Irish in Britain: a critique of the segregation/assimilation model', in R. Swift and S. Gilley (eds), *The Irish in Victorian Britain*.

93 Peach, 'The Irish in Birmingham', p. 218. The most convincing interpretation of the place and identity of the Irish in Britain remains that of David Fitzpatrick, 'A curious middle place: the Irish in Britain', in Swift and Gilley (eds), *The Irish in Britain*, pp. 10–59.

94 John Belchem, and Donald MacRaild, 'Cosmopolitan Liverpool', in Belchem (ed.), *Liverpool 800*, p. 338.

95 Mervyn Busteed, 'I shall never return to Hibernia's bowers: Irish migrant identities in early Victorian Manchester', *North West Geography*, 1:1 (2001).

96 Lynn Hollen Lees, *Exiles of Erin: Irish Migrants in Victorian London* (Manchester: Manchester University Press, 1979), pp. 22–23.

97 On the significance of this folk tradition in a garrisoned society, see Guy Beiner, *Remembering the Year of the French: Irish Folk History and Social Memory* (Madison, WI: University of Wisconsin Press, 2009).

98 John Belchem, *Irish, Catholic and Scouse: The History of the Liverpool-Irish, 1800–1939* (Liverpool: Liverpool University Press, 2007), pp. 201–202, 234–235.

99 Gaelic League of London, *Half-Yearly Magazine* (1904): 21. Art Ó Briain, 'Some notes on the history of the Gaelic League of London', *Capuchin Annual*, 1944: 116–126. On the highly gendered philosophy and participation of women in the Gaelic League, see D.A.J. MacPherson, *Women and the Irish Nation: Gender, Culture and Irish Identity* (Basingstoke: Palgrave Macmillan, 2012).

100 Tom Garvin, *Nationalist Revolutionaries in Ireland*, p. 108, cited in *Darragh Gannon*, 'Celticism in exile: the London Gaelic League, 1917–1921', *Proceedings of the Harvard Celtic Colloquium*, 30 (2010), 82–101.

101 Autohistory by Seoirse Ó Broin; Seán MacStíofáin, *Memoirs of a Revolutionary* (London: Gordon Cremonesi, 1975), pp. 2, 34.

102 See the contrasting positions of Alan O'Day and John Belchem in Donald MacRaild (ed.), *Great Famine and Beyond*.

103 Alan O'Day, 'A conundrum of Irish diasporic identity: mutative ethnicity', *Immigrants and Minorities*, 27: 2–3 (2009); Alan O'Day, 'Imagined Irish communities: networks of social communication of the Irish diaspora in the United States and Britain in the late nineteenth and early twentieth centuries', *Immigrants and Minorities*, 23:2–3 (2005).

104 David Fitzpatrick, 'The Irish in Britain: settlers or transients?', *Labour History Review* 57:3 (1992), 4.

105 John Belchem, 'Whiteness and the Liverpool-Irish'. *Journal of British Studies*, 44:1 (2005), 146–152; Bernard Canavan, 'Story-tellers and writers: Irish identity in emigrant labourers' autobiographies, 1870–1970', in Patrick O' Sullivan (ed.), *The Irish World Wide. History, Heritage, Identity Volume III: The Creative Migrant* (Leicester: Leicester University Press, 1994), pp. 154–169; Corbally 'Postwar immigration to the heart of Empire'.

106 Lance Pettitt, 'Phillip Donnellan, Ireland and dissident documentary', *Historical Journal of Film, Radio and Television*, 20:3 (2000), 351–365.

107 Birmingham Heritage and Archive Services MS 4000/2/107, 'The Crack' actuality transcripts, quotation from Tony Crumlin.

108 Birmingham Heritage and Archives Services, MS 4000/2/107, 'The Crack' music and lyric book.

109 On Donnellan's Irishness, see his unpublished autobiography, 'We were the BBC'; Pettitt, 'Phillip Donnellan', pp. 352–354, 358.

110 Birmingham Heritage and Archives Services, 4000/2/107, typescript quotation from T.A. Jackson, *Ireland Her Own*, pp. 22–23.

111 *What Is the Connolly Association? Constitution and Explanation* (Ripley, n.d. *c*.1965), pp. 2, 12.

112 Editor Pat Dooley described the paper, then entitled *Irish Freedom*, as 'more than a newspaper, it was an interpreter, an organiser, agitator and educator of the Irish in Britain'. P. Dooley, *The Irish in Britain* (Watford: Connolly Association, 1943), p. 18.

113 Birmingham Heritage and Archives Services, MS 4000/2/107, 'The Crack' actuality transcripts, p. 28.

114 *Ibid*.

115 Donald H. Akenson with Sean Farren and John Coolahan, 'Pre-university education, 1921–84', in Jacqueline R. Hill (ed.), *A New History of Ireland Volume VII* (Oxford: Oxford University Press, 2003), pp. 726–731; see comment in Canavan, 'Story-tellers and writers', p. 169, fn 39 and Birmingham Heritage and Archives Services, 4000/2/107, 'The Crack' actuality transcripts, pp. 4, 8, 14 for the limitations and consequences of this education.

116 Nicole McLennan, 'Irish connections: London's county associations', unpublished paper given to the Irish in Britain Seminar Series, London Metropolitan University 10 June 2009.

117 Dónall MacAmhlaigh, *An Irish Navy: The Diary of an Exile*, trans. V. Iremonger (Cork: Collins Press edn, 2008), pp. 39, 42.

118 *Birmingham Mail* (27 October 1965).

119 Anna May Mangan, *Me and Mine: A Warm Hearted Memoir of a London Irish Family* (London: Virago, 2011), p. 143 notes that 'essential for every London Irish family were a scroll of the Sacred

Heart of Jesus, a plaster statue of the Virgin Mary and a framed photograph of John F. Kennedy'.

120 Birmingham Heritage and Archive Services, MS1914/1/5/1/1 Sparkbrook Discussion Papers, 18 October 1962, p. 1. For similar comment, see Farrukh Hashmi, *The Psychology of Racial Prejudice* (London: Community Relations Commission, 1968).

121 Delaney, *The Irish in Postwar Britain*, pp. 158–159.

122 *Ibid.*

123 John Archer Jackson, *The Irish in Britain* (London: Routledge & Kegan Paul, 1963), p. 158. L. Harte, 'You want to be a British Paddy? The anxiety of identity in post-war Irish writing', in Dermot Keogh, Finbarr O'Shea and Carmel Quinlan (eds), *The Lost Decade: Ireland in the 1950s* (Cork: Mercier, 2004).

124 David Dabydeen and Nana Wilson-Tagoe, *A Reader's Guide to West Indian and Black British Literature* (Hatfield: Hansib, 1988), pp. 144–145.

125 Holmes, *John Bull's Island*, pp. 255–270.

126 Peter Fryer, *Staying Power*; David Killingray (ed.), *Africans in Britain* (London: Frank Cass, 1994).

127 David Eltis, 'Europeans and the rise and fall of African slavery in the Americas: an interpretation', *American Historical Review*, 98:5 (1993), 1419; Robin Blackburn, *The American Crucible: Slavery, Emancipation and Human Rights* (London: Verso, 2011).

128 For contrasting views on the significance of race see, for example, Bernard Porter, *The Absent-Minded Imperialists: Empire Society and Culture in Britain* (Oxford: Oxford University Press, 2004); Catherine Hall, *Macaulay and Son: Architects of Imperial Britain* (Yale, CT: Yale University Press, 2012). On Froude, and the limits of his appeal, see Koditschek, *Liberalism, Imperialism and the Historical Imagination*, pp. 189–205.

129 Figures are in Panayi, *An Immigration History of Britain*, p. 39.

130 Laura Tabili, *'We Ask for British Justice': Workers and Racial Difference in Late Imperial Britain* (London: Cornell University Press, 1994).

131 Holmes, *John Bull's Island*, p. 89.

132 Jenkinson, *Black 1919*.

133 Anne Spry Rush, *Bonds of Empire*; Bell, *The Idea of Greater Britain*; David Killingray, '"A good West Indian, a good African, and, in short, a good Britisher": black and British in a colour-conscious empire, 1760–1950', *Journal of Imperial and Commonwealth History*, 36:3 (2008), 363, 381.

134 For an overview, see Barbara Bush, *Imperialism, Race and Resistance: Africa and Britain, 1919–1945* (London: Routledge, 1999). On aspects

of formal and informal education, see Jim English, 'Empire day in Britain, 1904–1958', *Historical Journal*, 49:1 (2006), 247–276; Ian Grosvenor, 'There's no place like home: education and the making of national identity', *History of Education*, 28:3 (1999), 235–250. On documentary film and the imperial imaginary, see Marc Matera, 'An empire of development: Africa and the Caribbean in God's chillun', *Twentieth Century British History*, 23:1 (2012), 12–37.

135 Hakim Adi, *West Africans in Britain 1900–1960: Nationalism, Pan-Africanism and Communism* (London: Lawrence & Wishart, 1998), pp. 6–22.

136 Marika Sherwood, *Origins of Pan-Africanism: Henry Sylvester Williams and the African diaspora* (London: Routledge, 2011).

137 Estimates for the black press, that is publications owned, controlled or edited by black people, are in J. Voogd, *Race, Riots and Resistance: the Red Summer of 1919* (Oxford: Peter Lang, 2008), p. 133. Colin Grant, *Negro with a Hat: The Rise and Fall of Marcus Garvey and His Dream of Mother Africa* (London: Jonathan Cape, 2008), pp. 43–44.

138 Bush, *Imperialism, Race and Resistance*, p. 219.

139 Marika Sherwood, *Pastor Ekarte and the African Churches Mission, Liverpool 1932–64* (London: Savannah Press, 1994); Belchem, *Before the Windrush*, pp. 65–67; David Killingray, '"To do something for the race": Harold Moody and the League of Coloured Peoples', in Schwarz (ed.), *West Indian Intellectuals*, p. 60.

140 Cited in Killingray, '"To do something for the race"', 54.

141 Harold Moody, 'The Wilberforce Centenary Celebrations, Hull. July 23rd–29th', *The Keys*, 1:2 (1933), 22–23, 34; S. Sanmuganathan, 'The ancient civilisation of Africa', *The Keys*, 1:4 (1934), 79–81 and 1:5 (1934), 14–15, 27–28.

142 Carol Polsgrove, *Ending British Rule in Africa: Writers in a Common Cause* (Manchester: Manchester University Press, 2009), p. 38.

143 C.L.R. James, *The Black Jacobins: Toussaint L'Overture and the San Domingo Revolution* (London: Penguin, 1991 [1938]), pp. xviii, xx.

144 *Ibid.*, p. 304.

145 Cited in C. Hall, 'What is a West Indian?', *West Indian Intellectuals in Britain* (Manchester: Manchester University Press, 2003), p. 32.

146 Polsgrove, *Ending British Rule in Africa*, p. 37.

147 Jörn Rusen, *History: Narration, Interpretation, Orientation* (Oxford: Berghahn, 2005), pp. 2, 9–19.

148 On defining diasporic consciousness, see T.R. Patterson and R.D.G. Kelley, 'Unfinished migrations: reflections on the African diaspora and the making of the modern world', *African Studies Review*, 43:1 (2000), 14–15.

149 Nancie Sharpe, 'Cardiff's coloured population', *The Keys*, 1:3 (1934),

44–45, 61. H. Moody, 'The president's message', 2:3 (1934), 22; Laura Tabili's analysis sometimes suffers from the imprecision around the concept of ethnicity but perceptively concludes that inter-war 'Black Britons did not view themselves or their cultures as outside the British working class' ('Social networks and organization building in Britain's interwar black communities', in Gabriella Hauch (ed.), *Geschlecht, Klasses, Ethnizität: 28. Internationale Tagung der Historikerinnen und Historiker der Arbeiterbewegung* (Wien: Europaverlag, 1993), p. 181).

150	Michael Banton, *The Coloured Quarter: Negro Immigrants in an English City* (London: Jonathan Cape, 1955).

151	Polsgrove, *Ending British Rule in Africa*, ch. 2.

152	Rush, *Bonds of Empire*, pp. 128–132; David Killingray, *Fighting for Britain: African Soldiers in the Second World War* (Woodbridge: James Currey, 2010).

153	See, for example, the compelling testimony in Lambeth City Council, *Forty Winters On: Memories of Britain's Postwar Caribbean Immigrants* (Lambeth: Lambeth City Council, 1988).

154	Schaffer, *Racial Science and British Society*, p. 87.

155	Figures from Panayi, *An Immigration History of Britain*, p. 44.

156	W. Collins, *Jamaican Migrant* (London: Routledge Kegan Paul, 1965), p. 76.

157	Edward Pilkington, 'The West Indian community and the Notting Hill riots of 1958', in Pankios Panayi (ed.), *Racial Violence in Britain in the Nineteenth and Twentieth Centuries* (Leicester: Leicester University Press, 2003), p. 182.

158	'Four year terms for nine "Nigger-hunting" youths', *The Times* (16 September 1958), p. 4.

159	Dilip Hiro, *Black British, White British* (London: Eyre & Spottiswoode, 1971), p. 40.

160	'Editorial', *West Indian Gazette* (3:6 May 1961); 'Africa's true history unearthed', *West Indian Gazette* (3:1 January 1960); 'The teaching of West Indian history', *West Indian Gazette*, 3:6 (1961); 'Our Links to Africa', *West Indian Gazette*, 4:10 (1961).

161	Bill Schwarz, 'Crossing the seas', in Schwarz (ed.), *West Indian Intellectuals in Britain*, p. 15.

162	These consequences are many but for some examples, see Vijay Prashad, *The Darker Nations: A People's History of the Third World* (London: New Press, 2007), pp. 82–91; Mahmood Mamdani, *Define and Rule: Native as Political Identity* (Cambridge, MA: Harvard University Press, 2012).

163	Cited in Mark Meredith, *The State of Africa: A History of the Continent since Independence* (London: Free Press, 2005 [2006]), p. 29.

164 Rupert C. Lewis, *Walter Rodney's Intellectual and Political Thought* (Kingston, Jamaica: University of West Indies Press, 1998), pp. 7, 24–26.

165 Cedric J. Robinson, *Black Marxism: The Making of the Black Radical Tradition* (Chapel Hill, NC and London: University of North Carolina Press, 2000).

166 Lewis, *Walter Rodney's Intellectual and Political Thought*, p. 76.

167 Cited in Lewis, *Walter Rodney's Intellectual and Political Thought*, pp. 33–34.

168 Gerard Parsons, 'Filling a void? Afro-Caribbean identity and religion', in Gerard Parsons (ed.), *The Growth of Religious Diversity: Britain from 1945* (London: Routledge, 1993), p. 243.

169 Roswith Gerloff, *A Plea for Black British Theologies: The Black Church Movement in Britain and Its Transatlantic Cultural and Theological Interaction* (New York: Peter Lang, 1992); Clifford Hill, *Black Churches: West Indian and African Sects in Britain* (London: Community and Race Relations Unit of the British Council of Churches, 1971), pp. 13–20.

170 Stephen Howe, *Afrocentrism: Mythical Pasts and Imagined Homes* (London: Verso, 1998), pp. 63–64.

171 Kevin Myers, 'Faith in History: memory, multiculturalism and the legacies of Empire in postwar England', *History of Education*, 40:6 (2011).

172 Beckford, *Jesus Dub*, p. 60; P. Pemberton, E. Pemberton and J.R. Maxwell-Hughes (eds), *Pilgrims Progress: A History of the Wesleyan Holiness Church, 1958–1983* (Handsworth: Wesleyan Holiness Church District Office, 1983).

173 Malcolm Calley, *God's People: West Indian Pentecostal Sects in England* (Oxford: Oxford University Press), p. 144.

174 Calley, *God's People*, pp. 55–56.

175 Bill Schwarz, 'Afterword: the predicament of history', in Schwarz (ed.), *West Indian Intellectuals in Britain*, p. 256.

176 Eric Hobsbawm, *Age of Extremes: The Short Twentieth Century, 1914–1991* (Penguin, 1994), ch. 9.

177 Bill Schwarz, 'Unspeakable histories: diasporic lives in Old England', in P. Osborne and S. Sandford (eds), *Philosophies of Race and Ethnicity* (London: Continuum, 2002), pp. 82–85.

178 Malik, *The Meaning of Race*, pp. 183–193.

179 Schwarz, *White Man's World*; Stephen Heathorn, *For Home, Country and Race: Constructing Gender, Class and Englishness in the Elementary School, 1880–1914* (Toronto: University of Toronto Press, 2000); Sonya O. Rose, *Which People's War? National Identity and Citizenship in Wartime Britain 1939–1945* (Oxford: Oxford University Press, 2003).

180 Belchem, *Irish, Catholic and Scouse*, p. 66; Frank Boyce, 'From Victorian "Little Ireland" to heritage trail: Catholicism, Community and change in Liverpool's docklands', in R. Swift and S. Gilley (eds), *The Irish in Victorian Britain*, pp. 289–290.

181 The defence of slavery is in G. Chandler, *Liverpool* (London: B.T. Batsford, 1957), p. 306 and discussed by Roger Anstey and P.E.H. Hair, 'Introduction', in Roger Anstey and P.E.H. Hair (eds), *Liverpool, the African Slave Trade and British Abolition: Essays to Illustrate Current Knowledge and Research* (Bristol: Historic Society of Lancashire and Cheshire, 1976). The denial of discrimination is reported in various sections of Belchem (ed.), *Liverpool 800*, pp. 386, 442.

182 C. McGlashan, 'Growing up with Pinky', *Observer Review* (10 September 1967), p. 17; Bill Schwarz, 'Not even past yet', *History Workshop Journal*, 57 (2004).

2

History and humanism
(1968–1981)

> It is time we let the world know we are proud of our
> heritage and we stand as living monuments. For those who
> are afraid of who they must be are but slaves in a trance.
> (Len Garrison)

Introduction

On Tuesday 1 April 1969 the BBC broadcast a documentary programme
on Radio 4 entitled 'We Lived across the River'. Compiled by Dilip
Hiro, narrated by Stuart Hall and produced by Charles Parker, the
programme explored how 'after three centuries of the slave trade and
its aftermath, the black man is struggling for a distinct identity in the
white man's world'. Based on interviews and recordings conducted
by Hiro in the USA (Harlem and Washington, DC) and England
(Birmingham and Wolverhampton), and in the aftermath of the
assassination of Martin Luther King, the programme documented
what it called a 'resurgent striving towards identity, consciousness
and dignity' most obviously expressed in, but not contained by, the
Black Power movement. Hall went onto explain that this striving was
common to everyone of African descent in the Western hemisphere:

> The common history of these peoples reaches back into slavery.
> Separated by the Atlantic from their African past; they were also
> separated from their freedom, from the 'Promised Land'. The slave
> lived 'across the River'.[1]

The broadcast, the work of men loosely associated with the New
Left, explored topics and expressed views which were central to
migrant struggles for a past and to the specific themes of this chapter.

First, the pan-Atlantic design of the programme and the scope of the interviews are indicative of the growing influence of black struggles in the USA on both black and Irish communities in Britain. Radio, but especially television, brought the sights and sounds, the marches and songs, of the civil rights movement into the front rooms of homes in Liverpool, Birmingham and London; 'you could actually see what was going on' recalled activist and educator Ama Gueye, 'and you could hear and, you know, people were exchanging much more fluidly across the ponds'.[2] For a period in the 1960s, the language and demands of the civil rights movement could be heard both in Northern Ireland, where the Civil Rights Association campaigned for an end to anti-Catholic discrimination, and in England, where black people campaigned for a future free from racism. These were, in retrospect, moderate aims. But they were also to prove elusive ones that intensified the exploration of black and Irish identities among immigrants and their children in the 1970s.

A second theme of this chapter concerns the development of diasporic identities. 'We Lived Across the River' demonstrated the increasing significance of transnational identifications in black communities. It also showed that such identifications were partly dependent upon bringing to light a history of slavery that was forgotten in Britain and insisting, as one interviewee put it, 'on the continuing psychological, physical and economic oppression that slavery had imposed on black populations'.[3] The construction and distribution of histories of the Irish famine between 1845 and 1852 would eventually come to operate in much the same way. 'The fight over the interpretation of the famine was and remains a potent ideological issue' wrote sociologist Peter Gibbon in 1975.[4] Condemning what were presented as 'British, Malthusian and bourgeois' interpretations, Irish scholar activists championed the famine as a symbol of the colonial exploitation that explained the presence and experiences of Irish immigrants in England. In short, and for both Irish and black groups, particular historical memories became central to the definition of minority ethnic identities.

However, there were different chronologies at work here. The radio programme of Hiro, Parker and Hall was illustrative of the different mode of discrimination black people in Britain were subjected to. Interviewees described experiences of violent racist attacks, of discrimination in employment and housing and, perhaps most poignantly, of feelings of confusion about their identity. These feelings could combine a sense of nagging inferiority and a feeling of respect for the English that was explained by references to tangled relationships going back three hundred years. It could also, as one interviewee put it, result in becoming 'more aware of the fact that I'm black, because of the situations that one comes up against ... there's always something there that tells you you're not the same'.[5] Irish immigrants could report similar feelings but with, perhaps, less insistence, less experience of overt racism, with not quite the same sense of rejection as citizens of a newly independent republic and a closer proximity to home. In addition, and despite fulfilling the two essential criteria of an ethnic group laid down by the 1976 Race Relations Act, the Irish were not formally recognised as such by the Community Relations Commission until 1986. These factors, together with a stronger sense of transatlantic solidarities in emergent black communities, help to explain why it was histories of slavery that emerged first and most forcefully as a historical memory around which new forms of ethnic identity could cohere. It is also why this chapter focuses mostly, although not exclusively, on the struggles of black activists and campaigners.

A third important theme of this chapter concerns the ways in which first and second generation immigrants explored tangled sites of identification. Fanon's autobiographical account of becoming 'black with ethnic characteristics' on the streets of post-war Paris slowly took on a deep resonance for immigrant groups exploring and engaging with the past.[6] History had powerful potential as a site of identification, a possibility powerfully illustrated and explained by Hiro, Parker and Hall when they recounted at some length 'one of the most dramatic rediscoveries of African ancestry' by Alex Haley 'who, on a trip to Gambia found the village of his great grandfather and was celebrated as "one who had been long lost from us and returned"'.[7] Even if the accuracy of this story was immediately challenged, it functioned as both metaphor and therapy. In it, as in the subsequent and phenomenal success of Haley's novel, and its adaptation for television as the *Roots* series, were the imaginative resources for new sites of identification and new, seemingly more authentic, modes of identity.[8] If this was true for migrants from the Caribbean and from Africa, it was also evident among the Irish in England. Gaelic games enjoyed a renaissance, language classes boomed and the study of Irish history in schools became the subject of controversy. This was the period in which history, in other words, provided the resources for rejecting the national master narrative and the prescribed forms of identification that went with it. New and critical forms of historical consciousness were emerging from the reflexivity of individuals and their collaborative projects.[9]

This chapter traces the activities through which first and second generation black and Irish migrants identified, appropriated and utilised their historical heritage in the period between 1968 and 1981. This was a considerable task. Routinely misidentified, their real and imagined social and psychological problems were taken as evidence of the difficulties of living between distinct and tightly bound cultures. Their struggle against their categorisation as an alien people, a foreign body and a separate race, entailed an engagement with their heritage and with history. Migrants mobilised to write themselves as subjects into history, and to develop modes of identification outside racialised boundaries and outside of the assumptions of race relations research. In order to do so they formed formal study groups, conducted historical research and developed alternative forms of education. They explored their heritage in theatre, music and sport and they campaigned for public recognition of different histories and discussed and debated how to utilise historical knowledge in the present. The starting point for these projects was the state activities that rendered immigrants as alien and that understood their presence in England as posing race relations problems.[10]

Consolidating race relations

There were two major state responses to mass immigration in the post-war period. The first was to pass a series of legislative measures designed specifically to restrict the arrival of black immigrants from the commonwealth. The 1962 Commonwealth Immigrants Act withdrew the right of Commonwealth citizens to settle in Britain and made it conditional on the granting of a restricted number of work permits. The 1968 Commonwealth Immigrants Act and the 1971 Immigration Act further restricted right of entry to those migrants who had 'patrial' ties, or at least one grandparent, born in Britain. 'Patrial', as is now widely accepted, was a concept designed specifically to identify White Commonwealth citizens as within the national community, and black ones as problematic and subject to immigration control.[11]

This position was not inevitable and nor was it natural. Despite the legacies of Empire and the discernible retreat into a domesticated version of national identity, popular reactions to black immigration can best be described as mixed, for at least the two decades after the arrival of *SS Windrush* in 1948. Richmond's study of 1955, for example, categorised Britons as one-third tolerant, one-third mildly prejudiced and one-third extremely prejudiced. Other studies of the same period found broadly similar, or more positive, results.[12] Nonetheless, a certain degree of caution, and often outright hostility, about specifically black immigration was also evident for all of this period. Stimulated, no doubt, by 'a sense of White supremacy nourished over many years' and by a fear of visible difference, there were not only physical outbreaks of sustained violence, but regular experiences of prejudice.[13]

This ambiguous picture turned into a political consensus on the damages wrought by specifically black immigration because of mounting state concern at black immigration, an early determination to halt it and the realisation that this necessitated careful explanation and justification. One key element in official explanations of the necessity for immigration controls was a rewriting of history. It involved forgetting the traces of the imperial past, marginalising inclusive definitions of British citizenship and rendering of black British subjects as aliens posing specific problems that needed particular policy solutions. The inveterate amateur historian, anti-immigration campaigner and Conservative MP and influential member of the Monday Club, John Stokes, summed up his own responsibilities in an immigration debate as 'trying to keep all that is best in England and to be able to hand on to my children, as my father handed on to me, a country to be proud of, a homogeneous nation, sharing the same faith, history and background'.[14] When Enoch Powell voiced these sentiments in 1968 they were still considered controversial in political circles. However, when the Conservative party leader, Margaret Thatcher, echoed them in 1978, speaking of the dangers of being 'swamped by people with a different culture' and discussing the 'prospect of a clear end to immigration', the propositions had become widely accepted in Parliament and electorally popular.[15] In terms of immigration legislation, the national community had been defined as primarily white.[16]

Yet the racialisation of immigration, the ascription of race identities to particular groups as though they were fixed and immutable, occurred not just at the level of political debate or in the passing of legislation designed to control immigration. Studies of education policy and practice, of health care and policing also contributed to the ascription of specific identities to groups who, initially, were defined primarily in terms of their colour. The West Indian mother, the black child and the mugger youth became pathological subjects, with particular psychological profiles and specific needs that, whatever their intention, contributed to experiences of public services that were routinely discriminatory.[17] However, and while skin colour was undoubtedly treated as the major signifier of difference, it was not the only sign of outsider status.

The Irish may have escaped the constraints of restrictive immigration legislation but they continued to inhabit a marginal position in English society. 'In the nation but not of it' was John Archer Jackson's apposite phrase to describe a distinct section of the population frequently subjected to popular prejudice and official scrutiny.[18] Pejorative name calling was underpinned by older historical stereotypes that continued to ensure that the Irish settling in Britain struggled to find rented accommodation, to obtain employment outside manual and service occupations, to secure mortgages when purchasing property, and they were overrepresented in crime statistics even before the development of the euphemistically named Troubles in Northern Ireland in 1969.[19] The slow escalation of violence in the province between a Nationalist and Catholic minority and a Loyalist and Protestant majority was to have quite disastrous consequences for the Irish in Britain. The deployment of British troops on the streets of Northern Ireland and their widespread and indiscriminate use of internment without trial only encouraged the perception of an occupying power holding up a redundant and illegitimate Protestant state. The Provisional Irish Republican Army (IRA), founded in 1969 with the expressed aims of defending Nationalist Catholics in Ireland and of bringing an end to the imperialist occupation of Ireland by Britain, also turned public spaces in England into legitimate targets for guerrilla warfare. The Troubles brought with them persistent calls for immigration controls on the Irish, not only on the basis of national security, but also because, as Enoch Powell argued, the Irish, like New Commonwealth citizens, were 'aliens' who 'did not belong in the United Kingdom' and who 'did not identify themselves with the rest of the institution, community or nation'.[20]

These sentiments became more voluble in the aftermath of the worst terrorist atrocities in England. Bombs planted by the Provisional IRA in pubs in Birmingham, Guildford and Woolwich were designed to inflict maximum damage on the civilian population. The consequences of the bombing included a virulent anti-Irish backlash that, in Birmingham, encompassed verbal diatribe, physical assault and the petrol bombing of local Catholic churches.[21] As well as popular hostility, the 1974 Prevention of Terrorism Act made the Irish in Britain an officially suspect community, subject to sweeping powers of stop, search and detention, which were enthusiastically and violently applied by police forces around the country.[22] Such experiences undoubtedly encouraged and confirmed the ethnicisation of the Irish and their sense of constituting a community apart. As one journalist put it, just weeks after the bombings and having sought out conversations in Irish pubs, clubs and places of work, 'it is impossible not to sense that some people who have long since given up thinking of themselves as immigrants, are now beginning to feel "Irish" in a way that has previously been reserved for Christmas and St. Patrick's Day'.[23] Even Paul Harrison, whose social reportage was careful to stress class and generational differences among the Irish in England, thought that the bomb attacks have 'made most of those I spoke to feel less at home here, and more like aliens'.[24] Thousands of first and second generation migrants were taken into custody and six young men were convicted on the basis of forced confessions. Their seventeen years in prison were a personal disaster but they were also widely interpreted in the Irish community as symbolic of their status as a community apart, tolerated but not really belonging.[25]

Alongside the ascription of black and Irish identities, there was a second significant state response to the arrival of large numbers of immigrants in the period after 1968. Even if an official view persisted that British traditions of tolerance would ensure that any prejudice towards immigrants would dissolve over time, the establishment and development of race relations legislation expressed a different model of toleration.[26] Cumulatively, the Race Relations Acts of 1965, 1968 and 1976 recognised the existence of racial discrimination, outlawed it and created a body to identify and conduct the schemes of public education that would help to create a harmonious multicultural society. That body was the Community Relations Commission (CRC) which was founded in 1968 and which has been a target for widespread criticism in all of its various guises ever since. In the popular media its main task, to encourage the growth of 'harmonious community relations', was widely interpreted as an attempt to impose politically correct attitudes and to stifle free thought. Members of the CRC were crudely caricatured as do-gooders and busybodies, meddling in matters better left to the common sense of the public.[27]

Scholarly analyses tend to have rather more substance but have generally shared the sceptical tone of popular criticisms. Katznelson's influential critique, for example, regarded the CRC as an attempt by dominant political parties to create a 'racial buffer' designed to protect the political establishment from black demands for fundamental social and political change.[28] By co-opting black leaders, by showing rhetorical commitment to racial integration, by supporting a social welfare approach to migrant and minority communities, the CRC worked as a barrier to the development of black consciousness and served to depoliticise racism. Certainly, the CRC had serious weaknesses, some of which were evident from the start. Administratively, the CRC occupied an uncertain space between local voluntary organisations and central and local government, from whom it received both finance and other forms of support.[29] The CRC duty to promote 'harmonious race relations' was not clearly defined, there was an associated lack of clarity around policy implementation and the role of the CRC in commissioning research was hampered by the lack of financial resource.[30] In other words, there was substance to the wide criticism that the CRC received for its lack of vision, political clout and credibility with minority communities.[31] These early failures help to explain the drastic revision and strengthening of race relations under the terms of the 1976 Race Relations Act that included a new and wider definition of discrimination, that made both direct and indirect discrimination unlawful in public institutions and established a single body, the Commission for Racial Equality (CRE), to work towards the elimination of discrimination, to promote equality of opportunity and good relations between persons of different racial groups.

Notwithstanding these weaknesses, however, both before but especially after the 1976 Race Relations Act, the public education role of the CRC/CRE was important. Frequently neglected by scholars, the attempt to modify social attitudes and values was one of the first tangible and permanent manifestations of the new multicultural era.[32] In their educational and campaigning work, and especially in the pages of the CRC journal *New Community* launched in 1971, the CRC/CRE drew heavily on race relations experts. They accepted that the nation was a culturally and ethnically homogeneous unit and that immigrants formed cultural or national 'out-groups' who inevitably became the target for popular prejudice. If, in practice, these out-groups were initially identified almost exclusively by reference to skin colour, race ideas linked them to ethnicity and national origins in marking out the 'nation's others'.[33] In fact, and under the terms of the 1976 Race Relations Act, an ethnic group was defined as having seven key characteristics; 'a long shared history, distinct traditions and customs, distinct geographical origins, their own language, a distinct literature and a common religion'.[34] In defining these characteristics the legislation confirmed that all those who remembered and could articulate a point of origin overseas, or in a subsequent legal judgment 'a long shared history of which the group is conscious' and 'the memory of which it keeps alive' could form an alien body in British society that required recognition, understanding and protection, as well as new forms of educational work to aid their integration to British society.[35] On this basis some states in Western Europe, as well as those dominated by white settlement around the globe, tentatively drifted towards multiculturalism and created the conditions for the proliferation of ethnicity.[36]

Politicians, educationalists and commentators may have been slow to accept the existence of domestic 'colour prejudice' but as they began to do so black–white relations, rather than racism, were configured as a source of potential social conflict. Such analyses of prejudice remained individualised, mostly located in cognitive processes and tackled only by rather vague liberal statements about cultural communication and understanding.[37]

An instructive example was the foundation in 1968 of the Working Group on Education for the Eradication of Colour Prejudice (WGEECP) by John Hunt (Conservative MP for Bromley in London). Hunt, later assisted by Joan Lester (Labour MP for Eton and Slough), wanted to establish a group which would work towards the 'gradual eradication of colour prejudice through educational means with particular emphasis on the education of the school population as a whole, and not on immigrants as a separate group'. As an explicit response to Enoch Powell's Rivers of Blood speech, and indicative of a deliberately less hostile and less imperial Conservative response to immigration, Hunt saw the WGEECP as a kind of information and coordination body for parliamentarians, ensuring that colour prejudice got equal prominence with 'immigrant and coloured children's problems' and distributing important developments in the research field.[38]

However, influenced by race relations scholars, that research field continued to be largely a psychological and educational space that was devoid of the long-term historical perspectives beginning to emerge in black communities. Aside from politicians, those invited to speak to the Group, or work for it, were mostly psychologists with a sprinkling of educationalists. They included child psychologist James Hemmings, psychiatrist Antony Storr, Jack Wrigley and Keith Cooper of the Schools Council and the influential social psychologist, Henri Tajfel. Despite its stated aim of exploring relationships between groups in society, the WGEECP showed little interest in the constitution of those groups and struggled to move away from a focus on what Tajfel called, in a 1968 report to the Group, the 'cultural and linguistic problems of immigrant children' and the 'psychological attitudes of coloured children and other immigrant groups'.[39] This indicates how the founding assumptions of the WGEECP tended to come from social psychology and showed little interest in the processes through which immigrant children, and their cultures or ethnicities, were coming to be defined as a topic for research. By November 1969 the group had identified three priorities: the evaluation of present research projects; promoting better communication between academic disciplines and research projects; and, tellingly, research into the 'needs, methods and attitude formation for a multi-racial society, as distinct from research into the problems of minority groups'.[40] A year later, in November 1970, a Group newsletter reported, in rather plaintive terms, 'not more than a peripheral interest in our terms of reference and the actual Minutes reveal the very slow progress we have been able to record'.[41] 'A group of "reasonable, cautious, well-meaning liberal people"', containing 'no extremists' and with 'no money', 'it has achieved almost nothing' concurred an education officer at the BBC, before deciding it was safe to participate in a WGEECP conference on television, radio and the multiracial society.[42]

Parliamentary interest into research in education and prejudice may have initially proved disappointing but academics were nonetheless important in shaping state responses to mass immigration. This was because by the 1970s, a model of 'experimental public policy formation' had been established in which social science research was incorporated into government to an unprecedented degree.[43] As was noted in the last chapter, research work on immigration and race in the immediate post-war period was already a partial exception to the initially weak institutional position of the social sciences in Britain.

But it was strengthened further by the establishment in 1965 of the Social Science Research Council (SSRC), chaired by sociologist, Michael Young, which cemented relationships between social science research and government and which championed gradualist solutions to designated race relations problems. When the SSRC-funded centre, the Research Unit on Race Relations (RURR) was founded in 1970 under the directorship of Michael Banton, there appeared to be little theoretical interest in the formulation of the race relations problematic and an implicit agreement about the social ends that the RURR was to serve. Publicly at least, the RURR took for granted that races existed, that different race identities were a potential source of social conflict and that they would require mediation and management for the pursuit of social stability.[44]

Privately, every aspect of the work of the RURR was the subject of conflict and debate. Banton's Unit, based at the University of Bristol, was successful in developing applied research projects not just through the auspices of the SSRC but also through the mechanisms set up by central government to recognise and address the growth of urban deprivation. RURR contributions to government urban renewal policies, notably in the Urban Aid Programme and Community Development projects, outwardly suggest a confident research programme with growing influence. It was certainly becoming possible to find both funding and jobs, even if they were jobs without tenure and funding tended to be relatively short term. In public, the study of race relations appeared to be a vibrant area of growth. Internally, however, any kind of consensus on exactly what RRUR was supposed to be studying and how best to do so remained elusive. An early name change, from Research Unit on Race Relations to Ethnic Relations, was insisted on by staff who maintained that '"race" was not an accurate designation of what they were studying'. Their preference for Group Relations Research Unit was rejected by an academic advisory committee that included social psychologist Henri Tajfel because 'it did not clearly signal to the outside world and to Parliament, that relations between ethnic groups were the chief object of interest'.[45] This was an astute and revealing intervention. It demonstrated an early understanding that social science research was closely bound to particular definitions of social problems and it made clear that a key condition of funding was the assumption that British society consisted of different ethnic or racial groups with different psychologies or cultures or natures. Any research that cast doubt on that fundamental assumption, or whose immediate application was unclear, like Peter Weinreich's theoretical review of identity or Banton's desire to appoint a historian, for example, was open to criticism and critical review because it did not obviously or immediately support the emerging educational, cultural and therapeutic strategies that sought to build strong ethnic identities.[46] Indeed, Banton's directorship of the Unit ended in 1979 following Social Science Research Council criticism of the 'conceptualisation, content and conduct of much of its research'.[47]

The preference of state agencies and funding bodies for academic research into race relations is one of the reasons why it was Tajfel's social psychology that became influential in the 1970s and 1980s. Its mode of analysis insisted on a universal process of cognition that inevitably created clear distinctions between particular kinds of in-groups and out-groups. Arguably the single most influential text on education and race in this period was published by a student of Tajfel's, David Milner. Milner's *Children and Race* (1975) explored children's prejudices and focused both on black children's self and group images, and white children's attitudes towards ethnic minority groups.[48] The book, republished in 1984 in a substantially revised edition, would go on to achieve what Barry Troyna accurately described as 'reverential status' in academic and policy discourse.[49] A critical element in the development and practices of multicultural education in the 1980s, these identity studies concentrated on processes of social cognition in which an individual sought to establish a sense of coherence and continuity with wider society. The complexity of modern societies required mental schemata that classified and categorised; constructs like gender, race, religion and occupation were seen as helping individuals make sense of the world. Milner stressed that these categories, or social representations, had a history that required scrutiny and that they were also the basis of stereotypes which tended to accentuate the similarities within groups and the differences between them. However, because categorisation and stereotyping were not abnormal but a fundamental part of ordinary cognition, they were, more or less implicitly, also regarded as difficult to alter and perhaps even permanent.[50] Milner's work may have been located within a distinctly sociological social psychology but it was widely interpreted as demonstrating that, in a nation with a long imperial history, prejudices against identified out-groups, especially if they were black, was both natural and inevitable.[51]

Importantly, Milner's *Children and Race* (1975) seemed to show that black and white children expressed a preference for what were now called white identities. In doing so, claimed psychologists and educationalists, black children were said to be expressing a form of self-rejection, self-hate or a severe form of low self-esteem just like children in the USA where this kind of research had played a central role in the desegregation of schooling.[52] Milner was optimistic that the construction of a positive black consciousness would reduce the identity conflicts experienced by black children but his work was firmly located in a tradition of research that went right back to the Chicago School of Sociology. Indeed, Milner's research was crucial because it endorsed the widely held assumption that 'culture clashes' caused psychological distress for individuals and that modern migration posed unprecedented problems in race relations.[53]

The logical policy responses to the identity studies paradigm, and a key cause of their popularity, were to develop educational materials, and wider cultural and therapeutic strategies, that helped to promote a stronger sense of identity. If these responses were initially centred on black migrants and their children they would also come to be applied to the Irish in England, as evidence of their disproportionate tendency to suffer mental illness was taken up by activists and educationalists in the 1980s.[54] Alongside the tight controls placed on immigration, therefore, state policies encouraged a slow and contested movement towards multiculturalism. They did so by appealing to the idea of tolerance that loomed so large in the national imaginary and by slowly developing educational practices and policies that, in recognising the existence of ethnic minorities and of domestic prejudice, necessarily opened up a space for the discussion of histories outside the national master narrative. Yet, if these were new histories, or more accurately, historical memories, there remained limits on the types of stories they could tell. Ethnic memory was tolerated because of its assumed psychological benefits and, in particular, for its contribution to individual and collective esteem. It formed part of a therapeutic ethos, increasingly evident in the human sciences and with particular applications in education and mental health, which was ultimately concerned with the management of the self.[55] The focus on subjectivity, on memories, esteem and identities, would ultimately come at the expense of a convincing account of social change and material inequalities.

Memories, esteem and identities

By the late 1960s, policy documents, campaigning pamphlets and public discussions of immigration began to interrogate the national master narrative and they did so in a manner conditioned by social science research. A psychologised language of race relations, of ethnicity and identity entered the public domain and were increasingly the idiom through which claims for social and educational change were expressed. This was not only because they were flexible and capable of wide interpretation but also because they secured consensus around the need for educational and therapeutic interventions. A typical example was *Race Relations and the Secondary School: A Statement of Minimum Requirements*, a pamphlet produced by the Education Committee of the Ealing Community Relations Council. These minimum requirements amounted to the demand that all secondary school pupils needed to study the factors in personal and group psychology which predisposed individuals to racial and cultural prejudice, and that first and second generation immigrant pupils needed to have the opportunity to undertake a detailed study of the 'land of their forefathers because it is felt that a child sundered from his family roots and the language and atmosphere of his infant years risks psychological damage (rootlessness) and social damage (exacerbated culture clashes within the family)'.[56] In identifying twin educational needs, of a majority population predisposed to both racial and cultural prejudice and a minority population with a need for 'roots' in the land of their forefathers, the Ealing Community Relations Council, like countless others around the country, echoed both the educational ambitions beginning to be set out by the CRC and by the growing number of projects involved with researching the problems of multicultural societies.[57]

The CRC's self-help fund was established in 1974 and earmarked for 'organisations promoting self-help activities mainly but not exclusively among young West Indians' between the ages of 13 and 25 and whose 'level of alienation' and resistance to statutory authorities was interpreted as a problem that had to be solved. Grants were available for the provision of three basic needs: 'counselling schemes, supplementary education and/or literary projects and training facilities'.[58] Such projects were designed to promote minority cultures but, assessing progress in 1977, the CRC made it clear that more needed to be done to enable ethnic minorities to transmit their cultures and, in doing so, to establish a secure sense of identity that would enable minority children to withstand the damage inflicted by a racially discriminating society. As well as making curricula recommendations for schools, the CRC proposed that black studies be encouraged in the further education and youth sectors of social services.[59] The hope was that such projects would boost the self-esteem, assuage the anger and frustration of young West Indians and also, perhaps, to facilitate some form of vocational training.

The CRC was an important funder of educational projects that initially, and reflecting the racialisation of immigration, were largely confined to black community groups. In 1973, for example, the Wandsworth Supplementary Education Project received a grant of £1,000 as did the Kwame Nkrumah Supplementary School. In 1974 the Wolverhampton Community Relations Council received a grant of £2,495 for what was described as a Black Studies Series.[60] In urban areas across England projects promoting or invoking Black Studies began. Their precise content and actual practices could vary widely but Black Studies programmes were characteristically interdisciplinary and committed to understanding the contemporary position and the historical experiences of African peoples and the African diaspora. Established in the USA as part of the development of African-American political movements, they attracted considerable attention in England during the 1970s.[61] One of the reasons they did so was because of the growing influence and the broad assent that the identity paradigm could command. Even the CRC became involved in the promotion of one version of Black Studies in the belief if would address the low esteem of black youth and help them to develop a positive identity.

Sam Morris, born in Grenada in 1908 and a sometime teacher, army officer, civil servant, educational researcher and the last general secretary of the League of Coloured Peoples, was the deputy chief officer of the CRC in the early 1970s.[62] He also became a champion for a rather moderate version of Black Studies in England. In 1973 he helped to establish the 'Committee for Black Studies' that campaigned for the introduction of Black Studies in schools and on training programmes for teachers, youth workers, the police and others. In this Morris faced an unenviable task. Even though the acknowledgement of prejudice was becoming more commonplace, this was very far from a majority opinion, even within professional or policymaking circles. Even those sympathetic to multicultural education tended to deny the existence of racism and the necessity for black education programmes, which were often dismissed as divisive and dangerously radical. On the other hand, Morris was seen by activists of some local groups as too close to the establishment; an Uncle Tom figure whose association with the CRC and the League of Coloured Peoples marked him out as somebody out of touch with local communities.[63]

Morris was at least partly aware of this. At the CRC Annual Conference in 1973 he gave a paper on the 'Implications of Black Studies in Britain' that was subsequently published in the CRC's journal, *New Community*.[64] Somewhat vaguely defining Black Studies 'as an investigation in depth by black people (chiefly New World Africans) of themselves, a study of their past, an application of their present and their aspirations for the future', Morris attempted to present a moderate case for Black Studies. He stressed how it would provide 'recognition of black identity and black awareness where these are not already present, and it will strengthen them where they are' and approvingly quoted a passage from Roucek and Kiernan's textbook for Black Studies in the USA, *The Negro Impact on Western Civilization* (1970), to the effect that Black Studies could alter the ghetto consciousness of black people, 'alter their image of themselves, their motivations and their ability to achieve'.[65] As with other early literature, Morris also claimed that the introduction of Black Studies in schools, specifically Tulse Hill and William Penn, had been a remarkable success with beneficial effects for pupil motivation and behaviour. The broadcasting of a series of twenty Black Studies lessons on Radio London in 1972, organised with the help of Teachers Against Racism (TAR), and the slow development of Black Studies training courses for professionals around the country demonstrated the growing interest in the subject.[66] The time had come, Morris argued, to move beyond ad hoc arrangements and he urged for the Inner London Education Authority to take a lead in developing pilot schemes of work, and for the British Council of Churches, the Institute of Race Relations, the Runnymede Trust and the CRC to launch a drive to recruit and train future teachers.[67]

When Black Studies was presented as a programme to address problems in the self image or self confidence of black children, it could attract some support because, as Bridget Harris of TAR argued, it taught black children 'black history, a sense of their own value, past, and culture' and 'it not only greatly improved their learning capacity in the general school system, but also reduced race tensions in those schools'.[68] Of course, the focus of these interventions remained squarely on black children and, even then, proposed methods for Black Studies proved controversial. Sam Morris, for example, outlined for a curriculum of thirty six lessons began with ancient Egypt, ended with 'the Cuban experience' and covered Columbus's New World voyage, slavery, African colonisation, Third World politics, neo-colonialism and pan-Africanism in between.[69] Such a curriculum clearly had radical credentials and possibilities. 'For a growing number of Black Britons', noted the journalist Sandy Kirby in the journal *New Society*, 'it's not just a simple matter of knowing who they are; they want to know the structures that keep them where they are, the patterns of relationships that have stepped into colonialism's breach, and the place this society is prepared to cede them. Black studies thus becomes less a cultural than a wide political concept'.[70] If this unwittingly reproduced the idea that any interest in Black Studies placed individuals outside the nation, it also helps to explain the ultimate reluctance for educational authorities to develop curricula in Black Studies. Many politicians and education-alists worried precisely about the political concepts in Black Studies, the divisiveness of even the cultural versions of the curriculum and the ultimate damage that would be done to 'race relations'. Miss Garvie of the Association of Teachers in Colleges and Departments of Education worried, for example, that Black Studies would offend the sensitive nature of adolescent girls who did not want to be identified as different and many of whom wanted to pull away from their cultural background.[71] In a political environment in which assimilation and integration were routinely discussed as policy goals, declarations of difference continued to be interpreted as radical, and especially left-wing, challenges to English culture. This is certainly one of the reasons why Morris publically, but rather unconvincingly claimed, that 'to meet the demand for Black Studies a number of areas, partic-ularly in London, now run Saturday morning schools on the initiation of some Community Relations Officers'.[72] But the suggestion that the CRC-initiated Black Studies classes was certainly an exaggeration and it was one designed to assuage the anxieties of liberals and to confer on those projects a degree of official respectability.

In reality, of course, Morris was not a leader of educational change and there was no singular or unified black community controlled by a single leader or group. These were fictions that emerged in the media, among politicians and policymakers and in a general public now used to scare stories about the rise of black power and becoming familiar with the language of ethnic minority communities.[73] There were certainly influential activists, but there was never any sustained unity in the field of black politics, culture or education. As will become clear below, some educational projects were radical but the existence of rather more conservative attempts to boost academic attainment received little publicity. Instead, both the media and state bodies were continually haunted by the phantom spectre of black radicalism and its presumed impact on the attitudes and behaviour of black youth. In the demands for supplementary education, black history, and the wider pursuit of a black identity free of the assumptions of the national master narrative, state officials frequently imagined the presence of anti-white ideologues committed to promoting the kinds of 'race war' that they saw breaking out in the USA and various parts of the decolonising world. Moreover, and on some occasions, officials suggested that an educational philosophy of pluralism implied a wider recognition of difference because the 'psychological difficulties of young and old in a new land are not confined to those from one part of the world'. This explains why the Select Committee on Race Relations and Immigration was not attracted to, and failed to support, proposals for Black Studies and opted, instead, for an approach they called 'unity through diversity'.[74]

The identity studies paradigm that emerged in England in the 1970s was the vehicle through which the position of immigrants and their children in English society was discussed. Its interest in processes of categorisation made it consistent with an emerging language of ethnic minorities. The acceptance that prejudice was inflected by historical processes opened up the opportunity to discuss historical processes and their legacies for the present and future. This helps to explain its influence and adoption. However, the overriding concern among race relations scholars and policymakers was with inherent cognitive processes and the psychology of immigrant groups. As such, it was not difficult to appeal to the novel language of identity studies while taking some very traditional positions.

One apposite example of the flexibility of the identity studies paradigm was presented in the confidential paper 'Policing in Racially Sensitive Divisions' written by Kenneth Newman, Commander of the New Scotland Yard's Community Relations Branch in 1973.[75] The Yard may have been the elite of the British police but it was deeply embroiled in corruption scandals in the early part of the decade and it was developing a deserved reputation for subjecting black immigrants to sustained campaigns of hostility and harassment.[76] Organised and sustained campaigns against the police, for causing the death of homeless Nigerian David Oluwale or charging the Mangrove Nine with affray, for example, ensured that allegations of brutality or discrimination had begun to receive extensive press coverage.[77] Newman set out a fourteen-page analysis of the causes and implications of the 'tensions' developing between police and West Indian youths. It repeated many well-established and racist assumptions about the 'West Indian community'; that the 'Victorian severity of parents produced difficult behavioural problems in children' and that 'West Indian children have a poor record of performance in schools and teachers complained about their difficult behaviour, their violence, their inattentiveness and their slow progress'. Similarly, Newman claimed, unemployment figures for West Indian youths were above average because 'their expectations are frequently too ambitious and in excess of their capacity and qualifications', but they were 'unwilling to lower their sights' and engage in menial work. If these sound like the usual racist claims, there followed an important section, entitled 'History', in which it is possible to detect the influence of the identity studies paradigm. Here Newman argued that:

> History and the tradition of subjection to white supremacy left an aftermath of something akin to an inferiority complex in older West Indians. In an effort to free themselves from the shackling effect of this psychological hang-up, the idea that 'black is beautiful' has been promulgated for good and worthy motives. However, in black youth, pursuit of this concept often takes an aggressive form towards whites who appear to frustrate their aspirations and towards their parents whom they regard as having been too submissive. Many of them have a vague notion, exploited by the militants among them, that they are owed something because our ancestors 'exploited' theirs.[78]

A senior police officer's fleeting recognition that there are historical processes underpinning current social relations partly explains Newman's later reputation as a progressive police reformer. Yet any potential changes in police practices are lost first in the denigration, captured in the inverted commas, of the idea that a history of exploitation was real and had lasting legacies, and then in the observation that while attempts to alter the psychology of West Indian youth were good and worthy, they were doomed to fail because they were overtaken by an aggression and naivety that was exploited by unnamed militants. What remains is the idea that black youth have psychological problems, manifested in aggressive behaviour, whose origins may be found in a past that was definitively over. The long discussion of management and command policies that emphasised how black youth clubs required 'careful handling' was a more typical police analysis and consistent with Newman's later insistence that Jamaicans were 'constitutionally disorderly' and 'anti-authority'.[79] Coupled with a definition of subversion that incrementally moved from the 'overthrow of the state by unlawful means' to 'activities which threaten the wellbeing of the state', Newman's paper helps to explain some of the activities of both Special Branch and the Special Patrol Group and their destructive impact on the experiences of black immigrants and their children.

The dominant concern with the safety of the state also marginalised political reforms designed to tackle prejudice and promote positive forms of identity for black people. Successive governments and race relations scholars of the 1960s and 1970s regularly proclaimed that it was desirable that immigrant groups develop their own political and cultural organisations. These organisations would serve an integrative function in which political dialogue would develop a reciprocal understanding of the problems that immigrant communities faced and the ways in which political organisation and lobbying could address these needs. Yet, and in practice, state desire for democracy did not extend much beyond a circumscribed request for respectable representation that did not offend the analyses set out by race relations bureaucracy and endorsed by psychological and educational research. To take one pertinent example, the Home Office Response to the 1974 Report on Immigration and Race Relations thought it 'highly desirable that both the Government and the new Commission [for Racial Equality] should encourage the growth of minority group organisations, but that 'in considering appointments to such bodies as the Standing Advisory Council and the Commission for Racial Equality the Government is conscious of the need to select individuals of high calibre who can speak for the minorities with experience and insight'.[80] But, in the event, only certain experiences and insights, and those which centred on apparently practical tasks like English-language teaching and the provision of multiracial playgroups, were sought. Identifying domestic racism, promoting equality and building more inclusive identities, or what Chris Mullard called the 'real work of teaching black people their history, the institutionalised savagery of white racism, how to defend themselves, how to find and live with themselves', did not feature prominently on these kinds of agendas.[81] And when state bodies funded educational projects that they thought respectable but were worried about their activities, as in the case of the George Padmore and Albertina Sylvester supplementary schools in London, they could 'expressly ask[ed] that this project should not be publicised in the press'.[82]

Some radical CRC officers existed, and some of them certainly promoted Black Studies, but most were more cautious and framed their opinions and their expectations around what former community relations officer and anti-racist campaigner Ann Dummett called a 'national popular mythology'; the stories of decency and tolerance that helped to hide the facts of the past.[83] For Dummett, community relations work was a failure because it had no clear vision of how to advance the stated goal of a multiracial society. Instead, such work drew more or less implicitly on concepts, forms of organisation and practices inspired by movements in the very different circumstances of the USA.[84] These entirely ignored the very different historical conditions that shaped the practices of community relations in England. The existence of a global Empire, of a Commonwealth citizenship that was rhetorically inclusive and the absence of formalised segregation and discrimination between groups, were important influences on the ways in which people in England thought about themselves and others. Yet, as Dummett pointed out, their significance was completely lost in ahistorical programmes that too often ended up focusing on the problems supposedly caused by immigration or on teaching about race relations through the exchange of cultural information. The Schools Council's Humanities Project on Race, she argued, failed to put 'race into context. Everywhere it is isolated from other historical, social and political information. The effect of this selection is to emphasise that racial difference is itself a cause of problems – that is to accept an essential assumption of racism itself.'[85]

Indeed, and despite having a minimal goal of changing expressed attitudes, the scanty evidence that emerged from community and race relations projects was not encouraging. Too often they became a vehicle for the expression of prejudiced views, a source of deep frustration for activists, and one that became embroiled in controversies that often ended up with their withdrawal.[86] The reason, of course, was that early race relations approaches focused on cross-cultural understanding, on the exchange of information, on the teaching English, and on social mixing. It had very little space for discussing the dynamics or legacies of history. Race relations practitioners took national popular mythology, English tolerance and decency, as a fixed starting point and had little room for perceived dissent on the achievements of British civilisation. Historical narratives, and especially versions of black history, were sometimes promoted but more or less implicitly as a therapeutic, rather than analytical, resource. Focusing on the feelings and esteem of black children did not adequately explain structures of exploitation and domination and nor did they address the legacies of empire on the attitudes and identities of English people. Yet, in some religious movements and organisations, and especially those Christian institutions inspired by the social justice agenda emanating from the Second Vatican Council and the World Council of Churches, there were educational projects designed to address just these issues.[87]

In 1974, the British Council of Churches, concerned about claims of racism in society, established a Working Party on Britain as a Multi-Racial Society. The group was given a broad brief (examining and assessing impact of immigration on society; discovering the forces at work; articulating the principles revealed; describing the objective for a new multiracial society) and the freedom to explore particular issues and themes. In the final Working Party report Chair Gus John wrote that:

> A pronounced and almost cynical lack of attention to history on the part of white society has accounted for a situation where black people in Britain today are being regarded as if they are aliens from another planet suddenly transported to a society which has had no experience of a black presence and bears no responsibility for their troublesome presence now.[88]

Britain, John argued, was 'refusing to come to terms with its own history'.[89] The development of a multiracial society required a sustained and serious historical education that would explain the presence of black immigrants and explore and critique responses to them. John's vision, strongly influenced by the Marxist scholar Ambalavaner Sivanandan, was for a long-term historical and structural analysis, and one which was not confined to identifying cognitive processes or the emotionality of esteem in first and second generation black children. In practice, however, these attempts at historical education for multiracial societies struggled to find a language and a tone in which the investigation of historical processes could take place without resorting to a language of 'victim' and 'oppressor' and 'innocent' and 'guilty'. History was often imagined as a discrete set of experiences that belonged to either blacks or whites, a tendency reinforced by the loose application of concepts of race and ethnicity that saw history as determining feature of identity. In addition, racialised forms of public communication, in which the looming possibility of a race war was significant, made meaningful dialogue and reflection extremely difficult.[90]

The Zebra Project, established in the Methodist Bow Street Mission in London in 1975, attempted just this kind of dialogue. In the Project, history, or perhaps popular memory, was identified as a source of confusion, misunderstanding and, ultimately, racism. It, too, claimed that the course of British history was badly misrepresented and its legacies completely ignored. Quoting from a book of Aboriginal short stories, the Reverend Tony Holden argued that what used to be called 'the Expansion of Europe' was the 'saddest and most terrible theme in history' but it was important precisely because it continued to shape attitudes and behaviour in the present and was a direct obstacle to the development of new, pluralist societies.

'There is a sense in which', Holden argued, 'we are inevitably racist in Britain because we are an ex-colonial power'. While that sense was never clearly spelled out, it was loosely associated with black experiences of racism and discrimination and a refusal to understand or embrace the coming of multiculturalism:

> They want us to pretend it is not happening. They want, often, to turn the clock back to some imaginary time before our social bereavement as a nation, to a time when they falsely imagine there was only one way of being English.

Holden's analysis, clearly influenced by race awareness training in the USA, was strongly dialogic. This meant that rather than simply affirming the importance of developing a positive black identity and consciousness, he also insisted that whites had most to learn from these efforts. Revisiting the past held out the promise of unravelling a history of economic exploitation, colonisation and trade in human beings. White liberation meant freedom from untruth and required changes in the educational system. The purpose of eliminating racism from textbooks, of reviewing school curricula for a multiracial society, of introducing Black Studies, was not to accommodate black children. It had a far more fundamental aim; 'seeing the world with fresh eyes'.

The Project itself developed a short course called 'Face to Face' in which small groups of black and white Christians met together on five successive weekday evenings to agree a programme of events to promote understanding. Typically, a black speaker began by sharing something of the black experience. A second event consisted of a filmstrip or film about the black experience. A third event could involve a visit to a Pentecostal church. A fourth event was devoted to assessing what has happened and what has been learned.[91]

All this amounted to an ambitious project and it embodied the kind of meaningful dialogue that activists like John and Dummett were seeking. It sought to gather Christians together and it sought to promote knowledge of the impact of European colonialism on black people worldwide. Versions of it were practised in many of the big cities with significant Afro-Caribbean communities; in London, Birmingham and Liverpool for example.[92] But it also sat uncomfortably with the established idioms of British life; the public profession of racial discrimination, as either victim or unwitting perpetrator, was difficult in a country where personal privacy and a national reputation for tolerance were still highly prized. So there were practical difficulties. But there were also more conceptual ones.

The Zebra Project can be taken as further evidence of the influence of psychological theories of identity and race in the 1970s. Originating in the USA, these theories tended to locate racism and prejudice in the universal cognitive processes of individuals. For some social psychologists, these cognitive processes of social categorisation were inflected by particular historical and cultural circumstances which required study, dialogue and reflection to properly understand. However, and all too frequently, the attention to historical processes as important resources in understanding personal identities and the formation of social groups, was lost in favour of a generic black–white model of analysis. This was the case for the emerging body of race relations literature that drew inspiration from the USA and from the US psychologist, Judith Katz. Katz conceptualised racism as a psychological disorder that was deeply embedded in white people from a very early age on both a conscious and unconscious level and that 'being White ... implies being racist'.[93] This was because while there were inherent cognitive processes that always resulted in prejudice, racism was qualitatively different. Prejudicial thoughts or actions were purely individual but only some of those were taken up, translated into law, custom and common sense and thereby reinforced by a wide range of institutions into a systematic form of oppression.

The proposed solution was education. Despite being 'largely untested and unused' in the USA, Race Awareness Training (RAT) programmes were widely adopted in the 1980s, especially as part of local government attempts to tackle racism.[94] RAT challenged individuals to examine the origins of their attitudes and feelings and was potentially a space for discussing, for example, the significance of the British Empire in the formation of emotions and identities. In RAT training there were opportunities to discuss British imperialism and its consequences but the whole process was individualised and, in important respects, ahistorical. It was designed to correct individual attitudes that were the product of inherent cognitive processes but held up by normative social arrangements. Prejudice was seen as universal and inevitable and it was transformed into racism by a history reduced to simplistic story of white dominance over blacks. White racism, and the whiteness that it depended on was, as Sivanandan put it, a kind of original sin.[95] Those identified as 'whites' took the role of oppressors and were encouraged to develop a relationship to the past that was defined by the need to expiate the collective guilt of their forbears.[96] In other words, these were psychological renditions of the past that lacked both historical accuracy and sensitivity. Racism became a property of whites who always benefited from it. History was reduced to a simple prelude of the present. Long-term historical and structural analysis, with the possibility of change, was marginalised.[97]

In fact, and in practice, attempts to promote harmonious community relations in either formal or informal educational projects often resulted in an exclusive focus on the psychology of the immigrant. That they did so was partly to do with the growing influence of North American race relations model that relied on the conceptual framework provided by the psychologists Kenneth and Mamie Clark. These social–psychological accounts of identity formation and race were clearly apparent in Britain by the middle of the 1970s and travelled successfully because they were adaptable enough to appeal to educational authorities, to campaigning minority groups and the psychological and therapeutic professionals who were slowly becoming to be involved in dealing with the effects of racism. Social–psychological explanations accounted for the problems of black youth in terms of the damage to esteem inflicted by racism. This proved a durable explanation, despite research that found no differences in the self-esteem between groups of children categorised as West Indian, Asian and English, and it presented a field susceptible to the interventions of the social welfare approach of local community relations councils.[98]

The social psychology of identity sought to address the individual and social aspects of identity formation and rightly stressed the importance of identifying with and establishing a sense of belonging with a wider community. When this community was primarily and routinely imagined as white it was claimed to impose damage on those identified as black and inspired in them a search for historical roots, for that important sense of continuity that was the basis of personal and social identities. The difficulty was not with this as a theoretical account of identity formation but rather in its practical applications. These tended to move away from politics and history, and from the historical conditions that promoted race ideas and racism, and towards a concern with culture, and with individual and group esteem. As the Barbadian journalist Louis Chase complained 'well-meaning people' had encouraged 'youth clubs and exhibition centres for an emerging black sub-culture' that had become the 'subject of analysis by social psychologists, sociologists and ill-equipped and quasi-trained youth club leaders'. In Bristol, he argued, it was 'essential to look at roots' and to 'rediscover and publicise Bristol's involvement in the slave trade'.[99]

From the middle of the 1970s, it would become more and more commonplace for migrant activists to seek to establish secure identities by struggling for their pasts. Resisting the social and psychic alienation engendered by dominant national histories, seeking to confront and expose experiences of Western imperialism and recovering historical identities, became central to all sorts of political, educational and therapeutic practices.[100] These were, to be sure, marginal practices. As will become clear below, they were small in number, struggling for resources and dependent on the admirable commitment and determination of activists. In their struggles, activists understandably deferred questions about their ultimate aims and the longer term outcomes of their activities. However, such questions were never far away. When C.L.R. James accepted a visiting Black Studies professorship in the USA he told an audience at Federal City College Washington that he did not believe there was any such thing as

Black Studies and that the reading of history as 'some kind of ethnic problem is a lot of nonsense'. 'I only know the struggle of people against tyranny and oppression in a certain social and political setting and, particularly, the last two hundred years. It's impossible for me to separate black studies and white studies.'[101] That view was to become rarer as the past was increasingly deployed as a guarantee of contemporary identities in both formal and informal education. This was not necessarily the result of intentional action by scholar activists. Instead, and as they went about the work of researching and teaching a history that explained their experiences, scholar activists inhabited a space dominated by a philosophy of race relations. While their struggles for a past produced new forms of historical education, it did not, and could not, escape the ideology of race or fix the meaning of black and Irish ethnic identities.

Struggles for a past

On 1 December 1968 in Birmingham, Mihar Gupta, a 33-year-old teacher from Calcutta, told an audience of more than seven hundred, mostly South Asian, immigrants in Birmingham that Black Power was the successor to the anti-slavery and anti-colonial campaigns. One of the organisers of what was claimed to be the first national conference of black youth in Britain, Gupta declared a new historical era was at hand. Three hundred years of turning the other cheek were over, he said, it was time to slap back. A report in *The Times* noted, somewhat ominously, that the mood of the conference had been set by a formal, clenched fist, black-gloved salute, in the manner seen at the Mexico Olympics.[102]

US influences were also detected in at least some analyses of the tensions that erupted in Northern Ireland in the winter of 1968.[103] Committed to the non-violent means of the civil rights movement in the USA and adopting the hymn of cotton-picking black slaves, liberals and nationalists demanded an end to the sectarian discrimination against Catholics that was a defining feature of life in Northern Ireland. One early confrontation in the Troubles took place in Armagh in November 1968. Televised, and subject to a special report by the news programme *Panorama*, it featured an interview with the Reverend Ian Paisley who explained his successful attempt to prevent Protestants and Loyalists taking a stand in 'defence of their heritage' in a civil rights march.[104] That heritage was explained in the film as belonging to the seventeenth century and to the Counter-Reformation. Shortly afterwards, and perhaps not coincidentally, some commentators expressed concern that perceptions of Irish immigrants in England were stuck in the past, conformed to nineteenth-century images of the Irish as drunken, violent and stupid, which made the process of assimilation more difficult.[105]

If 1968 has become overwhelming associated with a youth revolution, and one often condemned for its hedonistic individualism, events in Birmingham and in Armagh signalled other processes at work. The continuing struggles for decolonisation and the emergence of civil rights movements fuelled a politics of recognition in which groups hidden from the master narratives of national and imperial history began to articulate what were presented as distinctive historical experiences. But what those experiences were, and what it meant to be black or Irish in England, were not straightforward but the subject of research and reflection and of discussion and debate. They were, moreover, just one element in the new social movements that also embraced feminism and gay rights and which were also concerned with issues of recognition, belonging and identity.

One forum for those issues remained the church. Even if religious authorities reported again and again that migrants, whether from the Caribbean or from Ireland, had found the temptations of materialist England difficult to resist, and their estimates of those who had lapsed varied from around one-fifth to as many as one-half, churches remained of crucial significance to questions around identity and belonging.[106] This could be true in a negative sense. One of the most popular explanations for the decline in migrant church attendance, and the cause of considerable angst and controversy in churches themselves, was their unwillingness or inability to welcome migrant co-religionists. The devotional Catholicism of Ireland, the cults of the Virgin Mary and St Patrick, public procession and a distinctly Catholic popular culture, were absent outside of the big areas of Irish settlement in England, with the result that 'even when migrants did attend [mass] the physical location of the Irish at the back of the church was symbolic of their marginal status'.[107] English Catholics, wrote one honest worshipper, were 'embarrassed by the neo-superstition of their Irish co-religionists' and at least some clergy worried that Irish mysticism had legitimated violence in Northern Ireland.[108] Similarly black worshippers were often treated with coldness and insensitivity in traditional Christian churches in Britain. They routinely reported being ignored, patronised or asked not to return. Experiences of outright discrimination were common.[109]

However, and while formal allegiance to established churches certainly declined overall in this period, historians may have been rather too quick to dismiss their continuing significance as sites which both constrained and enabled those turns to the past that were crucial to the formulation of new identities. This happened in different ways. Black Sunday Schools may await their historian but there is little doubt that they were significant sites of learning and empowerment for women and children. Women like Esme Lancaster and Pastor Smith were important in developing the social and educational programmes in which scripture and biblical hermeneutics were employed to construct a specific sense of black community.[110] Similarly, and even for those who no longer attended weekly mass, the Catholic Church continued as the 'mediator between the migrant and wider society', not least because the Church retained responsibility for the schooling of Catholic children and therefore the vast majority of the migrant Irish. It is certainly the case that Catholic schools did little or nothing to facilitate or encourage the articulation of Irish national or migrant identities. Bernadette Hyland remembered, for example, the agenda of her Catholic high school as being designed to 'forget your Irishness'.[111] Indeed, and for some writers, the aggressive and specifically Anglo-Catholicity of school teaching, was the continuation of an older strategy of denationalisation that facilitated the integration of the Irish into British society.[112] In both schools and churches where the majority of young people might be second generation Irish, there was often a clear reluctance to provide activities dedicated to Irish culture and classes in history, language learning and dancing were overwhelmingly organised and paid for by parents.[113] Even so, the proximity at school to other Irish Catholics meant that even a schooling committed to denationalisation could be experienced as distinctive, precisely because it was in some way Irish.[114] This might just have been the realisation that the class register was 'like a Dublin phone book with Murphys, Reillys, Kellys and McMahons', or it might be an implicit but powerful imaginative sympathy with an oppressed Catholic minority in the English Reformation.[115] It could mean certain curricula interests, a desire to explore Irish history, or invoking nationalist historical memories when singing the English Catholic reformation hymn 'Faith of our Fathers'. Those 'fathers, chained in prisons dark' and who were 'still in heart and conscience free' were easily imagined as contemporary nationalists rather than sixteenth-century martyrs.[116]

That pupils could bring wider meanings to church and school routines is an indication of just how decisively developing identities were dependent on the reflexivity, or what sociologist Margaret Archer calls the internal conversations, of individuals. The precise workings of these conversations may elude historians who must routinely infer mental processes from documented or observed behaviour. Yet, individuals certainly exercised their mental ability to consider themselves in relation to their contexts and vice versa. Archer offers a sophisticated and robust account of just why 'human beings have the powers of critical reflection upon their social context and of creatively redesigning their social environment, its institutional or ideational configurations, or both'.[117] This offers a very different conceptualisation of the internal mental processes to that proffered by the social psychologists of race in the 1970s. In place of universal processes, inevitably producing prejudice that resulted in specifically white racism, the thinking and evaluating subject is apparent. This subject is both liberated and constrained in their reflections by available linguistic, cultural and social resources. Historical narratives, episodes and images, form a critical part of these resources.

Feeling, being or becoming Irish was, therefore, dependent both on the concerns of individuals and their adoption of the cultural resources in the homes and associational culture of the Irish in Britain. This was less a matter of formal instruction than the simple routines of everyday life. Working-class children lived their lives surrounded by Irish people; they read Irish papers, listened to Irish music and were a vital part of the rapid expansion of sporting, cultural and educational groups that contributed to a clear sense of living in a distinctive community. In these activities, argues Breda Grey, were 'the beginnings of a more self-conscious and coordinated Irish identity in Britain' and a movement away from Catholicism and the Catholic Church as the dominant cultural and educational institution in Britain.[118] This shift may have been reflected both in the foundation of the Federation of Irish Societies in 1974 and, in the pages of the *Irish Post*, the first general newspaper for the Irish in England, whose first edition was published in February 1970 and whose coverage of sport, culture and education helped to develop and consolidate a sense of the Irish as a distinctive and recognisable community. The editor and co-founder of the *Irish Post* was Brendan Mac Lua, an emigrant from County Clare, a former GAA official and, as one obituary writer put it, an 'extraordinary Irish nationalist and bon vivant' who 'played a leading role in creating an activist Irish community'.[119] A tribute in the House of Commons judged Mac Lua to have 'raised the standing and self-worth of an immigrant population to that of a community proud of its roots, its language, sports and identity'.[120]

These tributes may be exaggerations, typical of the biographical distortions inherent in obituary writing. But they also hint at Mac Lua's conviction, expressed some years later, that the post-war Irish migrants looked 'backwards, to home and usually the west of Ireland' to where their 'dreams of return lingered for many years'.[121] The result was that the Irish in England clung tightly to old regional loyalties, invested little in settling down in England and, thinking of themselves only as exiles or migrants, lacked the confidence and self-sufficiency of other visible communities or ethnic minorities. This judgement was arguably clearer in retrospect than it was at the time. Yet, despite important developments in the Irish cultural scene in England it was, as Mac Lua realised, also fragmented. There was no effective political lobby for the Irish in England, relatively little organisation outside of established Catholic and GAA networks and, according to historian and journalist Peter Beresford Ellis, 'a vanishing cultural identity of the Irish migrant community in England'.[122] In addition, and for some of the more explicitly nationalist correspondents to the *Irish Post*, the quality of Irish cultural activities, amounting only to 'second rate country songs', was a disappointment that accurately reflected the failures of the Irish Republic.[123]

Irish immigrants displayed typical ambiguity on questions of identity and their orientation to the past. Interviewed for a feature on the Irish in Birmingham on St Patrick's Day 1970, the popular singer and former carpenter, Larry Cunningham, made it clear that he would not sing nationalist rebel songs. 'Those days are over', he averred because 'an audience like this don't like thinking of past troubles. They want entertainment with a touch of the green, not harrowing memories.'[124] Commercial considerations may have underpinned this assertion because the most recognisable Irish singer and television presenter of this period was the distinctly mainstream Country and Western star, Val Doonican. Propriety dictated that conventional music and performers should ignore difficult and painful history. Many first generation immigrants, especially middle-class ones, seemed happy to leave the past behind. Yet, and because identity is never fully achieved but a dynamic process involving continuous reflection, the past could not and did not simply disappear. 'A late Saturday night visit to many a London pub' was journalist Mary Kenny reported, 'to happen upon the sentiment and early conditioning of Irish education, as the rebel songs were sung and Mother Ireland wept once more and a thousand pledges were made again to set old Ireland free'.[125] A nationalist and sentimental history, captured in songs and dance as much as formal historical narratives, was an integral part of the homes, clubs and pubs of Irish immigrants. As one reveller told the *Birmingham Mail*, 'patriots' enjoyed tearful celebrations on St Patrick's Day because the 'Irish love a good cry over the past'.[126]

Translating this populist nationalism into something more tangible and assertive depended, however, on the second generation of Irish immigrants. These were the children of the immigrants of the 1950s and 1960s, born to one or more Irish parents or educated in England, sometimes educated at Catholic grammar schools, politically left wing and with Republican sympathies. They included Ivan Gibbons, who founded the journal *Irish Studies* in 1981, sociologist Mary Hickman, historian and politician Alan Clinton, teacher Naseen Danaher and the writer and activist, Bernadette Hyland. This new generation of activists drove the renaissance of cultural activities that more or less directly explored this past. GAA clubs, Irish language classes, traditional music and dance may have traditionally expressed some sense of what it was to be Irish but, there was an increasing demand that these activities include explicit reference to, or teaching of, the Irish history and culture the revival in Irish ethnicity. The Federation of Irish Societies (FIS), for example, came under criticism for a lack of vigour, imagination and their neglect of the children of the immigrants of the 1950s and 1960s. Correspondents to the *Irish Post* were fiercely critical of the FIS 'tea and welfare approach', their 'lower middle class values' and their 'extreme regard for respectability in the eyes of the British host community' made them 'afraid of politics' and 'unable to develop a sense of Irishness in our youth'.[127] Even within the confines of radical feminism Irish women could feel disenchanted in a movement whose 'mythical universalism' managed to ignore 'British colonial history'.[128]

Slowly, and especially after the foundation of the Irish in Britain History Group, and the Irish in Britain Representation Group, there emerged a concerted effort to launch programmes of historical research and education. Taken collectively, and as the next chapter will show, these projects worked to educate second generation Irish about the histories of Ireland and Britain, and to explore their tangled relationships. They championed Irish language learning. They provided evening classes and Saturday schools and developed a significant, if fragile, presence in the adult and higher education sectors. In doing so, they attempted to provide the resources for new forms of subjectivity for Irish migrants, but particularly for their children born in England. Moreover, this attempt was successful. Through language, dance, music and song, the Irish narrated their history. They constructed a symbolic world that made sense, that intuitively felt right and that articulated something intangible but essential. It should not be a surprise that this process was never complete and that identifications remained contested and dynamic rather than fixed. Fluidity and complexity are the very stuff of identity and of the processes of identification. If this was true for the Irish it was also true for those black migrants, and especially those from the Caribbean, who were undergoing a parallel process.

Black history and radical education

Founded in the summer of 1968 by the Nigerian Obi Egbuna, the British Black Panthers were explicitly modelled on the US Black Panther Party (USBPP). The USBPP aimed to develop an international anti-capitalist struggle in response to a four-hundred-year period in which the West had systematically oppressed peoples in Asia, Africa, the Caribbean and the Americas.[129] In the USA, with the experience of domestic plantation slavery fresh in familial memory, and sustained in the community by African-American political and cultural organisations, the Panthers were able to draw on a well-established pool of shared historical memories. In England, however, the significance and meaning of those four hundred years, especially for Caribbean migrants with a British education, could not simply be assumed. Egbuna's account of the development of the Panthers, written in prison, told a powerful, but also obviously didactic and moral tale. 'One of the saddest consequences of Negro history', he wrote, 'is that while every other racial group in America enjoys a cultural linkage with her past the Negro was brutally and suddenly cut off from his own'. Segregated and lynched, it slowly dawned on black Americans that integration was impossible and this became for the Negro a 'blessing in disguise':

> The cultural rebuff of the Whites galvanised him [the Negro] into a desperate quest for his past. And the emergence of New African nations, in his land of origin, brought to the open very telling historical facts about his past. Africa was never a cultural vacuum as alleged by Whites.

Egbuna reported the rise of the hyphenated, Afro-American and a new Afro-American pride, fostered and taught at Afro-American 'schools of culture' that had 'sprung up everywhere like mushrooms'.[130]

The British media displayed an enduring fascination with the arrival of the Black Power movement in Britain. If it initially proved difficult for black voices to be heard in the British media and Black Power leaders, who were the subject of sensationalist and hostile reporting, were presented as a sinister forewarning of a future race war. However, the foundation of the British Black Panther Movement (BBPM) was only the most notorious of the many different social movements that explored the meaning of black identity in the period after 1968. The Panthers were feared, partly because of the violent rhetoric that they employed, but also because their foundation seemed to provide further evidence of the importation of US race relations, and all its problems, to Britain. Jonathan Powers's documentary on Black Power, broadcast on the BBC's Third Programme in April 1968, reported in typically epochal terms that:

> Probably no two other words in the last few years have been so grossly misunderstood as Black Power. Yet their meaning, once revealed, is of the utmost significance. They denote a movement of ideas, of feelings, of human upheaval that will not leave one of us untouched. The American race problem, in which Black Power plays a central role, is too large to be swept under the carpet. In fact, it is of such a size as to influence the whole course of world politics: for if one thing is clear, it is that the major sources of conflict in the latter part of this century will be the twin problems of race and poverty and that America will, in one way or another, be at the hub of whatever conflicts do emerge.

The immediate effect of the programme, like so much press coverage of Black Power, seemed to confirm the impression, widely promoted in the popular media, that 'race problems' were being imported to Britain specifically as a result of black immigration. In fact, the programme tried hard to shift the focus of debate towards the attitudes and relationships engendered by Western imperialism. It made reference to the psychological research that showed that 'in the earliest drawings, stories and dreams of Negro children, there appears the desire to be white and to reject their own colour'. In addition, and in interview excerpts with the US novelist James Baldwin, space was given to the argument that Black Power was not a movement of hate but one whose origins and aims were directly related to the attitudes and assumptions generated by Western imperialism that, said Baldwin, 'assumed that millions of people had no culture worth preserving, and no identities worth respecting and they could be used by the Western powers for ever'. 'There was', Baldwin memorably declared, 'no hope for white people as long as they think they're white' and, in doing so, turned the complex and variable historical relationships found under imperialism into ones always and necessarily about relations between blacks and whites.[131] According to Egbuna it was the damage inflicted by white imperial identities, a kind of 'intrapersonal colonialism', that 'mutilated our personality and makes us intellectual hybrids', that led to the rise of Black Power.[132]

In its most inclusive guises, the BBPM attempted to take the diverse histories of colonialism, in the West Indies, continental Africa and South Asia, and present them as foundational moments in establishing a global black identity. This was a difficult task for peoples who came from different continents and who, in many cases, were themselves the products of imperial education. It required what was variously called 'self-help' or 'political or supplementary education'. Different forms of this education flourished in this period and the BBPM was just one of the movements seeking to foster black consciousness through reading history, making music, listening to poetry and watching film.[133]

Recent histories of the USBPP have stressed the importance of community and education programmes.[134] The same is true in Britain. More significant than the small membership and the provocative and stylish militancy were the Panthers', and the Black Power movement's broader educational projects that created a space for the exploration of black history. Classes in black history, politics and culture became an important aspect of the BBPM work and formed just one small part of an educational renaissance in the black community.[135] *Grassroots*, the newspaper of the Black Liberation Front, for example, reported the foundation of their own education and leisure programme that would 'provide extra lessons for black kids so as to give them a headstart in education'.[136] English, maths, science and art classes were planned in three age groups but it was always the search for historical identity, 'for the correction of the myth of the docile, slow witted Black, incapable of self-improvement', that was the priority. 'Black people, wherever we are, must see the importance of learning OUR history.'[137]

One early member of the BBPM in Brixton was the author, academic and activist, Beverley Bryant. Her account confirms a loose organisation eventually overcome by faction fighting, but accurately identifies a moment of possibilities based on a historical imagination that was to leave a long-term educational legacy. Linking up with socialist, feminist and black activists, many of them women as well as 'the more conscious men', Bryant helped to found a group that occupied a house on what was widely called Brixton's front line, Railton Road in Lambeth. The house became Sabarr Bookshop and was home to the influential scholar activists who comprised the Race Today collective.[138] A meeting point for writers and activists that facilitated the exchange of ideas and experiences, Sabarr sold a range of pamphlets and books that answered a growing but unmet demand for what was becoming to be identified as black material. That material emerged from a variety of sites and spaces because there was no single cohesive black movement in this period. Instead, there were highly localised and fluid groups that reflected the intellectual and political energies of the new social movements and the fierce debates that its agendas generated.[139]

Arguably the most significant of these groups were the people who gathered around Eric and Jessica Huntley, the founders of Bogle-L'Ouverture Publications Limited in 1969. Toussaint L'Ouverture and Paul Bogle were two heroes of the resistance movement against slavery and colonialism in the Caribbean and the naming of Huntley's publishing company was itself an intervention in historical memory. Working from a front room in Ealing, the Huntleys used Bogle-L'Ouverture to promote and distribute research into black history and black contributions to the world in academic, creative and social fields. Early publications, for example, included two texts by Walter Rodney, *The Groundings with My Brothers* (1969) and *How Europe Underdeveloped Africa* (1972) that, in different ways, sought to reclaim Africa's history from an Enlightenment tradition that had condemned it as the Dark Continent. Against dominant notions of a benign British Empire, both texts made significant contributions to anti-colonial politics and a movement for a diasporic black consciousness. *How Europe Underdeveloped Africa*, especially, was a global success and was translated into several languages. It became a mainstay of black history courses and rights sold to publishing houses in Dar-es-Salaam and Washington, DC.[140]

In fact, Rodney's publications hint at the emergence of a distinctive form of black politics that was dependent on, and reflected, a different generation's view of the past. Rodney's researches in African history are further evidence of that generational shift which had such an important effect on representations of the past.[141] African history and traditions now appealed. European civilisation, which for C.L.R. James and an earlier generation of pan-Africanists continued to exert considerable influence, was losing its grip on the historical imagination of a generation of migrants with direct experience of metropolitan racism, who had grown up with the demise of European empires and who were influenced by the energies of a politics self-consciously styled on youth. Instead, the Huntleys' publishing venture demonstrates a global vision of the black diaspora that would be united by a shared historical narrative of the kind promoted by the BBPM, made accessible and meaningful by the development and adoption of black history courses and by the materials that would support them, especially from the USA.[142] This was a profoundly historical and educational form of politics but it was also one based on the implicit assumption that black and white people had quite distinctive histories. It was often a short step to arguing that these distinctive histories created separate kinds of cultures that required sustenance and recognition through separate forms of education.[143]

Radical educator and activist John La Rose (1927–2006) traversed this line between an inclusive vision of social justice for all based on the politics of class and an anti-racism that sought to promote black identities. Born in Trinidad in 1927 he came to England via Venezuela in 1961.[144] Compensation monies paid as a result of an accident while working as a builder's labourer enabled La Rose and his partner, the historian, journalist and political activist, Sarah White, to start their publishing house New Beacon in 1966. Aiming to publish Caribbean literature and history for a British reading public, early volumes included a biography of Marcus Garvey by Adolph Edwards and a re-publication of John Jacob Thomas's *Froudacity*, a celebrated demolition of the idea of black inferiority proposed by the Victorian historian James Froude. Sociologist Brian Alleyne has argued that the republication of Thomas's book is suggestive not just of the general aims of New Beacon, establishing the existence of scholarly writing by black people in the colonies, but also to a specific context in which ideas about the restricted intellectual capacity of black children were commonplace.[145]

La Rose was also a founding and influential figure in the Black Education Movement (BEM) that played a key role in the protests against banding, or the racist placement of West Indian children in schools for the 'educationally sub-normal', and in the wider demand and long struggle for equality in schooling provision. It was an inclusive demand for social justice, and an argument that schools discriminated against not just black immigrants but also against white immigrants too. In 1969 La Rose was a member of the North London West Indian Association (NLWIA) that organised, alongside the Greek Parents Association and the Haringey Parents Group, a successful and high-profile campaign against Haringey Borough Council's policy of banding to distribute children to the comprehensive schools in the borough. The NLWIA was the lead organisation of a campaign that staged a mass demonstration, printed pamphlets, initiated the foundation of parents' committees and organised petitions.[146] Knowledge of the campaign circulated beyond London and acted as a mobilising agent among black parents. In the same year, the Caribbean Education Association (later the Caribbean Education and Community Workers Association, or CECWA) was established to campaign against the widespread practice of placing black children in schools for the educationally subnormal. La Rose was, with Jocelyn Barrow and Winston Best, organiser of an important three-day seminar held in August 1970 at Hughes Parry Hall with the title 'Talking to Ourselves' and its proceedings gives some indication of the range of cultural and educational questions now under consideration in this flourishing educational scene.

The seminar's focus was on the conditions and problems which the West Indian child experienced in British society. It began on the evening of Friday 28 August with a public lecture delivered by C.L.R. James. Entitled 'The meaning of the Haitian revolution for modern Caribbean Society', the lecture 'set the framework which must be our starting point in any thinking about West Indians' problems in Britain – the situation in the West Indies itself, and its historical roots'. James's argument was that just as the Haitian masses felt 'common identity as an oppressed people, so West Indians today, facing 'common Imperialistic ownership of their countries ... are showing a similar awareness'. Axiomatic for James was the idea that shared social identities were formed through the political and educational struggles of peoples located in, and conditioned by, historical processes. It followed that binary positions, of oppressor and victim or the inevitable and natural prejudice of white people about black people, were not employed as tools of historical analysis.

On Saturday morning Carl Campbell spoke about the disastrous impact of the education system in the West Indies; 'grossly neglected financially by the British Government and run by missionaries ... a bookish education, specialising in religious instruction and the arts, was largely irrelevant to the West Indian situation and needs for development'. The lively discussion that followed indicated a strain of thinking that saw merit in the current educational system in the West Indies, but there appears to have been little debate following Bernard Coard's hugely important paper entitled 'The problems of the West Indian child in an ESN school'. An exposé of the 'scandalous way in which West Indian children of average intelligence are being dumped in schools for educationally sub-normal children in this country', Coard's paper called for a range of measures to combat these practices, including the employment of black teachers, a programme of Black Studies to restore their self-respect and the development of black supplementary schools.[147] Overall, the seminar demonstrated a momentum developing in the black community in London with campaigns that sought redress against local grievances around schools, housing, policing and employment but also began to frame those issues in a broader historical perspective. Indeed, what sometimes inspired these campaigns, but what certainly developed out of them, was an historical imagination, global rather than local, seeking solidarities based both on class and on developing notions of diaspora that was to change the culture of history in the black community and to have significant educational, cultural and political consequences.

One of the most obvious and enduring consequences was the development of a Black Supplementary Schools Movement (BSSM). Different dates can be found for the foundation of the first schools but it is clear that an emerging system was in evidence from the late 1960s onwards with particular strengths in London but rapidly appearing in Birmingham, Liverpool, Bristol, Nottingham and Northampton.[148] A definitive list of these schools is not possible because many of them

were informal gatherings, they could be short-lived and many kept
no records. Other schools were celebrated and sustained over time. In
London, the Malcolm X Montessori School, modelled on a school of
the same name and philosophy in Compton, California, was opened
in May 1970 by Ajoy and Katherine Ghose with the help of Hakim
Tahar. Renting a room in Notting Hill, sixteen parents and their
children aged between 5 and 11 studied in the evenings, at weekends
and in the school holidays.[149] The Dachwyng Saturday School in
Peckham was established in 1975 by Nel Clark and, just five years
later, it was catering for 126 children.[150] The Josina Machel Black
Supplementary School in Newington Green opened in January 1976
teaching twenty-five children and there is evidence of the existence
of the Harriet Tubman Saturday School (opened 1977) and the Peter
Moses Supplementary School, founded by the Friends of Bogle group
associated with the publishers, in 1979.[151] Ahfiwe School, aiming
to develop in students 'the ability to think critically and politically
so that they are able to analyse intelligently that which relates to
their existence as an ethnic minority' was open every evening and
all day on Saturday and had a bookshop and library dedicated to
the exploration of the black experience.[152] These schools, and their
predominately women teachers, helped to stimulate further demand
for those educational publications and materials that enabled new
forms of identification for black youth in Britain.[153]

A loose alliance of educationalists and activists, the black supplementary school movement never developed a shared philosophy,
common methods or set of practices. This was a diffuse network of
people with different educational aims and political philosophies.
Some schools undoubtedly concentrated on promoting academic
attainment, especially for examination candidates. However, and
from the outset, most supplementary schools were concerned with
establishing a narrative of black history, exploring its significance
and utilising it as a resource for coming to terms with life as black
people in Britain.[154] At the 'Talking to Ourselves' conference 'the
general feeling arising from the talks and discussion was that the
formation and thriving of such groups reflected the increasing black
consciousness among West Indians in this country, and in turn helped
to further develop this consciousness'.[155] Similarly, in the journal of
the Ahfiwe School, co-founded by Trinidadian educationalist and
activist Ansel Wong, the first aim was to provide services that aided
the personal development of black youth, and 'their understanding

and appreciation of the black experience'. The programme would be wide and varied, cater for a wide ability range, promote academic excellence but stressed the importance of developing in students 'the ability to think critically and politically so that they are able to analyse intelligently that which relates to their existence as an ethnic minority'.[156] Similar emphases can be in found in the correspondence, publicity and funding applications that were a necessary part of the launch of the BSSM. John La Rose's handwritten notes confirm, for example, that the George Padmore School did 'not belong to a black elite' but was 'committed to social liberation of black people, and maximum literacy and numeracy through the study of Pan-African history and geography'.[157] Fostering a sense of the cultural and historical value of African societies was, argues sociologist Brian Alleyne, 'a major objective of the Padmore School' who quotes La Rose recalling an early lesson:

> The first time I gave a talk on African history and civilisation to the children at the Padmore school, some of them laughed loudly when I mentioned 'Africa'. I think it was partly a nervous, embarrassed reaction, because they, as black kids in Britain, were used to hearing Africa dismissed as a primitive place, and Africans as primitive people. Africa was something they were a bit ashamed of. So we had to change that.
>
> We had to teach them about the civilisations of Africa ... I don't mean we neglected the history of Europe, of classical Greece and Rome; that too was part of our history; it was part of my own education at St Mary's College in Trinidad. We did not neglect European culture – after all, the kids were growing up here in Europe – but we wanted them to learn about and develop pride in the African parts of their heritage.[158]

It was not only children who were catered for by the Black Education Movement. In 1973 the Centre for Extra-Mural Studies at the Polytechnic of Central London hosted a study week entitled 'Frantz Fanon: the reconstitution of black consciousness'. Consisting of 'connected lectures, music and poetry', it sought to relate 'the historical half-destruction of black consciousness by slavery and colonialism ... to the current movement for the reconstitution of an authentic black view of the world'.[159] The Community Education Trust, working in association with the City Literary Institute and, in particular with educationalist Pansey Jeffrey and novelist George Lamming, presented an eight-week course on history and racism.

Its promotional material suggested that it would use the 'disciplines of history, music and literature' to explore the continuing relations of Caribbean people and others of similar colonial experience to the former Colonial Powers, with special reference to the British'.[160] The syllabus included an exploration of West African societies before European intervention, an examination of the causes and consequences of slavery, a survey of the global movement of peoples in the formation of modern Caribbean societies and tracing, through personal histories, the experiences of Caribbean people and comparable minority groups in the period since 1930. In the major areas of black settlement similar educational projects, devoted to the construction and distribution of black history, could be found.[161]

These programmes for both adults and children inevitably stimulated a good deal of interest in radical pedagogy. Here too, it is not difficult to trace global influences. Arguably most significant, at least rhetorically, was the work of the Brazilian educator, Paulo Freire, whose vague style, as well his work for the revolutionary and anti-colonial Cabral government in Guinea-Bissau, helped ensure his popularity and adaptation among radicals, including the educationalist, historian and black activist Hazel Carby, who kept 'a much thumbed copy of Pedagogy of the Oppressed on my bedside table and using it in schools and adult literacy programmes'.[162] In Freire, they found a critique of the banking forms of education which were seen as part of a wider process of dehumanisation in which injustice, exploitation and oppression prevented the achievement of a full humanity. What radicals also found in Freire was a Hegelian Marxism in which historical consciousness, or praxis, held the key to social transformation. 'Only human beings are praxis', wrote Freire, and through their reflection and action 'men and women simultaneously create history and become historical–social beings'. Their reflection was necessarily historical because it was in the past that the oppressed found the origins of their dehumanisation. 'It is when the majorities are denied their right to participate in history as Subjects that they become dominated and alienated' and 'to supersede their conditions ... requires that people act, as well as reflect, upon the reality to be transformed'. That reflection required the interrogation of history and it fell to critically conscious revolutionary organisation(s) to 'pose to the people as problems their position in the historical process, the national reality and [their] manipulation'.[163]

Freire's revolutionary romanticism was not, of course, without problems but these did not affect the way in which his ideas were taken up. This was not, for the most part, in the manner of close studies of his ideas or detailed interpretations of his text. Instead, scattered references to his work display a working knowledge of some central themes but, ultimately, those projects relied rather less on a particular theory of learning and education, and more on a humanism that retained faith in people as learners and sought to transmit the power of their message in all available media. In 1974, for example, La Rose described a method mixing individual reading of shared texts, group discussion and spelling practice. The reading material consisted of texts used in Caribbean schools, *Marcus Garvey* for 12–13-year-olds, book three of the *People Who Came* series for 14-year-olds, and supplemented by C.L.R. James' *Black Jacobins and the Haitian Revolution*, 'a very important event in the history of Black people and the ending of slavery in Brazil, the USA and the Caribbean' La Rose told a senior community relations officer before adding that 'we urge the students to take their books home and to ask parents to read the same books that they are studying'.[164]

It is not easy, from fragmentary evidence, to estimate either the extent or the feel of these shared reading practices. La Rose's description of intensive and communal reading no doubt partly reflected the aspirations of a committed activist. Yet, there were certainly successes. Linton Kwesi Johnson's career as poet and artist began, for example, when he read Du Bois's *The Souls of Black Folk* with the Blank Panther Youth Section and scattered archival fragments reveal the commitment to historical education through shared reading.[165] In a 1973 survey refreshingly free of both moralising politics and community psychological analysis, University of Liverpool sociologist, Ilene Mellish, noted the 'overwhelming desire amidst the black community (but not limited to it and certainly not relevant only to it) to gain information about the history, literature, and culture of black people throughout the world. The quantity and sophistication of reading in this area and done by this community is great indeed.' Mellish proposed to further develop and formalise this reading activity by the establishment of a community college in Toxteth that would provide a:

> [F]ull program of courses, seminars and events dealing with the history, literature, and culture of the African peoples and their descendents

throughout the world, aimed at simply meeting the general interests of residents in the area, at exploring gaps in local history of significance and interest far beyond inner city Liverpool (such as a history of African settlement in Liverpool ...).[166]

Someway short of this demand, but important nonetheless, was the reading group sponsored by the Merseyside Community Relations Council (MCRC) who analysed racial bias in historical texts, and particularly those used in schools. The criticisms made of Derry and Jarman's *The Making of Modern Britain* are instructive of the philosophy and working methods of the MCRC. The group noted the sparse references to the slave trade, pointed to the omission of black immigrants in the sections dealing with migration, and recommended that the centuries-long growth of British communities of Chinese, African and West Indian origin be given much more prominence in accounts of the local and national past. A much praised exhibition, highlighting the deficiencies of history and geography textbooks, was mounted in the MCRC offices in 1974 and was an early attempt to expand the traditional national master narrative with a more global perspective.[167] An accompanying booklet features a significant quotation from Milton's *Areopagitica* on the front cover. Writing in opposition to seventeenth-century press censorship and comparing the power of books to that of Dragons Teeth, Milton's text endorsed a Renaissance humanism that was committed to dispelling myth and prejudice through a process of education that depended on the availability of relevant texts and the active interpretation of readers. Both presented problems for the nascent BSSM.

One key problem was the scarcity of relevant texts for Black Studies curricula. It would be easy to overlook the difficulties faced by black activists and educationalists who wanted to present and to teach a new version of British and world history. After all, printing remained a labour intensive and expensive process, heavily reliant on sales to recoup initial investment. It was also a business in which contacts counted. In both these areas ethnic minority activists and educationalists suffered. Activists frequently lacked the necessary networks that might facilitate the publication of their books and they were easily marginalised as a radical fringe with axes to grind in a publishing field that was both cautious and conservative.[168] Healthy projected sales figures might have helped smooth these difficulties but it was hard to imagine texts on black history selling commercially viable numbers in the early 1970s. As a result, only New

Beacon and Bogle-L'Ouverture offered realistic publishing options for authors in the UK.[169]

The scarcity of texts meant that teaching materials was a consistent problem for ethnic minority activists and educationalists. In 1972, for example, the West Indian Saturday School, in Handsworth, Birmingham, requested monies from the CRC to help purchase 'textbooks, readers and wall charts that would enable us to develop these classes as a really effective unit for helping the West Indian child'.[170] The local CRC education officer, Maureen Taylor, concurred that this was a difficulty and noted that 'books on Afro-Caribbean literature and history are not easy to obtain and are expensive'.[171] In these circumstances shared reading groups and the ethos of collective learning as a form of consciousness raising that a generation of activists, communists, trade unionists, and pan-African, had developed in earlier decades were crucial. Their reading and their discussion exemplified a historical imagination in which past and present were intimately related and which sought to understand contemporary conditions as the conjuncture of particular historical forces whose legacies continued in the present and which, more or less explicitly, challenged the chronologies and methodologies of the national master narrative.[172] It can also be argued that these reading practices were an important element in the construction of new kinds of historical distance in the post-war period.[173] Many radical reading groups sought a closer proximity with, and a new sensibility towards, events in the past. Against a powerful national master narrative, shared reading groups could establish new historical actors, antagonists and events. In place of a benign story of the English people, slavery, colonialism, migration and systematic racism were becoming the core events for a new black history.[174]

Technology played an important role in this process of education. The ability, still quite novel in the post-war period, to reproduce text quickly and cheaply through mimeograph technology, enabled activists not only to find an authorial voice but to be published. As Steven Clay and Rodney Phillips have pointed out in their history of the 'mimeo revolution', mimeo publishing was quick, could be undertaken without formal training and encouraged what they call 'collaborative sociality'; small groups of likeminded people could join together to write, edit, publish, collate, staple and mail.[175] Bounded together in a joint enterprise, this was a relatively democratised means of technological reproduction. It encouraged the formation of social movements because it gave campaigning groups a concrete means of debating their objectives, developing their agendas and reaching their audiences. The Afro-Caribbean Education Resource Centre (ACER), founded by Trinidadian historian and activist Len Garrison for example, devised and produced learning materials for use in schools. And ACER is only one example of the ways in which it was becoming possible to discuss and debate the legacies of history and to write, publish and distribute the materials that would, as Garrison later recalled, serve to 'memorialise ancestors' and act as the foundation for new forms of identity.[176]

In official circles such movements continued to be viewed with a mixture of fear and loathing. Local authorities, as well as central government and the more conservative local community relations councils, raised concerns about the quality of teaching in supplementary schools and worried that applications to support the publication of black history were designed, as Alderman Dawes of the Birmingham Education Committee bluntly put it, to teach the 'supremacy of the black'.[177] If this kind of accusation displayed a fundamental misunderstanding of the educational purposes of the curriculum and explained the surveillance of black educational groups by state security services, it also confirmed the power of the national master narrative.[178] For most of the 1970s, any attempt to explore the relevance of black history was interpreted as an attack on Britain and civilisation itself.

Even if there were no political, economic or educational obstacles to the teaching of black history, the diversity of the people and groups interested in exploring aspects of the black past presented further barriers to attempts to create a unified black education movement. For what constituted an authentic black identity, and the core historical events that made it, depended partly on idiosyncratic preferences but also on the fact that individuals accessed these ideas conditioned by class, gender and generation. Indeed, and arguably most importantly, was the emergence of a new generation of young people whose political beliefs, social attitudes and style owed much to the wider influence of the post-1968 youth culture. Politically radical and culturally distinctive through their consumption of fashion, music and faith, young black people in the 1970s sought new forms of identification and new relationships with the past.

Memory and black identity

Dorothy Kuya was born and raised in Liverpool. Her Nigerian father was one of the large numbers of black merchant seamen who worked through the ports of England during the Second World War. He was also a communist, influential in the local organisation of merchant seamen in the 1940s, and one of many who married a local white woman. These marriages, and the increasing numbers of mixed-race children in inter-war and post-war England, attracted not just popular prejudice but also official condemnation and, as was the case with the riots of 1919, were widely seen as justifying violent attack. 'The "half-caste" child', writes historian Lucy Bland, 'was deemed to inherit the worst features of both parents, namely immorality and laziness'.[179] Further, mixed-raced children were the subject of continued and acute anxiety because, it was widely assumed, especially by proponents of eugenics, by the police and by the male population more widely, that they could not belong to or in England.[180] 'Where are you really from?' was a question that the mixed-race future actor Paul Barber, also Liverpool born and bred but with a Sierra Leonean father, was repeatedly asked during his 1950s childhood. Being bleached by a foster parent during bath times in order to 'get white and blend in', while also being instructed to 'blacken' up with coal soot for entertainment purposes, demonstrated how belonging anywhere seemed impossible in this racist framework.[181]

Dorothy Kuya's childhood milieu, like Paul Barber's, was certainly shaped by the persistence of eugenic and racist thinking but it was also crucially influenced by her father's politics. Politics was often discussed in her childhood home in Granby, informed by the newspaper of the Communist Party, the *Daily Worker*, and guided by a pedagogical ethos in which the Party acted as teacher and guide to the masses and demanded distinctive forms of education in which reading, argument and disciplined study were considered duties. That education held out the promise that racial discrimination would cease in the socialist future and members of the Young Communist League, like Dorothy Kuya, were encouraged to invest much emotional and intellectual energy into the idea that they were '"conscious agents" of the emancipatory process, "conscious shapers" of history, conscious protagonists of the struggle that extends throughout society'.[182]

It was this kind of energy and this sense of history that Dorothy

Kuya was to bring to her own remarkable career, one which prefigured, but also drew on and helped to articulate, the experiences of post-war second generation migrants. Those experiences made racist discrimination, not race relations or culture clashes, the urgent social problem in need of attention. Kuya experienced this discrimination as both nurse and teacher before being appointed the first community relations officer in Liverpool. Writing in the Liverpool Community Relations Council report for 1973 she argued, in a telling turn of phrase, that 'Liverpool is a prime example of the "sins of the fathers visiting the children"' and warned readers that:

> The neglect of the problems of the original Non-white immigrant has led to many difficulties of the present day English Born Black Community. Racial discrimination is not a new phenomenon which came to Liverpool with the wave of New Commonwealth Immigrants in the 60s. Racial Discrimination has operated throughout the long period of time that Black People have lived in the city and reflects ideas that have prevailed in our society for many hundreds of years. It has been so much of our lifestyle that the white community has operated it without thought, and the Black Community on the whole have become complaisant about its own lack of opportunities.[183]

Kuya's perspective clearly emphasised the importance of recognising and discussing Liverpool's particular history to slavery and its legacies for both the black and white population in the city. Kuya, like her colleague and basketball coach Jimmy Young, saw it as crucial to the development of the whole community that the LCRC encouraged young people to be, as both 'self determining and self programming' and 'provided a service to help in their search for identity'.[184] Kuya stressed that it was the role of the MCRC to be involved in 'all forms of community action in helping our youth to achieve equality in society and in meeting and coping with their social, economic and cultural needs'. Kuya's activities were certainly testimony to her own vision as she took on multiple cultural and educational roles in addition to her salaried work. She was a governor at Arundle Comprehensive School, a manager of Windsor Street Primary School, a member of the Liverpool Trades Council Race Relations Committee, a member of the Black African Festival (1975) Committee and a member of the Multicultural Working Party in the Department of Education at the University of Liverpool. However, her vision for what community relations councils might achieve, covering the promotion of economic equality and the recognition of distinctive cultural needs based on particular histories, was far from universally shared either within her own organisation or more widely.

In the field of community relations, both nationally and locally, there were competing ideas about what constituted black history and how it might help different groups of people. In Liverpool, for example, the LCRC Annual General Meeting in 1972 reported in a rather confused fashion that Sam Morris (of the CRC) would be arriving to deliver a course on 'what are commonly known as Black Studies'. Appearing in the minutes under the heading 'Multicultural Studies', the weekend course was 'aimed at social workers, youth workers and teachers' and the subject matter was clearly identified by the title 'Some Historical Background to Commonwealth Immigrants'.[185] The ameliorative philosophy of community relations, and its consistent tendency to explain domestic intolerance as a temporary problem in an otherwise tolerant nation, discredited the MCRC in the eyes of local black communities and especially young people, who were long established in Liverpool and as Kuya realised, seeking new forms of identification as black Liverpudlians. For those young people, Black Studies were not about introducing or explaining black immigrants, and their supposed temperament, character, intellectual abilities or family structure. Instead, the independent growth of Black Studies courses and classes organised by local groups suggested a very different set of concerns and a particular orientation to the past which insisted on a global historical perspective designed to uncover silenced histories. At the same time, these courses and classes demonstrated the clear limitations of the community relations approach.

'Notes on Racism', written as a draft curriculum by the Liverpool Black Studies Group, began with a 'historical perspective' that covered the 'voyages of discovery, imperialism, the slave trade, colonialism (a racist practice) and unequal trade patterns'. It included a section on the struggle against racism conducted by slaves, in colonised countries, and by black ethnic minorities in New Zealand, Australia, Western Europe and Britain.[186] The draft constitution for the Group confirmed the centrality of history by listing in its aims and objectives the attempt to give 'Liverpool Blacks a stronger sense of identity', by 'study[ing] study the history and culture of Black Peoples', 'to understand the effects that colonialism and imperialism has on the Third world', and to educate 'ourselves and in the process dispel some of the myths regarding Black people and their history'.[187] Most

Black Studies classes shared these general aims but there remained significant disputes among black groups about both what to study and how to organise.

Practically, and characteristically for social movements, black groups of the period disagreed about whether an authentic black identity could be discovered and constructed in alliance with either the state or other political movements. The Liverpool Black Studies Group was content to identify other groups, including the MCRC, the Communist Party (and the *Morning Star*) and anti-racist campaigners, as potential allies not simply in a search of a stronger identity, but in the pursuit of an anti-racist public education. Contrastingly, the Liverpool Pan-African Committee resisted offers of financial and practical assistance from the MCRC because it was hostile to the 'community relations' approach and 'education' programmes of the MCRC and to the black groups who worked with them.[188] They criticised cultural programmes centred on 'limbo dancing' and 'steel bands' and condemned the bureaucracy and the funding from the CRC and local educational authorities that structured these activities. For many pan-African groups, such as the London-based Black Students' Action Collective, an authentic black identity could only be discovered and constructed outside the sphere of state intervention or other political alliances.[189]

How to position black struggles alongside the British New Left remained a dilemma to many activist young people. If, for the New Left, understanding working-class history and having an empathetic sense of working-class experience and culture became an important precondition of promoting political change, it was one that struggled to find room for migrant communities in Britain. Working-class culture was imagined as humane, dignified and democratic and as a resource of communitarian values that could build a new kind of social democracy. Yet this remained a resolutely national narrative that was largely silent on British imperialism and the settlement and development of migrant communities in Britain. Indeed, historian Geoff Eley has persuasively argued that the people's history that was represented in the folk revival, working-class autobiographies and oral histories, in the History Workshop movement and in the curriculum and pedagogical reforms of the Schools History Project had a 'latent ethnocentrism' at its heart.[190]

Birmingham's radical Banner Theatre of Actuality presented some of these ethnocentric dilemmas in their 1974 production *The Race*

Show. This was introduced to the audience with heavy irony as 'the story of how conquest and peaceful colonisation built up the world's greatest empire and brought the British way of life to every corner of the globe cannot fail to thrill all who hear it'.[191] The play's opening scene featured John Hawkins, widely acknowledged as a pioneer of the English slave trade because he was the first to run the Triangular Trade at the Court of Queen Elizabeth in 1563. Proceeding through what appears to have been a didactic and chronological narrative in the agitprop tradition, the play dramatised an Act of the Privy Council of 1596 banishing blacks from the kingdom and employing Casper Van Zeuden to transport them; the granting of the East India Company charter in 1600; English possession of Bermuda in 1609; the settlement of Surat in India in 1612; the 1711 Treaty of Utrecht and so on through the abolition of the slave trade to the Amritsar massacre, the imperial wars, the world wars, fascism and the arrival of immigrants in post 1945 Britain.[192]

The whole performance was structured through the character of Capital who appears as a 'super-man child', 'a dear hero who had to keep growing' and whose need for labour to secure a mighty expansion in trade and industry in the post-1945 world is articulated in the slogan 'Workers we need and workers we will have!'. Capital silences the complaints of the other major character in the play, a more ethical *Britannia*, but the performance ended with the suggestion that the legacies of the past would continue to haunt a post-imperial and firmly European Britain:

> And so our Island story comes up to the present day, and the glorious future that beckons us but now as part of a Europe strong and united as never before into one far flung Common Market. A new greatness awaits our erstwhile infant prodigy – now grown to full multi-national maturity, a peer among his peers, banding together to face new giants East and West. Ah indomitable Capital! But the past still comes to haunt our hero; try as he might memories persist of those golden days of Empire when the Englishman was Lord of the Earth.[193]

As a radical attempt to present a global history of British imperialism and to situate British identity within the experience of colonialism, the play nonetheless ended up presenting contemporary British racism as rooted in the abstract relations of capitalism. The existence of racism within the domestic working class, and the centrality of race ideas and images to the dominant narrative of British history, was not addressed. Nor was there reference to the agency of black migrant groups in constructing new forms of black consciousness through historical research and teaching.

Both liberal and radical attempts to promote a more pluralist Britain had limited appeal to a new generation of black Britons. Faced with discrimination and racist hostility at school, on the streets and in the labour market, increasing numbers of young black Britons were dissatisfied with those who preached piecemeal progress through patient communication with white society or else explained racism as secondary phenomena of capitalist relations. This sense of alienation helped explain the growth of the Rastafarian movement in Britain. In the words of historian and educationalist, Len Garrison, this represented not a withdrawal from society but 'an attempt at self discovery that constituted an important step in the rise of historical consciousness'.[194]

These processes may be best understood biographically and through the thirty-four in-depth interviews with black young people in Birmingham collected by the interfaith organisation All Faiths for One Race and published in 1978 as *Talking Blues*. The editors, the radical photographers and social activists, Derek Bishton and Brian Homer, framed the interviews firmly around the concept of identity deficit, and expounded the argument that Afro-Caribbean children were particularly vulnerable to psychological damage and to pathologies of self-hate, not because of the 'culture shock' attributed to recent immigration but to the cognitive consequences of long-term historical processes. In particular, slavery and colonialism meant that Caribbean societies lacked a distinct, cohesive, cultural identity to which migrant youths might attach themselves.[195] In some of the educational studies and training programmes that made use of *Talking Blues* this claim around identity deficit sometimes produced an image of young black people as wronged and passive victims inescapably damaged by history.[196] But other expressions of the argument left room for active resistance or responses to the past.[197]

This was exactly how Bishton and Homer interpreted the increasing popularity of Rastafarianism. Its growing attraction was illustrated in their long interview with Brian that is infused by a sense of history. Brian was fiercely critical of his schooling and his historical education because its litany of great figures consisted of those who had enslaved and oppressed black people. His disillusionment, widely shared in black autobiographies and oral testimonies of this period, meant a slow disengagement with formal schooling and a compensatory and auto-didactic search for roots and culture. The educational projects and publications of radical political groups were important in this process, as were biographical texts, on Marcus Garvey, Malcolm X and Martin Luther King. For Brian, scripture readings and 'groundings' with a local Rastafarian group, who gave long recitations of the historical atrocities of 'Babylon' and especially that of the Middle Passage, deepened his knowledge of black history.[198] Such recitations met at least some of the criteria subsequently set out by some historians for a process of collective remembering: a narrative of persecution to support the assertion and articulation of a new identity; a resistance to debate and ambiguity; and a commitment to the central meaning of the narrative.

Rastafarianism was, of course, a broad church running from religious doctrine to social protest movement. In its latter guise it was undoubtedly also helped by the phenomenal popularity of Bob Marley who toured England and Wales in the summer of 1976 and helped to make the 'history and memory of racial slavery into interpretative devices that could be turned towards innumerable varieties of injustice and unfreedom'.[199] Protest groups around the globe began to adopt what Paul Gilroy described, in an acute analysis of Marley's importance, as his 'universal poetics of sufferation and of hope'. Marley's music was taken up because it was a hybrid form of reggae, informed by US rhythm and blues, jazz and funk, and because, aided by the new technologies of reproduction and global networks of distribution and exchange, it became stylistically cool. Endlessly reproduced on posters, T-shirts and badges, Marley became 'the global patron saint of rebels and dissenters' and the soundtrack of the new international youth culture.[200]

Yet for many of the new generation of British-born black youth, reggae music, and a distinctly British sound system and deejay culture, was existentially rather than symbolically important. For them, Marley, and his link to Black Power and Rastafari cultures, were elements in the imaginative resources required for black identity. Sound systems were akin to mobile music libraries with giant speakers and complex forms of amplification that, together with local deejays, were the basis for a unique aesthetic experience.[201] It was, said the *Observer* journalist, Merrill Ferguson, valiantly trying to capture the feeling of a sound system, like an 'orchestra, artist, message, dance band, political platform and a night-out-on-the-town'.[202] For deejay and historian William Henry, reggae dancehalls were democratic spaces, where those who were harassed and marginalised gathered together the resources for alternative forms of collective identity.[203] Especially after the advent of toasting, a kind of improvised oratory set to instrumental reggae tracks that heralded the arrival of the reggae or dub poets, anyone could perform on a reggae dancehall platform. In practice, men dominated and they did so biographically, documenting 'an ongoing history into the present', that placed contemporary experiences of harassment and discrimination in a longer historical narrative of the African diaspora that was rooted in the memory of transatlantic slavery.[204] Call-and-response performances ensured that an audience participated in the creation and repetition of key episodes and memories. These were also often expressed in a Jamaican patois that further enabled the creation of identities outside allotted positions of 'voiceless, passive victims of a Eurocentric historical bias'. 'The deejay' argues William Henry, 'thus became the veritable keeper of memories, for once the word was performed, recorded and disseminated, it became an artefact; a historical document'.[205] These documents were dynamic, they proliferated quickly and they clearly had an impact and significance beyond the dancehall scene from which they emerged. *Grassroots*, the Black Liberation Front's newspaper, recommended a revolutionary reggae top 10 headed by 'History of Africa' by The Classics. In 1975 Birmingham's Steel Pulse, in an iconic track, demanded a 'History to recall the days of slavery'. John La Rose presciently realised the educational significance of 'record shops packed with black youths' that 'sharpens one's awareness that there is a constant to-ing and fro-ing to the Caribbean and back, in imagination, in consciousness as well as in actual fact'.[206]

In academic circles the importance of Rastafarianism continues to be a matter of some debate. Far from seeing Rastafarianism as contributing to the development of historical consciousness, historian Stephen Howe has argued that 'history has been the great missing element in the contemporary Caribbean impact on Britain. Rastafarianism, much reggae and rap orature have all espoused a mystical or eschatological rather than a genuinely historical consciousness'.[207] Howe's argument, and the distinction between eschatological and historical consciousness, should certainly be taken seriously but it also suffers from the insistence on a normative, and highly specific, concept of historical consciousness. History appears here exclusively as a reasoned account of the past based on linear passages of time that result in modern forms of consciousness. But Rastafarianism was important because it was one of the resources that second generation black migrants could employ to critique and reject the national master narrative. For if, as Jörn Rusen has argued, critical historical consciousness is about 'people's ability to say no to traditions, rules, principles which have been handed down to them', then Rastafarianism was crucial in enabling that active rejection.[208]

The second generation Afro-Caribbean migrants who made up the majority of adherents to Rastafarianism were attracted in part by the invocation of historical memories of suffering, repression and alienation. Yet these memories had to be made. As Brian's testimony revealed, they were the fruits of education in its broadest sense: listening, watching, reading; discussion and debate; publication and instruction. All of them sought in the past something intangible but important: roots, identity and a sense of self free from the prejudice and discrimination evident in post-war Britain. Whether religious, secular or sympathetic, Rastafarians had a belief in the power of historical memories as the source of identity and a vehicle for respect and recognition.

As Len Garrison and others realised, Rastafarianism could be an important part of the process of developing a black historical consciousness. But this was a possibility and not a guarantee. Many black youths, like interviewee Delroy, continued to be 'ashamed and afraid to be associated with the mythical and hidden past and accept[ed] nonsense labels on our persons instead of feeling proud and strong'.[209] Black narratives, images and heroes may have been a potential source of affirmation and pride but they could also be interpreted as having a soporific effect, and of distracting attention from political and educational struggles. As one young person put it, reggae and Rasta were 'meaningless things which offered consolation and justified a surrender to despair'.[210] Images of the black past may have provided new fragments of memory, a more complete sense of self and a kind of affirmation for some, but their appeal was not universal and the extent to which these cultural forms generated genuine historical consciousness remains a matter for debate.

For some activists there remained a clear dividing line between history as a form of consolation and an enabling history that produced new social identities. In Liverpool, for example, Dorothy Kuya was setting out a vision of an enabling kind of history. It was not enough, she argued, to substitute the missing histories of the local black population with an exclusive, and North American inflected, pan-Africanism. Instead, she demanded 'research work among the older black generation to document for ourselves the past resistance of our older black generations while they have been in Liverpool to photograph the struggle before we were born'.[211] Though it is difficult to judge the popularity of this historical education, or the scale of the research work undertaken, there is no doubt that this was an important period in the emergence of black history in Liverpool. The existence of some of the records of Charles Wootton College gives some evidence of this. Founded in 1974 as a form of community education, and in direct response to growing evidence of overt racism in schooling, historical study was an important part of the philosophy of the centre and its curriculum. During a move to new premises (on Upper Parliament Street) in 1978, students and staff researched the history of black people in Liverpool.[212] That research led to the renaming of the College and the publication, in 1979, of an eight page booklet entitled *Charles Wootton: 1919 Race Riots in Liverpool*. The booklet was written by activist and early member of the Black Studies Group, Louis Julienne, and it documented the murder of Charles Wootton by a racist mob. The text was launched to coincide with a fundraising week so that a commemorative plaque could be laid at Charles Wootton's unmarked grave in Sefton. The rediscovery of the riots, and the consistent engagement with Liverpool's black history at Charles Wootton College, marked a significant local intervention. Wootton became, as Gemma Romain has argued, 'an iconic figure and a symbol for the Black Liverpool community of a fight for recognition and equality'.[213]

Black people living in Liverpool may have been pressing for both equality and recognition but there were still no clear procedures for identifying who should be recognised or how. Indeed, the MCRC epitomised divisions that were reproduced elsewhere in England around the politics of history. For one consistent source of dispute was about how to recognise past injustices. Paul Sommerfeld, senior community relations officer at the MCRC in 1980, criticised Merseyside's ability to 'forget the existence of its fellow black citizens', reminded local people of a long history of local black settlement and cautioned that denials of contemporary racism failed to explain the fact 'Liverpool was the scene of one of Britain's earliest race riots in 1919'.[214] It followed that the educational functions of the MCRC were to champion public discussions about the history of empire but these remained sensitive subjects, routinely dismissed as the divisive agenda of political radicals. Local Justice of the Peace, Chair of the Pakistan Association and the CRC, Syed Safiruddin, was 'very uneasy' and 'uncomfortable' at the emergence of an overtly political MCRC and urged an 'unaggressive and unirritating [*sic*] approach' that saw missionary casework as an appropriate model for community relations work.[215] But missionary case work was less than keen to explore the origins of white prejudice and certainly not drawn to discussing the facts of slave-trading or its legacies for Liverpool's black people.

So who constituted the black community and who had the authority to identify their particular needs remained contested. Writing in 1980 the trade unionist and council employee, Eric Lynch, made an impassioned speech that the needs of Liverpool-born blacks could not continue to be ignored. The time had come, he argued, to act collectively, 'to take what is rightfully ours' and to achieve equal opportunities in housing, education and employment alongside the white working class. However, the collective invoked here was quite specific. Lynch objected to 'so-called Black West Indians put in places of authority over us' and argued that a positive black identity needed to be claimed by Liverpool-born blacks. But this was not a closely argued or careful speech. Instead, it was a passionate call for action that sought to bring the past into the present.

In it, Lynch asked:

> Then are we any less human beings because we were born in a White Society? Are we any less human beings because we through no fault of our own, were wrenched from our homeland; were educated in such a way that we alienated ourselves from that homeland? …
>
> We who are born outside of Africa, we the Black children of Africa, who now call ourselves Liverpool Born Black, we have no iron chains around our legs. We have no longer to wear the iron collars around our necks, and yet, we bear the chains of slavery mentally because through lack of understanding, through the lack of education, through the bigotry and racism which is handed to use and is fed to us by the White society in which we live, we are shackled and have been shackled since the first Black man or woman was so called freed of slavery.[216]

This is a particularly vivid example of the appeals to collective remembering which were circulating widely by 1980. These were narratives that identified golden ages in countries of origin, processes of exile, experiences of alienation and then a moment of recovery in the present that demanded political unity and action. The appeal of these narratives of collective remembering, as measured in the educational and cultural activities of the Irish and Afro-Caribbean, was widespread. Yet they did not, nor could they, fix the meaning of being black or Irish in England. Ethnic groups were in the process of construction. They had to imagine, research, reflect, debate and discuss the shared history that made them different. In doing so they were also discussing and debating, but also being conditioned by, the nation's master narrative.

Conclusion

Returning to England in 1979 after five years in Canada the cultural historian, Patrick Wright, was struck by the sensation that he had arrived in a museum. It seemed to him 'a country full of previous and imperilled traces – a closely held iconography of what it is to be English – all of them appealing in one covertly projective way or another to the historical and sacrosanct identity of the nation'. Not only was this historical identity sacred, it also had a champion in the newly elected Prime Minister, Margaret Thatcher, who was in the process of forging a set of political principles out of hindsight and on a governmental mission to promote and protect 'the transcendent and eternalised measure of an imperial national identity'.[217]

This was an aggressively nostalgic mission. The vision of the New Right that was embraced so enthusiastically by Margaret Thatcher was that the story of post-war Britain was one of decline. The foundation of the welfare state had encouraged dependency, nationalised industries promoted inefficiency and a liberal consensus attempted to excuse the problems caused by immigration, the collapse of standards in education and the alleged growth of sexual deviancy. The self-appointed task of the New Right was the restoration of a sense of national vigour, decency and purpose.[218] History was utilised for the purposes of exhortation and for examples of the great things that could be achieved by any individual in a free market society who did not wallow in the past. Of course, the New Right was not alone in these kinds of aims and England was not the only nation where the past became the object of political veneration and returning to some former golden age a more or less explicit aim of government policy. Indeed, history wars were common across the globe and have been seen as a general response to the rapidity of economic, political and social change in the last quarter of the twentieth century.

The New Right's championing of a restricted version of the white English, one that required the exclusion of black immigrants and relegated the Irish to a kind of second class citizenship, was only partially successful. For the cult of the past brought its own constraints. The discursive reliance on an imperial sense of national identity brought with it the rhetoric of freedom, tolerance and pluralism. This was, as David Feldman has argued, 'a ready history – one that combined empire and toleration, two central figures in the national imaginary' – that could be drawn upon to support pluralist solutions to policy debates.[219] Such solutions were always controversial and piecemeal but they were important because they encouraged and required the articulation of what were now being presented as the nations 'other histories'. The emerging and fragile framework of multiculturalism helped to create, in other words, a public space for the construction, recognition and affirmation of cultural differences that were ultimately guaranteed by specific historical experiences. In the social psychology of prejudice, in the furious debates on policing and in the myriad educational projects that sprung up to promote multiculturalism, Irish and black migrants began to struggle for their pasts. In doing so they promoted new perspectives on the national past and demanded a new reckoning of the global consequences of the British Empire.

The actual content of these histories could be very different in terms of their topics, their chronologies and their particular interpretative position. Many projects sought affirmation in the past but most demonstrated a belief in the power of history to spread enlightenment and to correct ignorance and prejudice. This was, in short, a profoundly progressive form of historical practice committed not only to the pursuit of cultural difference but to the investigation and demonstration of a common humanity. As the educationalist, writer and historian Mike Phillips put it when reflecting on this period, 'the impulse, the instinct was to create complex, nuanced, rounded versions of ourselves. To have black history, to look at its implications and to say "We are human beings like you" – with a history'.[220]

History was, in other words, central to the assertion of immigrant humanity. History, whether it was written, discussed, viewed, heard or imagined, was central to combating the essentialisms at work in popular culture, in the study of race relations and in the emerging educational policies of a multicultural society. History provided potential resources for alternative versions of black and Irish identity but these resources had to be mined and employed. The familial and public recounting of migrant stories are, after all, particularly vulnerable to official and unofficial forms of censorship that relegate memories of the past to a time and a place that is, in theory, left behind.[221] John Siblon was not unusual in learning nothing at all of his Guyanese ancestors at home. School history, which relegated 'Africans, Caribbeans, Arabs and Asians to walk-on parts in British imperial policy, usually as riotous mutineers in need of order or beneficiaries of Britain's so-called civilizing influence', was similarly uninstructive.[222]

Physically and verbally abused at school in Eltham, made to feel a foreigner in his own country and angry for having a darker skin colour, Siblon would not find out until the 1980s that there was a longstanding black presence in Britain that could help make sense of his imagined 'limbo-like existence half way between Guyana and South-East London'.[223] That he did so was at least partly due to the emergence of social movements whose campaigns against racism and prejudice began to explore and assert a heritage which would recognise and respect migrant identities.

Quite what those identities were was far more complex and less consensual than was implied by the political language of pluralism. Community identities, and their associated histories, were characterised by geographical, political, gender and generational divisions. Island loyalties were, for example, only slowly replaced by a collective identity as West Indian and it was a further challenge to inhabit a construct like Afro-Caribbean precisely because it required both a rational understanding of the effects of slavery as well as an emotional investment in the idea of a homeland or place of origin. So there was much to do and if men tended to lead political movements, women were prominent in the emergence of educational spaces and practices that developed just this kind of diasporic consciousness. In classrooms and front rooms, concerts venues, meeting halls, cinemas and churches, women taught, debated and discussed.

Whatever the differences and debates about authentic identities, it is perhaps not too speculative to suggest that one aim of Black Studies, the reconstitution of black consciousness through a study of history, literature and music, encapsulates a broader process in which immigrants and minority communities return to the past, recompose it and produce a heritage with which to live. This process was not confined to formal educational institutions or to written texts. It encompassed music, theatre, film, literature and history. In all of these media and in a wide range of institutions immigrant and minority individuals and groups were engaged in a process of learning. They recalled historical events, interpreted them and connected their own experiences with wider historical narratives. For black immigrants in Britain this might have meant reading and discussing Marcus Garvey, C.L.R. James, Sam Selvon or listening to the music of Bob Marley, Burning Spear or Linton Kwesi Johnson. For the Irish it might involve a study of the Irish language, of dancing and participation in Gaelic games or, in a different kind of mode, the reading of James Connolly or James Joyce or listening to the music of the Pogues (when their material was not banned or censored).[224]

Slowly, immigrant voices were being heard and their histories were being aired but this could be a profoundly disturbing phenomenon. In response to Charles Parker's 'We Lived Across the River' radio programme, one listener from a small village in Sussex wrote to the BBC and complained that she was

> shattered by your programme ... Even after all these days I cannot find adequate words ... to express what I feel about a programme which I believe was truly evil. Never have I heard such vitriol and hatred delivered completely undiluted before ... It could do more harm to race relations than anything I have come across in press, radio or public address so far.[225]

It is hard to be certain what it was, either in the radio programme or in wider society that produced such alarm. Newly assertive immigrant voices speaking about the violence of the British Empire offended deep sensibilities. It also indicated just why immigrants had to struggle so hard for their histories.[226]

Notes

1 Birmingham Heritage and Archive Services, MS 4000/2/129, broadcast script for 'We Lived across the River', p. 1.
2 Black Cultural Archives, Oral/1, Oral Histories of the Black Women's Movement, transcript of interview with Amy Gueye, p. 6.
3 Birmingham Heritage and Archives Services, MS 4000/2/129, script for 'We Lived across the River', p. 2.
4 Peter Gibbon, 'Colonialism and the Great Starvation in Ireland 1845–9', *Race and Class*, 17:2 (1975), 138. For an analysis of famine memories,

including those allied to modernist narratives of progress, see Peter Gray 'The making of mid-Victorian Ireland? Political economy and the memory of the Great Famine', in Peter Gray (ed.), *Victoria's Ireland? Irishness and Britishness, 1837–1901* (Dublin: Four Courts Press, 2004).

5 Birmingham Heritage and Archives Services, MS 4000/2/129, script for 'We Lived across the River', p. 3.

6 For an enlightening discussion of Fanon, and his determination to think dynamically about past–present relations, see Bill Schwarz, 'Conquerors of Truth: Reflections on Postcolonial Theory', in Schwarz (ed.) *The Expansion of England: Race, Ethnicity and Cultural History* (London: Routledge, 1996), pp. 13–23.

7 Birmingham Heritage and Archives Services, MS, 4000/2/129, script for 'We Lived across the River', p. 6.

8 'Responses to Roots' *Race and Class*, 19:1 (1977), 77–105. 'Remembering Roots', BBC Radio 4, 27 March 2007.

9 Rusen, *History*, pp. 11–12.

10 The theoretical starting point is Corrigan and Sayer, *Great Arch*, whose groundbreaking interest was the ways in which state activities regulated social life.

11 Bob Carter, Clive Harris and Shirley Joshi, 'The racialisation of black immigration: the Conservative government 1951–55', in Winston James and Clive Harris (eds), *Inside Babylon: the Caribbean Diaspora in Britain* (London: Verso, 1993), pp. 55–72; Ian Spencer, *British Immigration Policy since 1939: The Making of Multi-Racial Britain* (London: Routledge, 1997), pp. 143–151.

12 Richmond, *The Colour Problem*, pp. 240–241; Paul Foot, *Immigration and Race in British Politics* (Harmondsworth: Penguin, 1965).

13 Holmes, *John Bull's Island*, p. 262; Paul, *Whitewashing Britain*, pp. 155–161, 175–177; John Solomos, *Race and Racism in Britain* (Basingstoke: Palgrave Macmillan, 2003).

14 J. Stokes in Hansard (HC) vol. 941, col. 1065 (5 July 1976).

15 Thatcher Archive, Churchill College, Cambridge. Thatcher MSS (digital collection), TV interview for Granada *World in Action*, 27 January 1978. www.margaretthatcher.org.uk/document103485 (last accessed 21/07/14).

16 Schwarz, *White Man's World*; A. Dummett, *Who Is My Neighbour? The Race Question in the United Kingdom* (Liverpool: Institute of Socio-Religious Studies, 1977), pp. 19–23.

17 Bailkin, *Afterlife of Empire*; Grosvenor, *Assimilating Identities*.

18 John Archer Jackson, 'The Irish in Britain', *Sociological Review*, 10:1 (1962), 5–16.

19 Corbally, 'Jarring Irish', pp. 115–116.

20 [no author] 'Powell raises questions of Irish Republican citizens in Britain', *The Times* (28 August 1969), p. 2.

21 James Moran, *Irish Birmingham: A History* (Liverpool: Liverpool University Press), pp. 197–204; Paul Harrison, 'The Irish English', in P. Barker (ed.), *The Other Britain* (London: Routledge & Kegan Paul, 1982), pp. 76–83.

22 Mary Hickman, 'Difference, boundaries, community: the Irish in Britain', in Malcolm Miles (ed.), *City Cultures Reader* (London: Routledge, 2003), pp. 183–190; Paddy Hillyard, *Suspect Community: People's Experience of the Prevention of Terrorism Acts in Britain* (London: Pluto, 1992); Bernadette Hyland, 'My '70s: West of Ireland, East of Manchester', *North West Labour History*, 27 (2002), 43–44.

23 M. Holland, 'Feeling Irish and isolated', *Observer* (1 December 1974), p. 5.

24 Harrison, 'English/Irish', p. 83.

25 See, for example, Sister Sarah Clarke, *No Faith in the System* (Cork: Mercier, 1995); M. Hickman, L. Thomas, S. Silvestri and H. Nickels, 'Social cohesion and the notion of "suspect communities": a study of the experiences and impacts of being "suspect" for Irish communities and Muslim communities in Britain', *Critical Terrorism Studies*, 5:1 (2012), 89–106.

26 David Feldman, 'Why the English like turbans: multicultural politics in British history', in David Feldman and Jon Lawrence (eds), *Structures and Transformations in Modern British History* (Cambridge: Cambridge University Press, 2011).

27 This view is extended and argued for in Ray Honeyford, *The Commission for Racial Equality: British Bureaucracy Confronts the Multiethnic Society* (New Jersey, NY: Transaction, 1999). For a view from a visiting US scholar, see Lewis M. Killian, *Black and White: Reflections of a White Southern Sociologist* (Oxford: General Hall, 1994), ch. 14.

28 Ira Katznelson, *Black Men and White Cities* (London: Institute for Race Relations and Oxford University Press, 1973).

29 Home Office, *Organisation of Race Relations Administration* (London: HMSO, 1976); David Pitt in Hansard (HL) vol. 421, col. 217ff., 10 June 1981.

30 Estimates of expenditure on race relations research varied widely precisely because there was no single budget. Home Office, *Organisation of Race Relations*, p. 16 estimates the total research expenditure for 1974–1975 to be in the region of £290,000.

31 Phillip N. Sooben, *The Origins of the Race Relations Act* (Warwick: Centre for Research into Ethnic Relations, 1990); Community Relations

Commission, *Review of the Race Relations Act* (London: Community Relations Commission, 1975).

32 Feldman, 'Why the English like turbans'.

33 Race Relations HC Bill (1975–1976) [177] cols 35–40.

34 *Ibid*. See also B.J. Turner, 'Minority rights protection in the United Kingdom', in European Centre for Minority Issues (ed.), *European Yearbook of Minority Issues 2001/2* (Kluwer: The Hague, 2003), pp. 398, 402.

35 For historical background on *Mandla* v. *Dowell Lee*, see Gurharpal Singh and Darshan Singh Tatla, *Sikhs in Britain: The Making of a Community* (London: Zed Books, 2006), pp. 130–133; and for an analysis stressing the ways in which the legal judgement endorsed a deterministic notion of culture, see Anne Phillips, *Multiculturalism without Culture* (Princeton, NJ: Princeton University Press, 2007), pp. 107–110.

36 Stuart Hall, 'From Scarman to Stephen Lawrence', *History Workshop Journal*, 48 (1999), 187–197; John Breuilly, 'The historical conditions for multiculturalism', in John Eade, Martyn Barrett, Chirs Flood and Richard Race (eds), *Advancing Multiculturalism Post 7/7* (Newcastle: Cambridge Scholars, 2008).

37 See, for example, the series of articles in the 'community relations forum' published in 1972 and, particularly, P. Ray, 'The majority of the problem', *New Community*, 1:3 (1972), 212–214.

38 London Metropolitan Archives, MS 4462/P/01/40A, Report of the Working Group on Education and Race, 13 March 1969.

39 Wellcome Library, London, PSY/TAJ/5/34, Report of Special Meeting of MPs to Discuss Possibilities of the Elimination of Colour Prejudice through Education, 27 May 1968.

40 London Metropolitan Archives, MS 4462/P/01/40A, minutes of Working Group on Education for the Eradication of Colour Prejudice, 20 November 1969.

41 *Ibid*., newsletter by Working Group on Education for the Eradication of Colour Prejudice, November 1970.

42 BBC Written Archives Centre, R 108/25/1, 'House of Commons Working Group on Education for the Eradication of Colour Prejudice: March 30 Conference', by J. Rogers to DPA, 15 February 1971. The judgement was premature because the WGEECP continued to contribute to the formulation of policy. See, for example, Race Relations and Immigration Select Committee, *Education Volume 2* (HC, 1972–1973, 405–II), pp. 288–289.

43 Halsey, *History of Sociology in Britain*, pp. 104–112.

44 Wellcome Library, PSY/TAJ/550 SSRC, Revised Programme for Race Relations Unit, October 1970.

45 Wellcome Library, PSY/TAJ/1/1/3, Social Science Research Unit, Race Relations Unit Advisory Committee, Minutes of 4th Meeting, 9 March 1971.

46 Wellcome Library, PSY/5/52, Social Science Research Unit, Research Unit on Ethnic Relations Advisory Committee, 22 November 1976 for criticisms of Weinreich's identity programme and for the importance of historical work, see *Annual Report on the Research Unit on Ethnic Relations*, October 1976 and the section 'Forward look for 1978–83'.

47 N.A., 'Race post challenge', *New Society*, 47: 851 (January 1979), 180; John Rex, 'Race relations research in an academic setting: a personal note', *Home Office Research Bulletin*, 8 (1979), 29–30.

48 David Milner, *Children and Race* (Harmondsworth: Penguin, 1975).

49 Barry Troyna, '"Race" and racism: the limitations of research and policy', *British Journal of Educational Studies*, 39:4 (1991), 430.

50 Henri Tajfel (ed.), *European Developments in Social Psychology. The Social Dimension: European Developments in Social Psychology Volumes I and II* (Cambridge: Cambridge University Press, 1984); Marie Jahoda, 'The roots of prejudice', *New Community*, 4:2 (1975), 185.

51 Maykel Verkuyten, *The Social Psychology of Ethnic Identity* (Abingdon, Oxon.: Routledge, 2005), pp. 13–15; U. Flick (ed.), *The Psychology of the Social* (Cambridge: Cambridge University Press, 1998).

52 Herman, *Romance of American Psychology*, pp. 193–207; Alan Marsh, 'Tolerance and pluralism in Britain: perspectives in social psychology', *New Community*, 1:4 (1972), 282–289; 'Reports from correspondents: education', *New Community*, 1:5 (1972), 455–456.

53 For archetypal academic discussion, see, for example, J.L. Watson, *Between Two Cultures: Migrants and Minorities in Britain* (Oxford: Blackwell, 1977); and the important challenge by Robert Miles. 'Between two cultures? The case of Rastafarianism', *Social Science Research Council Working Papers on Ethnic Relations*, 10:1 (1978), 1–34.

54 Liam Greenslade, Moss Madden and Maggie Pearson, 'The "problem" of the health of Irish people in Britain', in L. Marks and M. Worboys (eds), *Migrants, Minorities and Health: Historical and Contemporary Studies* (London: Routledge, 1997), pp. 147–178.

55 Mathew Thomson, *Psychological Subjects: Identity Culture and Health in Twentieth Century Britain* (Oxford: Oxford University Press, 2006); Kenneth McLaughlin, *Surviving Identity: Vulnerability and the Psychology of Recognition* (Abingdon, Oxon.: Routledge, 2012).

56 Ealing Community Relations Council, *Race Relations and the Secondary School Curriculum: A Statement of Minimum Requirements* (n.p., Community Relations Commission, 1970), p. 1. From an extensive range of publications on community relations and multiculturalism, see,

for example, Community Relations Commission Great Britain, *Towards a Multi-Racial Society* (n.p., Community Relations Commission, 1970).

57 Community Relations Commission, *Urban Deprivation, Racial Inequality and Social Policy* (London: HMSO, 1977); Community Relations Commission, *Educational Needs of Children from Minority Groups* (London: Community Relations Commission, 1974); Hashmi, *Psychology of Racial Prejudice.*

58 National Archives, Home Office, HO 376/94, 'Community Relations Commission: conditions attached to the grant in aid to the Commission by the Home Office'.

59 Community Relations Commission, *Urban Deprivation, Racial Inequality and Social Policy* (London: HMSO, 1977), pp. 62–63, 69, 85, 100.

60 Details of grants are in NA CK/3/4 Community Relations Council, CRC Minute Book.

61 An extensive literature on Black Studies in the USA is reviewed in Jonathan Fenderson, James Stewart and Kabria Baumgartner, 'Expanding the history of the Black Studies movement: some prefatory notes', *Journal of African American Studies*, 16 (2012), 1–20. For examples of interest in England see, for example, BHAS, AFFOR, Box 4, memorandum by M. Taylor, 'Black Studies', August 1972.

62 National Archives, HO 376/102 has a curriculum vitae for Morris.

63 Mullard, *Black Britain*, p. 95.

64 National Archives, CK 3/28, CRC Annual Conference, All Saints College. Tottenham 4–7 September 1973, conference schedule and copies of selected papers.

65 Sam Morris, 'Black Studies in Britain', *New Community*, 11:3 (1973), 245–248.

66 Race Relations and Immigration Select Committee, *Education Volume 2* (HC, 1972–73, 405–II), pp. 57–58, 286.

67 Committee for Black Studies, *The Case and the Course: A Treatise on Black Studies* (n.p.: Committee for Black Studies, 1973).

68 Black Cultural Archives, Wong Papers, 2/29. Unpublished typescript by Bridget Harris, 'The question of Black Studies', p. 1. See also LRO, MCRC, 60/2 report by J.A. Rogers, February 1976, p. 1.

69 Morris, 'Black Studies in Britain', pp. 246–248.

70 Sandy Kirby, 'Black studies', *New Society*, 27:59 (28 March 1974), 773.

71 Race Relations and Immigration Select Committee, *Education Volume 2*, pp. 57–58, 286. Lord Ritchie-Calder in Hansard (HL) vol. 326, cols 1218–1219.

72 Morris, 'Black Studies in Britain', p. 248.

73 Robin Bunce and Paul Field, *Darcus Howe: A Political Biography* (London: Bloomsbury, 2013), ch. 7.

74 Race Relations and Immigration Select Committee, *Education Volume 1: Report* (HC, 1972–1973, 405–I), paras 101–104.

75 National Archives, HO/376/136, typescript memorandum by K.L. Newman 'The policing of racially sensitive divisions', unpublished paper, 1973.

76 Tony Moore, *Policing Notting Hill: Fifty Years of Turbulence* (Hook, Hants.: Waterfield Press, 2013).

77 Kester Aspden, *The Hounding of David Oluwale* (London: Vintage, 2008); Derek Humphreys and Gus John, *Because They're Black: Police Power and Black People* (Hardmonsworth: Penguin, 1972).

78 Newman 'Policing of racially sensitive divisions', pp. 11–13.

79 Newman, cited in Trevor Carter and Jean Coussins, 'Back to school? The police, the education system and the black community', in Ellis Cashmore and Eugene McLaughlin *Out of Order? Policing Black People* (London: Routledge, 1991), p. 159. On subversion see Clive Walker, *The Prevention of Terrorism in British Law* (Manchester: Manchester University Press, 1986), p. 3.

80 Select Committee on Race Relations and Immigration, *The Organisation of Race Relations Administration: Observations on the Report of the Select Committee on Race Relations and Immigration* (HMSO, London 1974), p. 6.

81 Mullard, *Black Britain*, p. 93.

82 George Padmore Library, BEM 3/1/4/1/30. Letter from Peter Tucker (CRC Director of Fieldwork and Administration) to John La Rose.

83 Ann Dummett, *A Portrait of English Racism* (Harmondsworth: Penguin, 1973) pp. 46–61.

84 H.L. Malchow, *Special Relations: The Americanization of Britain?* (Stanford, CA: Stanford University Press, 2011), ch. 7.

85 Ann Dummett, 'A. Dummett writes', *Race*, 13:3 (1972), 359. J. Bhatnagar, 'Teaching racial tolerance', *Race Today*, June (1970), 171–173; Race Relations and Immigration Select Committee, *The West Indian Community* (HC, 1975–1976, 47–i), para. 14.

86 For a contemporary critique of informal race relations work, see Dummett, *Portrait of English Racism*, esp. pp. 39–46, 62–89 and 123–130. For formal academic evaluation after a decade of practice, see L. Stenhouse *et al.*, *Teaching about Race Relations: Problems and Effects* (London: Routledge & Kegan Paul, 1982).

87 Michael Walsh, 'The religious ferment of the sixties', in H. McLeod (ed.), *The Cambridge History of Christianity Volume 9: World Christianities c.1914–c.2000* (Cambridge: Cambridge University Press, 2006); Dummett, *Who Is my Neighbour?*

88 British Council of Churches' Working Party on Britain as a Multi-Racial Society, *The New Black Presence in Britain: A Christian Scrutiny*

(London: Community and Race Relations Unit of the British Council of Churches, 1976), p. 12.

89 British Council of Churches' Working Party on Britain as a Multi-Racial Society, *New Black*, p. 12.

90 Gilroy, *There Ain't no Black*, pp. 104–110.

91 Tony Holden, *Black Consciousness and White Liberation* (n.p., Zebra Project, 1981), pp. 6, 12–16, 17.

92 Tony Holden, *People, Churches and Multi-Racial Projects: An Account of English Methodism's Response to Plural Britain* (London: Methodist Church Division of Social Responsibility, 1984).

93 Judith H. Katz, *White Awareness Handbook for Anti-Racism Training* (Duncan, OK: University of Oklahoma Press, 1978) pp. 14, 23.

94 Mohan Luthra, and Robin Oakley, *Combating Racism through Training: A Review of Approaches to Race Training in Organisations* (Coventry: Centre for Research in Ethnic Relations, 1991), p. 7. For one example, see the training materials developed by Birmingham City Council in David Ruddell, *Recognising Racism* (Birmingham: City of Birmingham Education Department, 1982); and for an angry denunciation, see Keith Thompson, *Under Siege! Racial Violence in Britain* (London: Penguin, 1988), pp. 120–121, 185–188 (fn 56).

95 Ambalavaner Sivanandan, 'RAT and the degradation of black struggle', *Race and Class*, 26:4 (1985), 24.

96 *Ibid.*; Raphael Samuel, 'A case for national history', *International Journal of Historical Teaching, Learning and Research*, 3:1 (2003), 89.

97 For some apt comment and evaluation, see Richards, *'Race', Racism and Psychology*, pp. 292–315.

98 Delroy Louden, 'Self-esteem and locus of control in minority group adolescents', *Ethnic and Racial Studies*, 1:2 (1978), 196–217; Delroy Louden, 'A comparative study of self-concepts among minority and majority group adolescents in English multi-racial schools', *Ethnic and Racial Studies*, 4:2 (1981), 153–174.

99 Louis Chase, 'Some of my grouses', *New Community*, 3:1–2 (1974), 111–112.

100 Small and Solomos, 'Race, immigration and politics in Britain', pp. 235–257.

101 C.L.R. James, *At the Rendezvous of Victory: Selected Writings* (London: Allison & Busby, 1984), pp. 194, 201.

102 S. Jessell, 'Unite and slap back', *The Times* (2 December 1968), p. 1.

103 Simon Prince, *Northern Ireland's 68: Civil Rights, Global Revolt and the Origins of the Troubles* (Dublin: Irish Academic Press, 2007).

104 http://news.bbc.co.uk/panorama/hi/front_page/newsid_7968000/7968671.stm (last accessed 12/09/13).

105 N. O'Connell, 'In the land of the stranger', *Catholic Herald* (31 January 1969), p. 9.

106 Delaney, *Irish in Post-War Britain*, pp. 159–168; Rex and Moore, *Race, Community and Conflict*, pp. 175–178, 190. Kevin Myers, 'Faith in history: memory, multiculturalism and the legacies of Empire in postwar England', *History of Education*, 40:6 (2011), 785.

107 Delaney, *Irish in Post-War Britain*, p. 163.

108 F. Chapman, 'Not to be spoken of in polite circles', *Irish Post*, 1 August, 1981, p. 6; D. Johnson, 'Why Catholics in Britain remain silent', *Guardian* (13 April 1974), p. 5; J.F.X. Harriot, 'Home thoughts on Northern Ireland', *The Month*, 7:4 (1974).

109 Hill, *Black Churches: West Indian and African Sects in Britain* (London: Community and Race Relations Unit of the British Council of Churches 1971), pp. 13–20. Hiro, *Black British*, pp. 28–31; Robert Beckford, *Jesus Dub: Theology, Music and Social Change* (London: Routledge, 2006), p. 40; University of Birmingham (hereafter UoB), Birmingham Black Oral History Project (hereafter BBOHP), Frank Scantlebury, part 36, p. 8 and Esme Lancaster, BBOHP, part 12, p. 12.

110 Valentina Alexander, 'A mouse in a jungle: the Black Christian woman's experiences in the church and society in Britain', in Delia Jarrett-Macauley (ed.), *Reconstructing Womanhood, Reconstructing Feminism: Writings on Black Women* (London: Routledge, 1996); Cadbury Research Library, DA6, BBOHP, archives, box 2, transcript of interview with Esme Lancaster.

111 Hyland, 'My '70s', p. 43; Delaney, pp. 158–159.

112 Hickman, *Religion, Class and Identity*, pp. 158–202; B. Walter. 'Celebrations of Irishness in Britain: second-generation experiences of St Patrick's Day', in Marie Clare Considère-Charon, Philippe Laplace and Michel Savaric (eds), *The Irish Celebrating: Festive and Tragic Overtones* (Newcastle: Cambridge Scholars Press, 2008).

113 N. Ryan, 'Irish are not well served by parish clubs', *Irish Post* (21 February 1981), p. 6; Walter, 'Celebrations of Irishness in Britain'.

114 Meg Maguire, 'Missing links: working class women of Irish descent', in Pat Mahoney and Christine Zmroczek (eds), *Class Matters: 'Working Class' Women's Perspectives on Social Class* (London: Verso, 1997); Mary J. Hickman, 'The religio-ethnic identities of teenagers of Irish descent', in M. Hornsby-Smith, *Catholics in England: Historical and Sociological Perspectives* (London: Geoffrey Chapman, 1999).

115 British Library, Sound Archive, C1371/60, History in Education Project Interview conducted by Dr Nicola Sheldon, Track 1.

116 Delaney, *Irish in Post-War Britain*, pp. 139–140; Shirley Chew and Anna Rutherford (eds), *Unbecoming Daughters of the Empire* (Hebden Bridge, Dangeroo Press, 1993), p. 17.

117 Margaret Archer, *Being Human: The Problem of Agency* (Cambridge: Cambridge University Press, 2000), p. 308.

118 Breda Gray, 'From "ethnicity" to "diaspora": 1980s emigration and "multicultural" London', in A. Bielenberg (ed.), *The Irish Diaspora* (London: Longman, 2000), p. 71.

119 N. O'Dowd, 'Death of a legend', www.irishcentral.com/gossip/Death-of-a-Legend-3982.html#ixzz24qEbm2ob (last accessed 18/09/12). On the significance of the *Irish Post* see Padraig Reidy, 'What the *Irish Post* did for Irishness' (5 September 2011) available on the *Guardian* Comment is Free website www.theguardian.com/commentisfree/2011/sep/05/irish-post-did-us (last accessed 16/09/13).

120 Early Day Motion 611, 2008–2009 session, tabled by Jim Dobbin.

121 Martin Doyle (ed.), *A History of the Irish Post* (London: Smurfit Media, 2000), pp. 16–18.

122 Peter Beresford Ellis, *Irish Post*, 4 April 1970; Dónall MacAmhlaigh, 'The middle nation', *Irish Times* (14 October 1970) ; Dónall MacAmlaigh, 'Social life and the emigrant', *Irish Times* (15 October 1970).

123 See letters from M. Corcoran and M. Callagher, 'Why pick on the Irish in Britain?', *Irish Post* (11 April 1981), p. 6.

124 A. Hastings, 'When the Irish laugh and cry', *Birmingham Mail* (18 March 1970), p. 8.

125 Mary Kenny, 'Being Irish in England', *New Society*, 34:68 (2012), 272; Gerry Smyth, 'Paddy sad and Paddy mad: music and the condition of Irishness', in Considère-Charon *et al.* (eds), *Irish Celebrating*, p. 60.

126 A. Hastings, 'When the Irish laugh and cry', *Birmingham Mail* (18 March 1970); D. MacAmlaigh 'The middle nation', *Irish Times*, 14 October 1970.

127 M. O Callanain and S. Timmons, 'Federation incapable of leading youth', *Irish Post* (3 January 1981), p. 6; see also, Working Class Movement Library, Irish in Britain Representation Group papers, undated typescript, 'History of the IBRG'.

128 S. and M. Lennon, '"Off the boat": Irish women talk about their experiences of living in England', *Spare Rib*, 94 (May 1980), 52–55.

129 Obi Egbuna, *Destroy this Temple: The Voice of Black Power in England* (London: MacGibbon & Kee, 1971); Robin Bunce and Paul Field, 'Obi B. Egbuna, C.L.R. James and the birth of Black Power in Britain: black radicalism in Britain 1967–72', *Twentieth Century British History*, 22:3 (2011), 391–414.

130 Egbuna, *Destroy this Temple*, pp. 88–89.

131 BBC, Written Archives Centre, R19/2, 073/1: Black Programme Script, 3 April 1968, pp. 1, 8, 25–26.

132 Egbuna, *Destroy this Temple*, pp. 46, 52–53.

133 See, for example, Kieran Connell, 'A micro-history of "black

Handsworth": towards a social history of race in Britain' (Ph.D. thesis, UoB, 2011), pp. 20–26; Paul Warmington, *Black British Intellectuals and Education* (Abingdon, Oxon.: Routledge, 2014), pp. 36–56; Anne-Marie Angelo, 'The Black Panthers in London, 1967–1972', *Radical History Review*, 103 (2009), 17–35; Hiro, *Black British*, pp. 108–109. BHAS, MS2141/C/4, Black People's Alliance and Black Power Groups, miscellaneous materials.

134 Andrew Witt, *The Black Panthers in the Midwest: The Community Programs and Services of the Black Panther Party in Milwaukee, 1966–1977* (New York: Routledge, 2007).

135 Farukh Dhondy, 'Teaching young blacks', *Race Today* (May/June 1978), 80–86; A. Dummett, *Portrait of English Racism*, pp. 128–130; Jessica Gerrard, 'Self-help and protests: the emergence of black supplementary schooling in England', *Race, Ethnicity and Education*, 16:1 (2013), 32–58; Bunce and Field, *Darcus Howe*.

136 [no author] 'Political and social action', *Grassroots* (4 September 1971), p. 10.

137 [no author] 'Black history and culture', *ibid.*, p. 8.

138 Black Cultural Archives, Oral/31, 'Oral histories of the Black Women's Movement'. Beverley Bryant transcript, pp. 99–10.

139 Brian W. Alleyne, *Radicals against Race: Black Activism and Cultural Politics* (Oxford: Berg, 2002); Burkett, *Constructing Post-Imperial Britain*; Angelo, 'Black Panthers in London', pp. 17–35.

140 Walter Rodney, *The Groundings with My Brother Brothers* (London: Bogle-L'Ouverture, 1969) and *How Europe Underdeveloped Africa* (London: Bogle L'Ouverture,1972). Publishing details in LMA 4462/ Bogle L'Ouverture Publications Limited, Catalogue.

141 Rupert Lewis, *Walter Rodney's Intellectual and Political Thought* (Detroit, MI: Wayne State University Press, 1998); David Austin, 'Introduction to Walter Rodney', *Small Axe*, 10 (2001), 60–62.

142 London Metropolitan Archives, MS 4462/D/01/141, course proposal and annotated bibliography (1973) by African-American scholar Robert A. Hill.

143 For a recent account of the Black Supplementary Schools Movement that identifies and explores different cultures of blackness, see J. Gerrard, *Radical Childhoods: Schooling and the Struggle for Social Change* (Manchester: Manchester University Press, 2014), ch. 5.

144 For a summary of La Rose's life and work, see Brian Alleyne, 'John La Rose' *History Workshop Journal*, 64 (2007), 460–466; Gus John, 'La Rose, John Anthony (1927–2006)', *Oxford Dictionary of National Biography* (Oxford: Oxford University Press, January 2010; online edn, January 2011) www. oxforddnb.com/view.article97081 (last accessed 21/01/13).

145 Alleyne, *Radicals against Race*, pp. 42–43.

146 George Padmore Library, BEM 4/7/1/6 letter from (unidentified signatories) to Mr Chapple, PPS to Edward Short. On the background to the campaign and the relationship to the emerging Black Supplementary School Movement, see Gerrard, *Radical Childhoods*, pp. 127–134.

147 George Padmore Library, BEM 2/2/2/3/39–40, no author, 'Talking to ourselves: report of the Caribbean Educationalists Association's weekend seminar, 28–30 August 1970', pp. 11–12. See also BEM 3/1/4/1/42 Caribbean Education and Community Workers Association, newsletter no.1 (1971).

148 Gerrard, *Radical Childhoods*, pp. 117–181; Diane Reay and Heidi Mirza, 'Uncovering genealogies of the margins: Black Supplementary Schooling', *British Journal of Sociology of Education*, 18:4 (1997), 477–499.

149 Hilary Arnott, 'School of the streets', *Race Today* (March 1971), 94–95.

150 Nel Clark, 'Dachwyng Saturday School', in Ashok Ohri, Basil Manning and Paul Curno (eds), *Community Work and Racism* (London, Routledge, 1982); C. Faulder, 'The people who like school on Saturdays', *Guardian* (5 May 1981).

151 George Padmore Library, BPM 4/2/3/1 Harriet Tubman School, information sheet [n.d]. Peter Moses Supplementary School, information sheet [n.d].

152 Black Cultural Archives, Wong 2/2/1/1, *Journal of the Ahfiwe School and Abeng*, no. 1; BCA, Wong 2/2 [n.d.]; *Journal of the Ahfiwe School and Abeng*, no. 2 [n.d].

153 Gerrard, *Radical Childhoods*, pp. 144–146.

154 Gerrard, 'Self-help and protests', pp. 34, 52.

155 George Padmore Library, BEM 2/2/2/3/39–40 Talking to Ourselves: Report of the Caribbean Educationalists Association's weekend seminar, 28–30 August 1970, p. 3.

156 Black Cultural Archives, Wong 2/2/1/1, *Journal of the Ahfiwe School and Abeng*, no.1 [n.d].

157 George Padmore Library, BEM 3/1/2/6 [undated 1974?] handwritten notes, 'The Ideology and Outlook of the School'.

158 Brian Alleyne, 'Anti-racist cultural politics in post-imperial Britain: the New Beacon Circle', in Mark Cote, Richard J.F. Day and Greig de Peuter (eds), *Utopian Pedagogy: Radical Experiments against Neoliberal Globalization* (Toronto: University of Toronto Press), pp. 207–226.

159 George Padmore Library, BEM 4/2/2/2, Education courses: various, 20 September 1971–6 January 1976; Polytechnic of Central London,

Centre for Extra-Mural Studies promotional materials for 'Frantz Fanon: the reconstitution of black consciousness'.

160 George Padmore Library, BEM 4/2/2/2, City Literary Institute, Community Education Trust, syllabus for 'History and racism' course; LMA 4462/01/039C, undated pamphlet on courses in history organised by the Community Education Trust.

161 Harry Golbourne, 'Africa and the Caribbean in Caribbean consciousness and action in Britain', David Nicholls Memorial Lectures, no. 2 (David Nicholls Memorial Trust, Oxford: University of Oxford, 2000); BEM 4/2/2/2, course promotional materials including Black Studies at Holloway Institute. BEM 4/2/2/6, Syllabus I for 'History and culture of African and Caribbean peoples', 1973–1974 and 1974–1975.

162 Hazel Carby, 'Lost (and found?) in translation', *Small Axe*, 28 (2009), 36.

163 P. Freire, *Pedagogy of the Oppressed* (London: Penguin, 1996 [1970]), pp. 81, 82, 111, 130.

164 George Padmore Library, BEM 3/1/2/6 [undated 1974?] handwritten notes, 'The ideology and outlook of the school'.

165 Roxy Harris and Sarah White (eds), *Changing Britannia: Life Experience within Britain* (London: New Beacon, 1999), pp. 55, 126, 207–208, 217.

166 Liverpool Record Office, Liverpool Community Relations Council, 60/2, I. Mellish 'Some notes on Action Research in Liverpool 8', February 1973, p. 10 (underlining in original).

167 Liverpool Record Office, Liverpool Community Relations Council, Minutes of the AGM 22 June 1972.

168 Carol Polsgrove, *Writers in a Common Cause* (Manchester: Manchester University Press, 2009).

169 Sarah White, Roxy Harris and Sharmilla Beezmohun (eds), *A Meeting of the Continents: The International Book Fair of Radical Black and Third World Books, 1982–1995* (London: New Beacon, 2005).

170 National Archives, CK 3/87 'West Indian Saturday School', letter from Roy Clarke to Development Section, Community Relations Commission, 28 March 1972.

171 National Archives, CK 3/87 letter from Maureen Taylor to Development Officer, Community Relations Commission, 9 November 1972. See also Black Cultural Archives, Dadzie 1/1/30, Black Teachers Meeting, minutes, 1 March 1979 for Sabarr bookshop's decision to move away from selling 'general literature into supplying libraries and schools and into providing books specifically for the black student population'.

172 Stuart Hall (interviewed by Bill Schwarz), 'Breaking bread with history: C.L.R. James and the Black Jacobins', *History Workshop Journal*, 46: 2 (1998), 20–21 for the origins of this historical imagination and its

place in radical social movements. For one participant account of how historical thinking, and an understanding of the historicity of human life, informed various political and intellectual projects of the post-war period, see Richard Johnson, 'Historical returns: transdisciplinarity, cultural studies and history', *European Journal of Cultural Studies*, 4:3 (2001), 261–288.

173 Mark Salber Phillips, 'History, memory and historical distance', in Peter Seixas (ed.), *Theorizing Historical Consciousness* (Toronto: University of Toronto Press, 2004).

174 Kevin Myers and Ian Grosvenor, 'Birmingham stories: local histories of migration and settlement and the practice of history', *Midland History*, 36:2 (2011), 149–162.

175 Steven Clay and Rodney Phillips, *A Secret Location on the Lower East Side: Adventures in Writing, 1960–1980* (New York: Granary, 1998).

176 Cited in Zhana, *Black Success Stories: Celebrating People of African Heritage* (London: Zhana, 2006), p. 80.

177 J. Bergman and B. Coard, 'Trials and tribulations of a self-help group', *Race Today*, 4:4 (1972), 112–114.

178 See, for example, the materials, including evidence of Black Panther community and educational work, collated in the case against the 'Mangrove 9', in National Archives, Metropolitan Police Records, 31/21, 'Black Power demonstration: original statements and newspaper cuttings, 1970–1973'; Tony Bunyan, *The History and Practice of the Political Police in Britain* (London: Friedman, 1976).

179 Lucy Bland, 'White women and men of colour: miscegenation fears in Britain after the Great War', *Gender and History*, 17:1 (2005), 33.

180 Mica Nava, *Visceral Cosmopolitanism*, pp. 75–94; Schaffer, *Racial Society and British Society*, pp. 86–88, 157–161; Rich, *Race and Empire*, ch. 6.

181 Paul Barber, *Foster Kid: A Liverpudlian Childhood* (London: Sphere, 2007), pp. 33, 35–36, 77; Dave Clay, 'The changing face of community participation: the Liverpool black experience', *Participatory Action and Learning*, 58 (June 2008), 88 recalls hearing a very similar story and the frightening implications of it.

182 Raphael Samuel, *The Lost World of British Communism* (London: Verso, 2006), p. 49.

183 Quotations and details of Kuya's activities are in Liverpool Record Office, MCRC 75/2, 'Dorothy Kuya's Annual Report 1972–73', p. 19.

184 Liverpool Record Office, MCRC 75/2, Jimmy Rogers's Annual Report 1972–1973, p. 3.

185 *Ibid.*, minutes of LCRC Annual General Meeting, 22 June 1972, p. 8.

186 Liverpool Record Office, MCRC/80/2, handwritten note on 'racism' [n.d, 1975?].

187 *Ibid.*, 'Draft constitution for Liverpool Black Studies Group' [n.d., 1975?].

188 Liverpool Record Office, MCRC/60/2 'Merseyside Community Relations Council: report to the executive', October 1977.

189 Farukh Dhondy, 'Teaching young blacks', *Race Today* (May/June, 1978), 82.

190 Geoff Eley, *A Crooked Line: From Cultural History to the History of Society* (Michigan, MI: University of Michigan Press, 2005), p. 139.

191 Birmingham Heritage and Archives Services, MS 1611/B3/1, script (with annotations) for *First Race Show* [n.d., 1974?], p. 1.

192 Baz Kershaw, 'Alternative Theatres, 1946–2000', in *The Cambridge History of British Theatre Volume III: Since 1895*, ed. Baz Kershaw (Cambridge: Cambridge University Press, 2004), pp. 349–376.

193 Birmingham Heritage and Archives Services, MS 1611/B3/1, script (with annotations) for *First Race Show* [n.d., 1974?], pp. 7–8, 13, 18.

194 Len Garrison, *Black Youth, Rastafarianism and the Identity Crisis in Britain* (London: ACER, 1979), p. 39.

195 Derek Bishton and Brian Homer, *Talking Blues: The Black Community Speaks about Its Relationship with the Police* (Birmingham: AFFOR, 1978), pp. 88–89. On AFFOR and the tensions within local anti-racist and community activist groups, see Connell, 'Micro-history of "black Handsworth"', pp. 108–117.

196 Birmingham Heritage and Archives Services, MS 2220, General Files Box 4: 'Talking blues follow up', miscellaneous correspondence.

197 See, for example, Ivor Morrish, *The Background of Immigrant Children* (London: Unwin, 1971).

198 Bishton and Homer, *Talking Blues*, pp. 14–17.

199 Paul Gilroy, 'Could You Be Loved? Bob Marley, Anti-Politics and Universal Sufferation', *Critical Quarterly*, 47:1–2 (2005), 239. Jason Toynbee, *Bob Marley: Herald of a Postcolonial World* (Cambridge: Polity, 2007).

200 Gilroy, 'Could You Be Loved?', p. 238.

201 Connell, 'Micro-history of "black Handsworth"', pp. 180–197.

202 M. Ferguson, 'The ghetto sound', *Guardian* (18 September 1976), p. 8.

203 W. 'Lez' Henry, 'Reggae, Rasta and the role of the deejay in the black British experience', *Contemporary British History*, 26:3 (2012), 353–373; Gilroy, *There Ain't No Black*, pp. 163–164.

204 Dave Ward, 'Putting down roots: an interview with Levi Tafari', in M. Murphy and D. Rees-Jones, *Writing Liverpool: Essays and Interviews* (Liverpool: Liverpool University Press, 2007), 252–264.

205 Henry, 'Reggae, Rasta and the role of the deejay', p. 364.

206 La Rose, 'All are consumed', in Parekh, *Colour, Culture and*

Consciousness, p. 121; Garrison, 'Black youth', pp. 22–23; Gilroy, *There Ain't No Black*, pp. 207–209.

207 Howe, 'C.L.R. James', pp. 169–170.

208 Rusen, 'Historical narration: foundation, types, reason', *History and Theory*, 26 (1987), 92.

209 Cited in Garrison, *Black Youth*, p. 7.

210 *Ibid.*, p. 34.

211 Liverpool Record Office, MCRC/76/6, File on 'Local black radical groups' containing early newsletters [n.d., 1975/1976?].

212 Birmingham Heritage and Archives Services, MS 2192/C/B/2/1, Charles Wootton Centre for Further Education, prospectus 1988/89.

213 Romain, *Connecting Histories*, p. 209; 'The roots of racism in city of many cultures', *Liverpool Daily Echo* (3 August 2005).

214 Liverpool Record Office, MCRC 64/2 Letter from Somerfeld, Mufti, Williams and Chopra to William Whitelaw, Secretary of State for Home Affairs 9 May 1980; Paul Somerfield, 'Race Relations and M.C.R.C.: ten years of concern', in MCRC, *10th Annual Report*, pp. 13–15.

215 MCRC, *10th Annual Report*, pp. 1, 3; Belchem, 'Before the Windrush', pp. 263–266.

216 Eric Lynch, 'Transcript of speech given by E. Lynch in 1980', in Gifford *et al.*, *Loosen the Shackles*, p. 248.

217 Patrick Wright, *On Living in an Old Country* (Oxford: Oxford University Press, 2nd edn, 2009), pp. 22–23.

218 Phillip Dodd. *The Battle Over Britain* (London: Demos, 1995), pp. 26–27.

219 Feldman, 'Why the English like turbans', p. 298.

220 Kevin Myers, interview with Mike Phillips, transcript in possession of the author.

221 Mary Chamberlain and Selma Leydesdorff, 'Transnational families: memories and narratives', *Global Networks*, 4:3 (2004), 229. Alistair Thomson, 'Moving stories: oral history and migration studies', *Oral History*, 27:1 (1999), 28.

222 John Siblon, 'A Mistaken Case of Identity', *History Workshop Journal*, 52 (2001), 259.

223 *Ibid.*, 257.

224 MacAmhlaigh, *An Irish Navy*, pp. 39, 42, 62.

225 Birmingham Heritage and Archives Services, MS 4000/2/129, post-transmission correspondence to Charles Parker, 13 April 1969.

226 Kevin Myers, 'Cultures of history: minority histories and the politics of the past in post-war England', in I. Glynn and J. Olaf Kleist (eds), *History, Memory and Migrant Incorporation* (Basingstoke: Palgrave Macmillan, 2012), pp. 33–48.

3

Pluralism, politics
and the uses of the past (1981–2000)

There must be a respect for the past. (Rhodes Boyson, 1980)

Introduction

The year 1981 was a tumultuous one for black people in England. It began ominously, when thirteen young black people attending a birthday celebration died in a suspicious fire at 439 New Cross Road in London. Although the cause was probably arson, the perpetrators of the fire were never caught and the complacent response of press, government and police confirmed, for many, that racist attacks on black people were acceptable and a direct result of their status as an alien wedge in British society.

These events would, no doubt, have been uppermost in the minds of the Liverpool Teachers' Association when it sat down to write a pamphlet, *Before the Fire*, that identified what it called a race relations crisis in the city and warned of future violent clashes unless immediate action was taken.[1] The pamphlet went ignored and its astute analysis, condemning a complacent city council for ignoring police harassment, racist attacks and discrimination in education, was unheeded. By the spring of 1981 the consequences of that complacency became clear.

Over the weekend of Friday 10 April to Sunday 12 April serious rioting broke out in London after a policeman had attempted to come to the aid of a young black man who had been stabbed by assailants. Such was the level of trust in the Metropolitan Police that a gathering crowd assumed the policeman to be the attacker. The injured youth was 'rescued' by the crowd and a riot protesting against an imagined police assault ensued. This level of mistrust had deep roots but it also had one specific, and more recent, cause: the Metropolitan Police's Special Patrol Group (SPG) and their 'clampdown' on petty crime. Codenamed Swamp 81, 'a tactless echo of Mrs Thatcher's 1978 interview on immigration' argues historian Mark Garnett, it consisted in the stopping and searching of London citizens, the vast majority of whom turned out to be black.[2] So when SPG forces arrived in Brixton on the afternoon of 11 April there was widespread anger and resentment. Full-scale riots, in which white youths were also prominent and active, followed; 279 police and 45 members of the public were injured. There was widespread damage to buildings and vehicles.[3]

A pattern had been set. Stop-and-search operations precipitated riots in Toxteth and Norris Green in Liverpool over the space of a month in July 1981. Almost 800 police were injured despite the deployment of CS gas for the first time in England. On 9 September the arrest of a young black man, following a police stop-and-search operation in Handsworth, Birmingham, resulted in two full days of rioting and resulted in the death of two local brothers, Kassamali and Amirali Moledina, injuries to 122 others and damage to property estimated at £7.5 million.[4] Although the riots would be widely attributed to problems in local race relations, organisations on the ground, like the local Birmingham Community Relations Council (BCRC), were united in arguing against the claim that there was a 'race problem' in Handsworth. Young people, the BCRC declared, were 'united racially' and there 'were no anti-white feelings amongst them'.[5]

The riots of summer 1981 are most accurately seen as symptoms of the difficult transition to a post-Fordist society. The slow and painful decline of industrialism, the closure of shipyards, car plants and factories, set in train a whole series of social and political changes; a transformation in urban landscapes; a shift in both the nature and the patterns of work; an associated, and loudly proclaimed, death of the manual working class and a clear shift in social and political imaginaries.[6] Nations and classes, the staple categories of identification for much of the twentieth century, seemed no longer sufficient to capture the depth of social change and the complexities of modern societies. They also seemed incapable of invoking the sense of belonging or directing the activism of at least some of the young people rioting on the streets of England. The social identities of young people became more dynamic precisely because they began to deploy the heritages, once hidden, forgotten and excluded by the national master narrative, but increasingly available in the spaces of radical education and popular culture.

The power of social identities expressed in racial or ethnic terms came from, and was asserted through, the past. Sophisticated analyses used a precise and historically informed vocabulary and sought to discuss, debate and educate. Scholar activists and their communities of practice, their supplementary schools, their publications, their teaching and their activism, sought to explain the lack of jobs, the anger and alienation, and the perceived lack of patriotism to England that so many second generation immigrants experienced. Their topic was the power of the past in the making of contemporary life chances. However, in a racialised public sphere, debates about the continued impact of the past on the Irish, but especially on black, immigrant groups, could easily lapse into a primordial language in which ethnic minorities were understood in a permanent and ahistorical fashion; as emotions, experiences, origins or natures that eluded those not included in the group but which required recognition and understanding. As this chapter demonstrates, ethnic difference in the present was to be explained by the invention of ethnic pasts and experiences that were tacitly assumed to be the basis of enduring historical identities. The resulting ethnic minority histories, which were initially championed by municipal multicultural policy and later recruited to combat social exclusion, may have effectively challenged the dominant national narrative but they also entailed their own silences and simplicities. Nowhere was this clearer than in sometimes acrimonious debates around what constituted 'indigenous culture' or 'authentic history' and in which the historical sensibility promoted by earlier scholar activists had all but disappeared.

Ethnicising the past

Urban rioting in 1981 is best understood in the context of the transformation of the British economy. Despite the preoccupation, in political and policy debate, with decline, the British economy grew for the whole of the post-war period and this growth helped to deliver real and sustained improvements in living standards. Measured by the average real gross domestic product per capita, living standards were, for example, 2.6 times higher in 1997 than in 1950. This, according to one economic historian, amounts to 'unparalleled historical success and of an economy transformed'.[7]

Abstract growth measures say nothing at all, of course, about either the actual distribution of wealth gains or the feelings and experiences of ordinary people. Even if the economy continued to grow over the post-war period, it did so slowly compared with other developed market economies and it entered a phase of acute instability after the first oil price shock in 1973. Accelerating inflation, rising unemployment and industrial relations unrest were exacerbated by structural changes to the economy. Some of these were a matter of intentional policy, most notably in the shift from an imperial/ commonwealth economy to a European and globalised one, others came as part of a wider process of technological revolution, as in the replacement of manufacturing by services as the largest employer in the economy and associated changes to available jobs, the labour force and wage rates. Unemployment figures surpassed the psychologically important figure of one million in 1975 and exceeded three million, or 11.3 per cent of the working population, by 1985. Even for those in work, the explosion of wage inequality that began in the early 1980s made the rewards of employment feel much less than in earlier decades. In the late 1970s, disorientation and insecurity abounded. Poverty, mass unemployment, squalor and instability, all of which were widely thought to be have been conquered by the post-war welfare state, spectacularly reappeared.[8]

The impact of these changes was not, of course, equally shared. As several studies have now shown, first and second generation ethnic minorities suffered higher rates of unemployment and lower wage rates than British-born white counterparts. These disadvantages were particularly acute and sustained across generations for both male and female black Caribbeans.[9] The location of black Caribbeans (especially men) in the manufacturing sector, which halved in size between 1970 and 2000, was clearly part of this story.[10] So too, despite the claims of some economists, was discrimination.[11] This meant that black Caribbeans and black Britons were most likely to be concentrated in the urban areas that spiralled into decline as a result of employment and population loss. Though it is more difficult to trace the experiences of the Irish because of the construction of ethnic minority data (see below), it is likely that they remained overwhelmingly located in construction (men) and in personal services and professional employment (women) where employment opportunities remained relatively stable.[12]

Notwithstanding these group differences, however, the structural changes to the economy helped to set in train significant social and political processes. Socially, as manufacturing plants and jobs either closed or moved overseas, significant depopulation occurred and crime rates increased. In Liverpool between 1966 and 1977, 350 factories closed or moved out, 40,000 jobs were lost and employment in the city fell by 33 per cent. As Jon Murden bleakly, but accurately concludes, for young black workers living in Liverpool 8 at the end of the 1970s 'the prospect of even an unskilled job was virtually nil'.[13] In Birmingham, the majority of foundries and engineering plants located in and around Handsworth, shut down or were relocated throughout the 1960s and 1970s.[14] At the time of the riots the unemployment rate for those below the age of 24 was 50 per cent.[15] Similarly, and in the area served by the Brixton Employment Office, the estimated unemployment rate for black males below the age of 19 was 55 per cent.[16]

Unemployment, police harassment, a lack of hope and a sense of alienation for young people are the contexts in which the summer riots of 1981 are best understood. Uprisings, argued historian and Birmingham educationalist Carlton Duncan, happen 'if society makes some of its members feel they don't belong [and] they haven't got a claim on anything'.[17] Governmental reaction was pragmatic. Rhetorically at least, Margaret Thatcher's Conservatives responded by denouncing acts of criminality, wrongly identifying them (as John Stokes did) as 'something new and sinister in our long national history' and misrepresenting them as the inevitable problems caused by 'multiracialism'.[18] In the immediate aftermath of the Brixton riots in April 1981, Home Secretary William Whitelaw pointedly praised the many 'coloured people' who have 'taken on the responsibilities of our country as well as the rights' but confirmed that 'a large number of those concerned came here between 1957 and 1962'.[19] 'Race relations' he argued, were 'a crucial strand' in explaining the rioting.[20]

In these responses, immigration was unambiguously signalled as a source of national decline and the arrival of large numbers of people who were identified as not belonging to England as a source of conflict. Such claims can be partly explained by an avowedly historicist reading of British history and one which was understood through the prism of race ideas. In English history there were centuries of domestic progress, imperial greatness and of tolerance towards those minorities, like Jews, who demonstrated a willingness to adapt to national culture.[21] 'Children must learn', argued educationalist and Conservative Minister for Education Rhodes Boyson, 'that they are heirs of a great cultural tradition, which must be nurtured. Attacking it will not bring about a better civilisation; it will merely sow dragon's teeth, and anarchy and destruction of law and order will follow'.[22] This was the singular meaning of the past and it provided roots, inspiration and identity in the present. It was also a past that was finished. There was nothing to be gained by revisiting the past or apologising for it. There were no structural legacies emerging from it. Anybody could succeed in Britain if they worked hard and assimilated to the demands of national culture. Thus, and for Margaret Thatcher's Conservatives and their mixture of aggressive modernity and nostalgia, the regular invocation of imperial history was accompanied both by some practical proposals designed to reawaken pride in being British and a thoroughly presentist philosophy that refused to accept historical processes as shaping contemporary society.[23]

The National Heritage Memorial Fund was established in 1980 and sought to encourage the preservation of those objects and artefacts thought to be important and to have significance for the nation. In practice, this entailed financial and other forms of support for the maintenance of cathedrals, castles and country houses, gardens, thatched cottages and statues of the famous. Elite culture was to be celebrated and consumed as though it were a common tradition.[24] Similarly, and even though these proposals became mired in a politics of history, the attempt to introduce a new and compulsory history curriculum in schools was a direct intervention in the social processes of memory. The nation's island story, Secretary of State for Education Sir Keith Joseph declared, should be continuously told and celebrated in schools, to foster the shared values and pride that were a direct consequence of properly understanding national progress and greatness.[25] Joseph also stressed the importance of teaching different interpretations of the past and of the sensitivities that were required in teaching children of different social, cultural and ethnic backgrounds but, and significantly, this was important for explicitly therapeutic reasons and because it promoted the 'self-confidence' and 'self-esteem' of children from ethnic backgrounds.[26] Overall, Joseph's intervention has usually been interpreted as an attempt to reassert a singular national narrative.[27]

Thatcherism's obvious concern for history, and its conviction that it offered the basis of a secure national identity, stimulated prolonged and sometimes bitter debate on both heritage and the politics of curriculum history. Raphael Samuel, a founding member of the consciously radical History Workshop at Ruskin College in the late 1960s, was a prominent and astute commentator in both debates. The singular island story was, he recognised from the outset, an active work of imagination; 'the national "we" is always in some ways a fiction' and he argued for a more pluralist politics, 'one which starts from a recognition of diversity' and arguing, like the conservative philosopher Edmund Burke, that it was through attachment to the 'little platoons' that we become 'members of the great society'. The diversity he had in mind was discussed at the History Workshop held in Oxford in 1994 and illustrated in the volume *Minorities and Outsiders* which explored the histories of different migrant communities, faith groups and sexual orientations. Samuel took delight in the ways in which these heritages began to enter the public domain through the cultural and educational programmes of local government. Curriculum projects, museums, galleries, exhibitions, displays, theme parks and shopping experiences 'left any unified view of the national past, radical or Conservative, in tatters'. Yet, the more radical or plebeian form of national identity, a kind of left-wing patriotism, that Samuel saw emerging did not challenge the basic assumption that ethnic identities were made and determined in the past. Moreover, and as Samuel was beginning to realise, the cultural meanings attached to the past were beginning to change.[28] No longer anchored to nations or classes, more affective uses of history were emerging in which, argues historian Carolyn Steedman, the past was primarily 'a place of succour and strength, a kind of home' and 'in the project of finding an identity through the process of historical identification, the past is searched for something (someone, some group, some series of events) that confirms the searcher in his or her sense of self, confirms them in what they want to be and feel in some measure that they already are'.[29]

Heritage debates both drew on, and helped to stimulate further, a concern with how identities were formed through historical processes and were retained or modified through the production of social memory. In some of the new social movements, and in the undisciplined spaces of universities, where immigrants and their descendants were disproportionately employed in the interdisciplinary study of areas, cultures and genders, the postcolonial moment had arrived.[30] Voices and experiences, once largely confined to radical spaces of education and political activism, were beginning to enter the political and academic mainstream. If this was initially organised around the study of gender, analyses of racism slowly began to argue that being or imagining oneself, as English (or British) was underpinned by powerful racist ideologies.[31] Racism, argued a groundbreaking text from the Centre for Contemporary Cultural Studies published in 1982, had 'to be located historically and in terms of the wider structures and relations of the British state'.[32] The actual empirical demonstration of these structures and processes might have remained sparse for at least two more decades but significant shifts were taking place in relationships to the past.[33] Against the Conservative championing of a nationalist culture guaranteed by a past that was over, one set of responses to the riots of 1981 insisted that the depth of discrimination against minority groups could only be understood and challenged by revisiting and reworking national history. Like other former colonial nations, Britain was beginning to confront its imperial pasts, to hear the voices of its imperial citizens and to debate just how an imperial past might be connected to the fractious present.[34]

Thus, and alongside the discursive emphasis on curtailing immigration and promoting integration and loyalty, it was recognised by some government ministers, that positive measures were required that would prevent the continued alienation of young black people in society.[35] Of course, this was not new. Similar arguments had been made in the 1970s and the previous chapter explored some of the projects that were indirectly funded by government at either central or local level. Yet, these remained marginal activities that were tolerated rather than championed and were dependent on local groups remaining moderate and compliant with the will of particular political administrations.[36] Martin Loney's analysis of the funding of community development projects, for example, made clear that when local projects began to reject notions of poverty as social pathology, and began to carry out historical studies designed to explain how economic conditions were rooted in the development of class relations, their funding was cut.[37] Even after the riots the particular disadvantages young black people faced, in housing, education and employment were only erratically acknowledged. Instead, complex factors were said to be at work. These were sometimes social and economic but, in political and policy discussion, they were also located in the minds and emotions of ethnic minority youth.

The major social and educational investigations of the period are typical in this respect. The Rampton Report identified low teacher expectations and racism in wider society as possible explanations for ethnic minority underperformance, but it did not attempt to challenge the validity of IQ testing and continued to discuss lower measured IQ in the context of cultural traditions, difficult conditions and family disruption.[38] Similarly, Liberal MP for Liverpool, David Alton, indulged in the customary praise for Liverpool's 'racial tolerance' that had allowed for the assimilation of ethnic communities but identified 'a paranoic [*sic*] hatred of the community towards some police officers' as one of the causes of the Toxteth riots.[39] Even Justice Julius Silverman's generally more astute analysis of the Handsworth riots of 1985 reflected pointedly on the fictive '*feeling* of being discriminated against' that was 'an important part of the social and psychological background of Handsworth'.[40] Historian Jed Fazakarley is right to identify, in elite reports, a sustained attention on a supposedly flawed black psychology, now clearly differentiated from that of Asians, and which was marked by 'ambivalent and inexplicable emotionality, intense and dangerous paranoia and easy susceptibility to rhetoric'.[41] While these were not groundbreaking racist ideas, the urgency of the moment meant that they were given renewed attention in the educational efforts to ameliorate the anger and alienation that had prompted the riots.

As a consequence central government increased funding available to local authorities with large ethnic populations to provide employment, training and funding for community projects.[42] Municipal authorities, especially those who claimed some form of left-wing identity, tentatively began to develop multicultural policies that promoted anti-racism, equal opportunities and the recognition of ethnic minority difference. Typically, these consisted of serious consideration to the statutory obligation of local authorities to eliminate racial discrimination and the promotion of equality of opportunity under the 1975 Race Relations Act. In London (1981–1986), Liverpool (1983–1987) and Birmingham (1984–2003) Labour administrations came to power and grappled in distinctive local ways with the definition and promotion of multiculturalism. At one extreme was Liverpool where the Trotskyist

Militant Tendency led the local council between 1983 and 1987. Viewing multiculturalism as a distraction from class politics and as a method for dividing the consciousness and interests of workers, racism went unacknowledged, campaigns for race equality treated with hostility and the black history that might have helped explained contemporary conditions was ignored.[43] The silences imposed by this particularly dogmatic version of the 'forward march of labour thesis' would continue well into the 1990s.[44] In contrast, Ken Livingstone's leadership of the Greater London Council (GLC), heavily influenced by Democratic affirmative action and equal opportunities policies in the USA, set an agenda for progressive local authorities.[45] Nine radical councils in London established ethnic minority units and, through them, conducted consultations, adopted equal opportunities statements and established permanent race relations units that would perform advisory, monitoring and consultation roles around race equality.[46]

It is important not to exaggerate the material significance of these political developments. The budgets of race relations (or later ethnic minority) units could be substantial but they were also short term and proved vulnerable to cuts to local government expenditure introduced in the 1980s. In terms of the everyday machinations of local politics, race relations units acted only in an advisory capacity and they had little formal or direct power to implement change. They continually had to battle with the elements of the national master narrative and, in particular, with the idea that the English were a tolerant people and that colour blindness offered the best route to national solidarity.

However, even if there were distinct local factors at work that resulted in different chronologies for implementation, and even if there were clear limits to the effectiveness of local authority race relations units, the development of municipal multiculturalism was important because the local machinery of government was beginning to consolidate a set of discrete ethnic identities. In naming ethnic minority communities, in collating data, in conducting consultations with them, by publishing documents on their profiles and funding identified needs, local government operations simultaneously encouraged particular kinds of identification. Becoming West Indian or what later became Afro-Caribbean, or Irish, became a publicly available identity. It was a way to be.[47]

Yet, becoming an ethnic minority did not attract universal assent. The widespread opposition to the creation of an ethnic origin question on the census was certainly stimulated by its potential as a tool for discrimination but also because it created a kind of second-class citizenship for people who were already British subjects. 'As British citizens and Nationals we do not consider that a question of ethnic origin is essential' wrote one Afro-Caribbean community group to the Home Affairs sub-committee, whilst another Asian group thought that ethnic questions only 'divide the community whereas we are trying to create a mixed society'.[48] These objections, and others that explicitly rejected ethnic data gathering as practised in the USA, continued to imagine a more inclusive notion of social justice that, whilst recognising the existence of deep-seated racism, was based on a notion of a common good and an insistence that black people be recognised not as special, different or second-class citizens but, as Clem Byfield of the Association of Jamaicans (UK) Trust put it, as 'part of humanity', and as part of the 'human race'.[49] Yet the considerable weight of state institutions was slowly moving towards the creation and measurement of officially recognised ethnic minority communities that were defined, in part, by their historical heritage.

The claim that ethnic minority communities were constituted by specific historical experiences, ones which were unrecognised and somehow formative, required both evidence and explanation. It was a task tacitly taken up by newly formed race relations units who began to commission, research and publish histories of, or 'guides' to, ethnic minority communities. In 1986, the two municipal multicultural authorities, in London and Birmingham, published similar histories. The Ethnic Minorities Unit of the GLC published *A History of the Black Presence in London* and Birmingham City Council Race Relations Unit published profiles of the Chinese and Vietnamese communities.[50] The former drew on a two-year programme of archival research, part of it funded by the GLC but part of which was conducted by volunteers. Their declaratory introduction captured something of the importance and optimism of the moment. Black history was, it argued, 'undoubtedly the most significant single area of historical research, not only because it discloses information about a new area of the black diaspora, but also because of its profound challenge to the popular misconception of Britain having been a racially homogeneous i.e. white society'. This popular misconception of white British homogeneity not only did theoretical violence to British history, it also resulted in actual violence visited upon black people in its name.

The racial hostility that is the everyday experience of black people, is in this regard informed by two major factors. Firstly, a general ignorance of the histories of black peoples, and in particular, of their long association with Britain; and secondly, widespread misinformation about black people which has tended to marginalise the black community and preclude any real understanding of what the black community actually represents in Britain. These two factors have encouraged the majority of people in Britain only ever to perceive black people as an 'immigrant' community. Attendant with the synonymity of 'blacks' with immigration has been that immigration, and therefore the immigrant, is a problem. Given the perceptions of post-war black immigration to Britain, black people are not only blamed for present economic ills, but are given no credit for – nor are believed to have made any positive, useful, or productive contributions to Britain whatsoever.[51]

This passage serves as a reliable summary of the purposes, aims and themes of the minority histories that started to be published under the auspices of local authority funding in the middle of the 1980s. In identifying widespread historical ignorance, and in seeing that ignorance as causal in the discrimination suffered by immigrants and their children, these were histories that made particular claims about the power of the past. When they appeared in text form they were deliberately written for a wide public audience, often specifically for schools, and were necessary, argued historian Sylvia Collicott, because of the need for 'new material to address the issue of omission in history' and because 'people need the power of self knowledge and past history'.[52] History was a key plank of the radical cultural policy, advocated by Parminder Vir and Alan Tomkins of the GLC, which would help people, retain 'some sense of self-identity because it would have at its core the celebration, production and preservation of working class, women's, black and youth histories'.[53] At their most instructive, as the previous chapter demonstrated, these histories told the stories, and explained the position, of people experiencing unemployment, poverty and discrimination. They had the potential to undermine the tendency in political discourse to condemn those detrimentally positioned by social change and, more specifically, those who were victims of racism. For the most part, their original aim had been to claim a common humanity and they could regularly be found in local educational and community projects, as well as in novel or interdisciplinary areas of university study.[54] The first International Conference on the History of Blacks in Britain, held at the University of London in 1981, demonstrated the range and rigour of this work.[55]

However, something subtly but significantly different was emerging from the histories sponsored by local authorities in the 1980s and 1990s. In imagining cities inhabited by a discrete number of ethnic communities, local authority race relations policy was in the process of ethnicising their localities. *A History of the Black Presence in London* implicitly contributed to this process by restricting its interest to people of African-Caribbean descent. The more expansive definition of 'black' that had attempted to unite peoples of Asian, West Indian and African origins in campaigns against racism was in the process of being marginalised. In its place came a more restricted version of black identity and one which was now supported by historical studies of a particular black experience that was increasingly presented as unique and as necessary to explain black identity or black needs in the present. These ideas were taken up by some black activists who identified alienation as the quintessential colonial condition and whose Afro-centrism, or their promotion of particular versions of Black Studies, was an act of resistance against it.[56]

Even in otherwise persuasive historical research, the framing of black community was, as Gundara and Duffield put it in an important early collection, around the idea that 'as soon as they were established in sufficient numbers, they developed their own social as opposed to purely individual and atomised responses to the pressures they faced in a generally hostile society'.[57] This was crucial because, with the demise of biological theories of race, it was these social responses to hostility that forged black community and this particular history that made contemporary (Afro-Caribbean) ethnic identities. This history (or experience and tradition) had much to deliver. Whilst demonstrating hostility towards black people was not difficult, identifying social responses that constituted an inclusive black identity and underpinned black community was more demanding. For contemporary ethnic identification to work, it was necessary for the historical record to demonstrate that the responses to racism that constituted black community were more important and more enduring than other potential sources of social unity. Ethnicity had now to be read back into history and it had to constitute a stable and significant site of difference.

One of the unintended consequences of writing ethnic histories was to situate those histories, and the people in them, outside of the nation.

An implicitly historicist philosophy, one that defined individuals and groups by historically located cultures, was championed. The idea that contemporary identities were made and fixed in the past, an idea entirely consistent with New Right philosophy, was not rejected or modified or overcome. It was moved. Most immigrants and their children, especially if they were black, now belonged primarily to ethnic groups who, in official publications, were routinely lauded for the positive, useful or productive contributions they made to British national life. The difficulty was not in the factual accuracy of this kind of claim; in the mundane routines of life, migrants and their descendants have certainly sometimes contributed to the public good. Instead, it was in the political imperative that immigrant agency, pursued for reasons of economic gain, personal pleasure, political advancement or the public good, must be interpreted as a contribution to national life. The implicit message was that some groups of immigrants, and certain numbers of those groups, should be tolerated and celebrated because of a contribution to national life made by their ancestors.

This was a conditional version of national inclusion. It presupposed that immigrants could be categorised into a number of discrete ethnic groups whose difference was constituted by a history that required recognition in the name of social justice. Retrospectively, it is perhaps easier to see that the efficacy of this form of pluralism depended on the shared understandings, and the historical imagination, of a generation of scholar activists. In their hands, these histories of minorities could emphasise historical agency and inform a political strategy for the present. Outside of their influence, and overtaken by wider economic, social and political changes, these histories could become an empty celebration of difference entirely consistent with the conditions of late capitalism. The discovery and celebration of ethnic roots could be a profoundly emotional experience and one through which individuals and groups could feel more validated and more secure, but, as scholar activists could attest, the assertion of difference could be historically inaccurate and it did not necessarily promote the social justice for which they struggled.

The 'indigenous culture' of the Irish

The publication of local authority-sponsored histories of minority communities signalled the arrival of what some scholars have called 'liberalism 2'. In piecemeal, uneven and contested fashion, the central and local state gradually committed itself to the protection of individual rights whilst also recognising specific community rights and identities. Those communities and identities were not, however, self-evident. In politics and popular culture, there was the tendency to interpret community identities as meaning simply black or white. Yet, and as was clear from the previous chapter, race relations legislation made ethnicity a condition open to all groups with a long shared history, distinct traditions and customs. The decision of the GLC to recognise the Irish as an ethnic minority who qualified for the relatively generous funding on offer for these marginalised groups was therefore highly significant in the ethnicisation of the past. The first local government Irish Liaison Office was appointed by the GLC in 1983 and a policy report on the Irish that followed, in 1984, highlighted widespread discrimination against the Irish in housing, employment, education and the media. Arguing that the Irish should be 'recognised unequivocally as an ethnic minority with a unique and identifiable cultural heritage', the key recommendations of the report demanded greater provisions for the preservation of Irish culture and identity in Britain.[58]

The Irish in Britain History Group (IBHG) was founded in London in 1980 with the aim of organising a conference on the history of the Irish in Britain. The conference that followed was held at North London Polytechnic on 25–26 April 1981, in the shadow of the hunger strikes undertaken by Republican prisoners in British jails. Attended by between three and four hundred people, and consisting of twenty-two papers, the conference explored the impact made by the Irish on the socio-economic and political life in Britain, the diversity of the immigration experience and the emergence of distinct Irish communities in the nineteenth and twentieth centuries. Among the delegates was historian and artist Bernard Canavan who reflected that even if it was often claimed that the Irish 'are the victims of too much history', the conference was actually an attempt to address the ignorance around Irish immigration and the nostalgic character and outlook of Irish organisations in Britain. 'Neither the occasional reference to the Irish Question nor the nostalgic feeling of their parents for the Ireland they remember, declared Canavan 'go very far in providing an understanding of Irish history or identity'.[59]

This marked a period of sustained historical activity by Irish migrants and their descendants in Britain. In London, the IBHG launched a project to record popular experiences of migration and community life with funding from the Greater London Council. Two full-time researchers were employed to develop this work by hosting monthly seminars, founding the Archive of the Irish in Britain and publishing an important bibliography that would facilitate further historical research.[60] History research groups were established with similar programmes in Manchester and Glasgow in the 1980s. This work was closely connected to the appearance of papers on the history of the Irish in History Workshops in 1984 (Leicester), 1985 and 1986 (both Leeds). Tellingly, the IBHG sustained its activity by defining its aims in a manner consistent with the developing politics of liberalism 2. It provided 'a resource of the Irish experience in Britain', highlighted the positive contribution made by the Irish in Britain, documented an 'area of popular history' and gave 'a voice to those people whose history would otherwise be lost and, in doing so, help to change the negative attitude which exists about the Irish in Britain'.[61]

The IBHG reflected not only a defensive response to discrimination but an increasingly articulate concern for the identity of the community. In the twice yearly journal, *Irish Studies in Britain*, also found in 1981 in an attempt to make the community more tangible, editor Ivan Gibbons argued that 'more and more Irish people living in this country are becoming aware of what is loosely called their heritage or their culture, that set of inherited experiences and traditions which somehow makes them feel slightly different from their English neighbours. Furthermore, many English (and Scottish and Welsh!) people have become aware of the different heritage and development of the neighbouring island and would like to know more about it.'[62] Demographic changes, and the decline of the Irish-born population in Britain, meant that these inherited traditions could no longer be assumed, but would have to be consciously fostered, promoted and taught. The Irish in Britain Representation Group (IBRG), was founded in late 1981, to address and tackle this situation and at the outset it appeared as a predominately a cultural and educational body. Writing in the *Irish Post* in December 1981 Michael Sheehan, the Acting Secretary of the IBRG, argued that, if Irish-born immigrants had not been successful in passing on their culture and values to their children, it was because of Britain's 'homogeneous culture' which allowed no pluralism, the 'long standing conflict between Britain and Ireland', and experiences of racism that had 'sapped the self-confidence' of the Irish and made them insecure and afraid to articulate their identity.[63] However, Sheehan argued, Britain was becoming a multiracial society and there was now both a need and an opportunity to transmit a sense of Irish identity to the British-born members of the Irish community.

The second national conference of the IBRG in 1983 affirmed its commitment to historical research and education by adopting a resolution that sought to 'encourage and foster a sense of identity and an understanding of Irish cultural inheritance among people of Irish origin and their descendants'.[64] In broadly defined cultural and educational activities the IBRG, and its Education Officer Naseen Danaher, sought to development supplementary education projects for Irish adults, young people and children, as well as the application of specifically Irish perspectives in the formal school curriculum. Danaher called on delegates to 'check the policy of their local authority, ask to see the school syllabus, and the books in the libraries. It was also possible to liaise with Roman Catholic schools and contact other Irish cultural organisations. Courses, for example, the Irish language and Irish history could be provided (through night classes if necessary).'[65]

The cultural and educational renaissance that can be detected in the foundation of the IBHG and IBRG rested on the promotion of shared historical memories. In specialist archives, in scattered local government files, newspaper reports and autobiographical accounts it is possible to trace the development of language classes, Saturday schools, history courses and research projects, reminiscence work and literacy, literacy and drama projects flourished.[66] A good deal of this activity centred on London and, because it was promoted and funded by the GLC, it was obliged to meet criteria that spoke to the strengthening of ethnic identity.

The Camden and Harrow branches of the IBRG were founded in 1982–1983. Funding applications to the GLC presented the groups as apolitical. References to some of the wider aims of the IBRG, campaigning against the Prevention of Terrorism Act and for republican prisoners in British gaols, were removed from funding applications and wider promotional literature. Instead, local branches of the IBRG promoted themselves as exclusively cultural and educational bodies that aimed to develop a 'a positive sense of Irish identity in the borough, a fair share of air time on local radio stations; Local Authority [classes] in Irish studies and the inclusion

of such studies in multi-racial school curricula'.[67] Access to Irish
culture, history and language would, it was claimed, combat the
negative effects of derogatory Irish stereotypes, promote a positive
sense of Irish identity and prevent the alienation of young people from
family and community that had recently prompted the involvement
of young Irish in fascist politics.[68] The GLC's race relations adviser
noted the cultural and educational programmes and approvingly
observed how language teaching, displays of Irish history and oral/
video reminiscence work was a method of 'strengthening the cultural
identity of the Irish community'. The IBRG was deserving of GLC
support because it helped in 'maintaining Irish cultural traditions'
and 'promoting experience of their [Irish] indigenous culture'.[69]

Experience was a key word here and it carried a heavy weight in the
intellectual and political debates of the period. New social movements
had been committed to recovering the silent voices of contemporary
societies and, in order to do so, were committed to identifying the
actions, thoughts, emotions and perceptions of the working class,
women, immigrants and a whole host of other minorities. These
political movements were stimulated by, and drew energy from, the
diverse intellectual currents summarised in the term post-structuralism.
Now most clearly associated with the work of French intellectuals
Michel Foucault and Jacques Derrida, post-structuralisms shared a
concern for deconstructing those intellectual traditions, and their
categories of thought, that served to classify, order, dominate and
discriminate. The European Enlightenment, far from launching a
new era of reason, science and political progress, was premised on the
intellectual and political domination of marginal peoples in European
nation states and in their empires. Postcolonial theorists, and a small
number of historians, demanded closer scrutiny of history and the
ways in which its assumptions and procedures, silenced the voices and
experiences of ordinary people.[70] National master narratives helped
to exclude and discriminate against women and children, the ill and
insane, real and imagined foreigners and homosexuals. Recovering
their voices and including their experiences in the project of the
nation was a key part of radical and social democratic politics.[71]

However, this project of recovery was understood to be particularly urgent for indigenous, enslaved and colonised peoples and
for their descendants touched by the long hand of colonialism and
imperialism. Quite what this recovery might entail was the subject
of prolonged and sometimes bitter debate. One strand of thinking

supported a broadly multicultural approach with an emphasis on strong ethnic identities, cultural transmission and the exchange of information. This was evident in some of the local IBRG activity and, to take another example, in the constitution of the London Irish Commission for Culture and Education (LICCE) founded in 1984, and which declared that 'any man content in the knowledge if his identity, history and heritage makes a far, far greater contribution ... to the benefit of the whole society. The Irish, for centuries, have been net contributors, cultural creditors, to the western European experience. We continue to have something special to offer this society given the opportunity and special facilities required to meet our special needs as an ethnic group.'[72] In contrast to this kind of ethnic boosterism, a more consciously anti-racist position stressed the value of historical study in terms of its ability to identify racism as a structural feature of capitalist and imperialist economies. This was basically a Marxist or neo-Marxist argument, heavily inflected by a particular reading of history that sought to develop links between 'colonial minorities'.[73]

The opinions and operations of local authority race relations advisers may not have featured prominently in these debates around historical recovery. Nonetheless, when such advisers began to recommend 'the maintenance of Irish cultural traditions' and promoted 'the indigenous cultures' of immigrant groups, they began to make powerful statements about the importance of history to contemporary well-being.[74] Such statements, as illustrated above, tended to be brief and to consist of assertion rather than detailed explanation, but they also assumed the positions that were becoming increasingly influential in social psychology.[75] More specifically, and as the increasingly influential work of Henri Tajfel put it, 'minorities were established partly through their association with negative stereotypes'.[76]

Negative stereotypes of the Irish may have induced some individuals to try to assimilate (or pass to a dominant group) but others who actively rejected anti-Irish hostility instead sought to establish a new and positive social identity. As Philip Ullah wrote in an early and influential study of second generation Irish youth in Britain, heavily influenced by Tajfel, those who had identified themselves as Irish 'had managed to reject the negative stereotyped images of the Irish and derive a sense of pride in their ethnic origins'. This pride was 'closely linked' to the social and cultural activities generated in the Irish community, it provided a 'cognitive alternative' to negative stereotypes and it helped second generation Irish youth to develop 'a sense of identity which was powerfully attached to their Irish origins'. In the stress on social organisation of Irish language, history and dancing classes, as well as more informal methods of imagining oneself as distinctively Irish, Ullah's study indicates something of the social character of historical knowledge. Young people actively drew on the historical images, ideas and associations available to them in community organisations. This sense of heritage, Ullah's 'cognitive alternatives', were the fruits of social organisation.

However, in a slippage typical of the ways in which identity studies were popularised and applied, Ullah also went on to observe that this powerful attachment to origins resembled in many respects the notion of paternity, or the 'recognition of putative "biological origins"' advanced by the US sociolinguist Stanley Fishman.[77] Fishman had identified this notion of paternity as something primordial and biological; 'an essence or experience passed on from generation to generation in a bio-kinship sense'.[78] The two senses of difference at work here, one a defensive response to discrimination based on an active historical imagination developed partly in conjunction with social organisations, the other concerned with a descent-related and biological experience, are a typical example of the confused constitution and distribution of ethnicity in the emerging conditions of liberalism 2. Ethnicity was represented both as a choice, as the conditioned and defensive reaction to widespread experiences of discrimination, and a requirement of particular biological essences or experiences based on common origins.

In politics and policymaking, in popular discussion and in the work of race relations advisers, the crucial distinctions between these quite different concepts were lost. This is easily understood since, in everyday conduct, the status and utility of social concepts is not a priority. Yet, for understanding the ways in which history as social process operates, and the legacies it creates, the distinction between instrumental and primordial notions of identity is extremely significant. Without this distinction, what existed were races as independent and ahistorical essences or experiences. As such, they did not require the reflections and activities of historical subjects with significant consequences for understandings of both past and present.

Identifying those consequences presents some challenges. Debates and discussions around ethnic identity proliferated quickly so that it became a routine feature of national and local politics, of educational debate and mass media reporting. At once presupposing and reinforcing the idea that the world was organised into discrete ethnic groups, the historical claims supporting Irish ethnicity, or indeed any ethnicity, were rarely explicated outside a specialised press or activist circles. When they were, complained historian David Fitzpatrick in 1992, it was clear that selective evidence pertaining to the social, geographical and residential marginality of the Irish in Britain was transformed by deploying a 'hazy and dubious concept of community' that itself was bolstered by a recent tendency 'to depict the Irish as belonging to the community of the oppressed'. 'The Irish community in Britain is a metaphor with a primarily political function' declared Fitzpatrick and although he may have underestimated the imaginative properties of communities, he had accurately identified political influences on the writing of history.[79]

Despite both evidential and interpretative weaknesses in arguing for distinctive experiences of a bounded Irish community in Britain, it was widely assumed that ethnic minorities were, in effect, different races, existing outside the national community, whose distinct needs as an indigenous people were the symbols and practices of cultural nationalism; Irish dancing, Gaelic sports, language learning and a broad outline of Irish history in which the disastrous consequences of British imperialism featured prominently. Engaging in indigenous cultural practices boosted self-esteem, promoted familial and community bonds and enabled the realisation of an authentic and ethnically located, inner self.

After attending an in-service training course on 'education for multicultural society', schoolteacher Joan Inglis embarked on a close reading of Irish history. Images and stereotypes from the past acted, she reflected, as a 'perceptual prison' which could only be broken for children by 'returning to their roots and perceiving the truth of their situation'.[80] Those roots were in Ireland and the truth of their situation lay, in a distinctly psychoanalytical reading of the past, in accessing forgotten or repressed historical memories. For the Irish Studies academic Liam Greenslade, bringing those memories to consciousness and understanding the historical relationship between England and Ireland, 'enables me to realign my sense of myself in the present with my experiences in the past. It ennobles, in an odd sense, my self-perceived status as the victim of forces based on a cultural and economic system beyond my control.' This was akin to a moment of catharsis, to an imaginative identification with a past that, once owned and understood, was emotionally satisfying. Imagining a return to this past was ennobling and enlightening because it affirmed but also explained the subjective condition of being Irish in Britain. This was a profoundly historical mode of understanding. Although it clearly could be emotionally satisfying, its primary objective was not affirmation. It did not simply seek from the past consolation even if it helped individuals to name and understand powerful feelings and emotions; 'the purpose was the recapturing of historical circumstances in order to create a future'.[81]

The sentiment expressed here, 'reclaiming the past to create the future', could sometimes degenerate into political sloganeering but it actually expressed a specific, elaborate and convincing understanding of historical processes. This understanding was broadly materialist, at once historical and sociological and, in its anti-colonial idioms, heavily influenced by the work of Frantz Fanon. It insisted on understanding social change as the result of the interaction between historical structures and conditioned agents. Its vision was of people as fully historical subjects, simultaneously placing themselves in a socio-historical process but also engaging in constructions about that process.[82]

Perhaps only in retrospect is it possible to see how the construction and distribution of a dynamic historical theory was a crucial resource for second generation immigrant groups. Its influence was also diffuse. It had been discussed and debated, nurtured and distributed in new social movements, in radical educational spaces and in the 'undisciplined' university social sciences where immigrants and their descendants were disproportionately to be found.[83] It was present in religious projects inspired by liberation theology whose praxis saw religious truths as emerging from concrete historical situations and redemption as possible only with the recognition and redress of historical injustices. The New Left's 'history from below' was based on the central premise that the people had been written out of history. With it, scholar activists could resist the temptation of sliding into racialised cultures or experiences that could celebrate the nativisms that were actually the consequences of imperialism. To do so, argued the hugely influential Edward Said, was 'to leave the historical world for the metaphysics of essences like negritude, Irishness, Island or Catholicism is to abandon history for essentialisations that have the power to turn human beings against each other'.[84]

Those that situated themselves in the particular historical process of British imperialism campaigned to extend their understanding and to develop the politics that emerged out of it. Education was a primary target. The IBRG sought to develop a shared consciousness amongst minority groups that would reject the version of multiculturalism that was emerging in local authorities. Exchanging information about food, dress and culture did nothing to identify the shared antecedents of Irish and black groups in British imperialism and nothing to challenge the racist practices that constituted a form of internal colonialism. This could only be achieved by promoting anti-racist strategies that explained contemporary patterns in housing, education and mental health as the result of historical structuring. Campaigns and projects designed to change this followed. In the educational field, this amounted to demands for inclusion of an Irish dimension in formal education and a greater presence for Irish Studies in the informal and tertiary education sectors.[85] Mirroring the demands and activities of Black Studies campaigns of the 1970s, the Irish Dimensions in British Education conferences brought together delegates determined to produce and apply curriculum material that would 'counteract stereotyping, give Irish pupils a sense of identity, to keep them aware of cultural roots, to give them materials to which they could relate'.[86]

In their campaigning activities the IBRG sought to promote knowledge and understanding of the historical circumstances that could explain anti-Irish discrimination in Britain. This discrimi-nation took many different forms but it was increasingly evident as a result of the conflict in Northern Ireland and its impact was beginning to be measured in studies of psychological and psychiatric health and of housing, employment and education.[87] Such data were often explained in individualistic terms, as a matter of individual choice and responsibility or by reference to ethnic or cultural behaviour (to drinking, Celtic temperament, unhealthy diet and lifestyle).

This was why historical research and education was so highly valued by scholar activists. Eschewing both individualistic and ethnic explanations, the IBRG saw history as important precisely because it revealed the structural conditions that constituted contemporary Irish difference and explained the position and experiences of the Irish in the present. It was an example of what sociologist Patrick Baert has called 'collective second order reflection'; the process through which previously tacit presuppositions, in this case about the Irish and their behaviour, were made explicit and challenged through the reconstruction of the past.[88] This was a collective process. Enabled by the slow emergence of liberalism 2, the Irish constituted themselves as an ethnic minority and began to publicly discuss and debate the legacies of the past. Those legacies were not stable and there remained significant disputes around the aims and purposes of promoting Irish culture and learning Irish history. But IBRG activists were not necessarily seeking identities, affirmation or consolation in history, even if there was a kind of psychological security to be found in it. They did not only seek their 'indigenous culture' but a society free from discrimination that required, in turn, a coming to terms with a colonial past.

Yet, in the insistence that Ireland's modern history, and *their* history, was to be understood primarily as a story of the damages inflicted by British colonialism, some IBRG activists, and others in the wider community, began to claim ownership of a past that belonged to them and, without which, they were alienated and incomplete. Although this was not a consensus position, it was increasingly articulated in social science research on the Irish in England and it was expressed by Liam Greenslade in the 'long-range strategy of re-connecting us as communities to our historical experience, to give us back not merely our voice but our memory of who we are and what we might become'.[89] The problem was that 'communities', 'experiences' and 'memories' began to be understood as properties of distinct ethnic groups and their importance was considered psychological and therapeutic. The slide into competing claims around the ownership and authenticity of ethnic histories had begun and, as they did so, discussions around the structural legacies of British colonialism for contemporary society and life chances began to wane.

An authentic black history

Colonialism, or the political rule and direct control of subjugated states and areas, had been marginalised in the post-war and domesticated renditions of national history. It was the achievement of minority memory makers to bring it back, to extend further its application and to bring into the public arena a history of empire from the point of view of the dominated. However, what constituted that point of view, whether it was singular or multiple and how it was to be consolidated, remembered and distributed, remained controversial matters.

In October 1981 the Training Working Party of the Black Parents' Movement (BPM) finalised a series of recommendations around the education and training opportunities for workers in supplementary schools. These opportunities were at once practical, political and philosophical. School workers, the Training Working Party recommended, should develop skills in fundraising, report writing and bookkeeping. Liaison and mediatory skills were also required in order to deal with local educational authorities and conflicts between children and their parents and between families and mainstream schools. Yet the Training Working Party also made clear that it saw the development of individual skills as meaningful only in the context of the wider aims and objectives of the BPM. Supplementary school workers, it argued, should be politicised so that they could more effectively develop black consciousness through their knowledge and understanding of black history and culture. This was underlined when a specific training objective was to develop a 'black historical perspective of our struggle' through the provision of 'black social and economic history, early black civilisation, the history of supplementary schools themselves and broader perspectives as they relate to the total black struggle (e.g. youth resistance, police–black relations)'.[90]

In the context of urban rioting (or uprisings) of the 1980s, black history also witnessed a renaissance that challenged the silences in the national master narrative. In Liverpool Ian Law and June Henfrey, both officers with the Merseyside Community Relations Council, produced the pamphlet *A History of Race and Racism in Liverpool 1660–1950*. An unflinching exposure of local racism, the research for the pamphlet had been designed and conducted as part of Law's Ph.D. research into racism in local housing policy and provision. Employing a historical materialist methodology, and specifically inspired by E.P. Thompson and other Marxist historians, Law utilised a wide range of primary sources to produce a convincing account of racialisation in Liverpool. The pamphlet was written in a deliberately accessible style, aimed at a local audience in schools and community education venues, and in keeping with a philosophy of 'research activism', aimed, in the words of Ian Law, to 'identify and articulate a sense of history, a sense of the historical, established, long standing hatred of the black community' and to challenge it.[91] Similar research and publication projects were undertaken in towns and cities of black settlement around England, including Bradford, Bristol, Nottingham and Wellingborough.[92] In addition, campaigns for multicultural or anti-racist approaches to education were successful in winning funding for projects that investigated and promoted the teaching of black history. In Birmingham, for example, the Afro-Caribbean Teaching Unit produced a series of black history posters and, perhaps more significantly, developed a school examination course (or O-level) in West African and Caribbean history for 14–16-year-olds.[93] Yet the aims and purposes of black history, like the wider black struggle, were always open to contest. Those radical groups closest to the political left in Europe continued to insist that blackness was a site of struggle against racism. African, Caribbean and Asian immigrants and their children were united in an anti-racist struggle and, indeed, there were joint protests, marches and meetings with Irish campaigners.[94]

However, this form of historical research and education was, as in the case of the Irish, challenged by more experiential, cultural and primordial forms of understanding. Even the attempt by the BPM to politicise supplementary school workers can be seen as a strategy designed to promote common histories that would consolidate radical political struggles in the present. The increasing tendency was for black to equate with ethnicity and, for the historical experiences that constituted ethnic minorities, to slowly become more specific. The foundation, in 1981, of the African People's Historical Monument Foundation (APHMF), organised and chaired by Len Garrison, provides one important example of this process in action. Dedicated to the 'collection, documentation and dissemination of the culture and history of African people in the diaspora' and a related, cultural, social and educational programme, the aim was to develop the kind of historical infrastructure that enabled the study of black history in Britain.[95] Garrison argued that this historical knowledge was beneficial for all young people, black and white, who were denied access to black people's history by the forces of racism and who were, as a result, susceptible to prejudice and intolerance. The APHMF did not aim just to produce publications or teaching materials aimed at black children but was an attempt to reshape the infrastructure of historical study. Establishing a physical building with archives and reading rooms, collections and cataloguing policies and a programme of public education, the APHMF set an ambitious and radical agenda dedicated to the reformation of social memory. For historical knowledge was a requisite of historical understanding and a more accurate and complete version of the national past. It was axiomatic that this history would be consistent with, and supportive of, social justice in the present.

It was not necessarily contradictory to argue, at the same time, that black history was required as a remedy to the identity crises facing young black people. Yet Garrison's own historical writings on pan-Africanism and Rastafarianism, and his associated promotion of black history, were increasingly framed around ethnicity and culture as antidotes to alienation. In 1981 Garrison's met with the famous African-American activist Audley Moore and he recalled being impressed with her vision of race relations and the existence of the Schomburg Center for Research in Black Culture in New York. The Schomburg Center promoted research and scholarship in African-American culture and Garrison was attracted to the idea of establishing a similar facility in Britain. 'Black people', he argued, 'had spent so much time distancing and denying our own history than we don't even know what belongs to us'.[96] The 'we' invoked in this ownership of the past was, however, not always clear and it prompted a further engagement with the politics of historical experience.

Experience was a central and deeply contested term. It simultaneously reached inwards, towards a unique psychological domain of feelings and emotions that were constitutive of persons but also outwards, towards events and processes seemingly more material and more tangible. The category of experience, memorably employed by the English historian E.P. Thompson, was used to transcend the divide between subjective and objective processes. It was at once empirical, used to investigate forgotten or silenced historical events, but also analytical, employed to advance claims about the impact of historical processes on the feelings and emotions, and, ultimately, the life chances of first and second generation immigrants in England. Experience was, in short, a tool for locating people in historical processes and for reflecting on and reworking the meaning of past events.[97]

Implicit in arguments that centred on the category of experience was that there were more or less authentic ways of remembering the past. Scholar activists had consistently argued that the national master narrative, race relations analyses and the identity studies paradigm had objectified black culture and ethnicity. Post-war social science contributed to the processes through which black people were identified as an alien body and, unwittingly, part of the problem that it sought to resolve. Active management and intervention, whether through multiracial friendship groups, race training or multicultural school curricula, was partly designed to avoid what were understood as 'race problems', but also to correct the deleterious positions assigned to black people in society.

History was an important resource in the response to this position. It offered the potential for black people to understand themselves and their position in England anew, outside of the ideas and ideologies that positioned them as alien and which damaged them materially. But this was only a potential. Its fulfilment depended on people not only reflecting on the stories circulating around them, and the emotions they helped to induce in them, but in articulating and organising responses to these feelings and emotions. Whether agents articulated and organised, and how they did so, partly depended on their location in historical time and space.

By the middle of the 1980s, and accompanied by the emergence of a more cultural politics, generational changes in immigrant communities and the context of a developing municipal multiculturalism, there developed a powerful argument that black people knew, felt and understood black history better than anyone else. Intuitively this was a history that black people felt they owned because, judging by the tone of responses to it, it induced powerful and visceral emotions that touched something within individuals. Reading Peter Fryer's *Staying Power*, a groundbreaking history of the black presence in Britain, was for John Siblon a 'revelation'. Linton Kwesi Johnson, responding enthusiastically to the television version of *Roots* ('perhaps one of the most creative and important imaginative historical documents of the twentieth century') identified a new sense of identity and belonging, a new feeling of racial pride and a basis for answering of the question: how can I as a black person place myself in the modern world, in the twentieth century?[98] Identifying, discovering and studying historical narratives could be important resources in the fashioning of personal identities and in the struggle for forms of social belonging that were not restricted by racism. Black history was deeply felt, necessary and potentially transformative precisely because it provided the materials from which black people could respond to racism, to transform themselves and their place in society.

Yet, the relationship between owning a past and developing a black identity was far from simple. For what constituted black history, how it should be researched and taught and how it connected with wider historical narratives were all matters that stimulated sustained and rancorous debate throughout this period. In November 1979, for example, the innovative Manchester Studies Unit of Manchester Polytechnic hosted the annual conference of the Oral History Society whose foundation and growth was itself testimony to the attempts, inspired by the History Workshop Movement, to democratise the practice of historical research. The conference focused on researching and teaching black history and was connected to an innovative project, funded by the Manpower Services Commission, which collected oral history interviews and photographs from Manchester's black community. Nonetheless, in some lively conference debates that mirrored conversations that would occur around similar history projects, some black scholar activists challenged the democratic goals and assumed outcomes of black history.[99] A report in the *Guardian* newspaper quoted the feminist author and activist Amrit Wilson as arguing:

> Because you are white you can never understand the black experience. All you can do is study us from a distance. But this turns us into objects and our culture, through your work, into a commodity, taken away from us for use by the state.[100]

There was nothing new in attempts to 'own' history. 'History', as Carolyn Steedman and a number of other post-colonial authors have argued, 'is always somebody's story'.[101] Those identified as proprietors of the past included (as we have seen) the nation, the capitalist elite, the people, Europe and the West. Black people generally, and Len Garrison's APHMF more specifically, thus joined a long list of potential owners of a past whose respective ownership rights were increasingly contested in the public sphere. Accusations of partisanship and fanaticism that continued to accompany demands for black history or Black Studies, and which were contrasted with the objective reason of the facts of the past can therefore be easily dismissed. The writing of history is always political and the 'active construction of conceptions of the past' are, as Bill Schwarz has argued, 'a continual and defining moment in political practice'.[102] In insisting on the contemporary legacies of past history, scholar activists like Garrison and Wilson were helping to open up the past, to move it into the present and to make visible the centrality of empire, and its ideologies of race, to contemporary national life.

Nonetheless, debates about the ownership of black history could, as the Manchester Oral History conference clearly demonstrated, easily slide into antagonistic and ultimately futile debates on the authenticity and ownership of black history. The scholar activists who campaigned against racism in the 1970s had widely regarded blackness as a political colour which sought to unite Asian, African and Caribbean peoples in their struggles against racism. Blackness, in this sense, was a deliberate mechanism for overcoming the geographical and cultural differences between these communities which, as the historian and activist Stella Dadzie would later recall, was made easier by a historical imagination in which slavery and the Middle Passage provided a point of origin and belonging. It was the study and remembrance of slavery that provided 'a connectedness with global politics that was rooted in what has happening to us'.[103] This was a global, inclusive and utopian vision of global justice. It sought to connect global decolonisation struggles in Asia, Africa, the Caribbean and Latin America with local, class-based and anti-racist politics in England. It was, above all, a moment of possibilities. Infused by the spirit of 1968 and an internationalist ethos, activists in the 1970s looked from the past to the future. History was the basis of their utopian dreams.[104]

However, the debate at Manchester Polytechnic in 1979 signalled how these dreams could be constrained by race ideas. The assertion that there was a black historical experience that was unintelligible to white people implicitly depended on race ideas. In these formulations black was no longer a political colour designed to encourage social solidarity but an inherent property of those included in particular definitions of ethnic groups. The developing practices of municipal multiculturalism, based on the social psychological study of identity, saw the value of history as primarily therapeutic and as a response to the damaged self-esteem of black children. In this view, it was entirely appropriate for black history to be considered a property of black people for their study, reclamation and celebration. This was because black history was primarily considered in terms of emulating role models and exhorting the achievements of black people. It was an agenda designed to boost academic attainment and one that tended to align itself with cultural nationalism and the separatist traditions significant in US politics. Focused on the promotion and celebration of black heritage, history could become part of a promotion of difference and presented as a panacea to long-standing criticisms of West Indian families and the wider black community. Explaining the philosophy of one supplementary school a former teacher explained

We tried to give the West Indian child a flavour of their background, where their parents came from and why they came here. Because I think, and I feel that I am right, that their parents were afraid to tell their children about their background and why they came here and that sort of thing. And I suppose it was better coming from members of the community, which gave the parents then courage to talk about it themselves.[105]

Silences around familial histories were not uncommon in migrant families. Fear may explain these silences but it was a fear often driven by a sense that familial histories in countries of origin, the habits and customs they recalled and the guides to action they invoked, were somehow irrelevant in Britain. The resulting silences were (and are) treated as a problem in the psychologised literature of culture shock. Not being socialised into familial and community history was, as for the Irish, identified as a reason for intergenerational tensions in immigrant communities, for low self-esteem in children and an explanation of the incomplete socialisation of immigrant children.[106] A specific version of black history was increasingly imagined and presented as a key educational and therapeutic tool that would correct the failure of black parents to socialise their children adequately into their cultural past.

As all of this suggests, by the 1980s black history was no longer routinely presented as a resource for understanding racism or as appropriate for study by all children. Instead, and in a manner which unwittingly reproduced those exclusions that scholar activists had been seeking to challenge, black history was often presented and understood as the exclusive property of black people. The past may have been reclaimed but a principle of ownership was reasserted. Yet, the binary divide between white and black histories not only belied the complexities of the past, it also constrained the potential for understanding contemporary society. Writing six years after the riots of 1981 and in the aftermath of more rioting at Broadwater Farm in London, community activist Stafford Scott hinted at these limitations when he observed an increased public willingness to 'extol our idols and heroes, especially after their deaths – men such as Marley and Martin Luther King Jnr., and to some extent Malcolm X yet you don't heed their words or messages' and the myth continued that 'black advancement had to be at the detriment to white people'.[107] British colonialism had gone and Scott pointedly reminded readers that there was nothing to fear from the fact that black people simply wanted to live their lives as equal human beings. But a language of equality and inclusivity was compromised against a concern for difference and in the conviction that there were separate black and white histories that should be recognised, respected and celebrated in pursuit of individual and ethnic well-being.[108]

The first Black History Month (BHM), held in October 1987, offers further evidence of the manner in which historical memory was affected by the development of multiculturalism. BHM sought to 'promote knowledge of Black History and experience, disseminate information on positive Black contributions to British society and heighten the confidence and awareness of Black people in their cultural history'.[109] Initiated by the London Strategic Policy Unit, and the idea of Akyaaba Addai-Sebo, Black History Month was inspired by activities in the USA and designed specifically to address and reverse examples of self-hate in young black children.[110] Yet the aims of BHM continued to imagine black history and experience as situated outside the national past and, in the stress on their contributions to national life, sought not only psychological recompense for racism but also an image of a model minority who deserved tolerance. Race ideas, rather than racism, became the focus of much of its historical education and there developed a powerful strand of argument that BHM was an African heritage event only.[111] A Heroes Day held at Langham School that celebrated black historical figures defined as a 'strictly an Afrikan families occasion'; the continuing conflicts between African and Caribbean communities and the difficulties of mixed race activists to identify with, and be accepted by, increasingly specific campaigning groups speak to this fracturing of the inclusive historical imagination.[112] As municipal multiculturalism continued to employ a race relations language of indigenous cultures, there was a tendency for cultural and educational projects became smaller and dedicated to restricted linguistic, national or ethnic groups.[113] As they did so, recalled historian and educationalist Beverley Bryant, the unifying focus on British colonialism broke down and, under the funding instructions of local race relations units, was 'decomposed' into the claims of different ethnicities who began to articulate their specific needs.[114] Retrospectively at least, there is no shortage of activists and commentators who appear to agree with Pratibha Parmar's judgement that the shift to ethnic forms of belonging and to 'authentic subjective experience' became 'destructive, divisive and immobilising'.[115] And even as they seized on the language of ethnicity, and saw its propositions and data proliferate, many scholar activists warned about the constraints it would place on how individuals and groups thought about their pasts, present and future.[116]

History and ethnic absolutism

Historical knowledge is contingent. It is produced in concrete time and space and so inevitably has connections with the wider world in which it is produced. As historian Mary Fulbrook puts it 'the discipline of history is in considerable measure shaped by the circumstances in which historical knowledge is produced and received'.[117] If this is the case for academic history, it is doubly so for the 'public history that is concerned with the popular presentation of the past to a range of audiences'.[118] Public history is, as the geographer Brian Graham has influentially argued, 'a knowledge, a cultural product and a political resource [that] possesses a crucial socio-political function'.[119] That crucial function is to provide one key source of identification in contemporary societies. Through its narration of the past, in its identification of historical actors and processes, public history is an essential element in the construction of those ideas, images and chronologies in which people situate themselves and their social identities. In monumental architecture, commemorative presentations, theatrical performance, history curricula, archival routines and a myriad range of cultural and educational practices, public history provides a framework within or against which individuals and groups remember. In the selection of historical periods and events for commemoration, in the provision of the themes, images and languages of historical recollection, public history provides the raw materials for processes of identification.[120]

Municipal multiculturalism, contested and piecemeal though it might have been, slowly began to commission, publish and promote what were, by the middle of the 1980s, coming to be recognised as 'ethnic minority histories'. The community profiles, published by ethnic minorities units, fleshed out historical narratives of the arrival and settlement of different ethnic groups. Oral history projects in areas of migrant settlement recorded the testimonies of individuals who belonged to selected immigrant groups, most typically Irish, Afro-Caribbean and Asian but also Vietnamese, Chinese and Polish.[121] Black and multicultural history curricula were developed by local education authorities and the support units established in response to the criticisms of teacher racism and the exclusive and nationalist curriculum contained in the Rampton Report.[122] Much of the work in formal educational spaces was funded through section 11 of the Local Government Act (1966) which awarded additional funding to local authorities with 'substantial numbers from the Commonwealth whose language and customs differ from those of the community'. Some of it was supported by the Commission for Racial Equality, by the Home Office (Urban Aid Programme) and others by the Manpower Services Commission's Community Programme. Such activity remained piecemeal, was often time-limited and existed in an environment in which it was opposed by successive Conservative governments and was routinely ridiculed in the media.[123] Notwithstanding these far from propitious circumstances, the scholar activists who protested, organised and campaigned and who were important influences on the emergence of municipal multiculturalism edged the national imaginary towards a version of pluralism in which ethnicity became a key source of difference. This pluralism would eventually come to be captured in the phrase 'community of communities' and in the idea that the nation, like its towns and cities, consisted of a number of communities that may overlap and be interdependent, but were also distinctive because of their race, ethnicity, culture and history.

The public histories that were a component part of municipal multiculturalism thus had specific purposes. Although immigrant histories were complicated, and although immigrant experiences were widely diverse according to class and gender, political imperatives packaged them together and promoted ethnicity, and ethnic minority history, as the defining feature of the lives of immigrants and their children. Ethnicity became a privileged point of departure in explaining social change. In London and in Birmingham and, eventually in Liverpool too, local histories became organised around themes of cultural change and ethnic diversity. First emerging in oral history testimony, in pamphlet form and in school curricula, this sense of historical change began to shape the language and practices, not just of local politics but also of educational practices.

In these popular histories, ethnic communities arrived fully formed, brought strange customs and practices with them but quickly settled down, fitted in and strived to contribute to the local economy and society. What Malcolm Dick argued for Birmingham, that 'without migration, Birmingham would not have emerged as a significant industrial and cultural centre, secured a range of retail and leisure opportunities or staffed its health and welfare services', would also be argued for other cities with significant post-war immigration.[124] All this was undoubtedly accurate. It was also a defensive reaction to a conservative rendering of the national past and to the insistent but ahistorical claims that associated immigration with unemployment and excessive welfare expenditure. Yet historical narratives organised around 'ethnic contributions to national life' unintentionally confirmed both that ethnicity was a source of enduring difference and that acceptance of ethnic communities in the national community was conditional. It left untouched a national imaginary in which the English were quintessentially moderate and decent and tolerant towards immigrants and refugees. As a result, histories of ethnic communities had the effect of focusing on discrete ethnic communities and their behaviour. Some of the more critical perspectives that had identified and challenged domestic racism began to disappear.

The commissioning and publication of ethnic histories were championed by scholar activists who in Birmingham and London became important influences on the formulation of municipal multiculturalism.[125] Some reached positions of influence as Members of Parliament, councillors, race relations advisors, educationalists, journalists and commentators.[126] This was important because these scholar activists carried in their personal biographies and in their heads an acute understanding of struggles for social justice. This was a distinctive generation of scholars, campaigners and activists, all of whom had been influenced by their own familial migrant histories, by the emergence of the New Left and by global processes of decolonisation. Even though they did not share a single ideology, even though their work was diverse, and even if their impact was conditioned by local circumstances, they sought to construct, promote and apply the historical perspectives they had learned in spaces of informal education.

Some of these scholar activists saw the championing of ethnicity, and their demand for state recognition and respect of ethnicities, as a temporary tactical measure. It was, in Stella Dadzie's words, a 'necessary phase of struggle' towards social justice for all.[127] A full humanity, not ethnicity, was their demand. The recognition of ethnicities was part of a wider attempt to secure a more equal society because it promoted discussion and understanding of the histories that explained migration to Britain and the life chances that immigrants and their children were allotted. These scholar activists took it for granted that contemporary attitudes and practices were conditioned by the past and that any strategy for social change had to identify and challenge historical injustices. Writing the histories of ethnic communities was part of this strategy but it was a strategy of transformation. The recurrent warnings issued by scholar activists against forms of ethnic essentialism, and against the tendency to read historical processes through simple stories of ethnic difference, confirm that ethnic history writing was originally configured as a continuation of the kinds of consciousness raising that had been such a feature of the 1970s.[128] It was against ethnic essentialism that some of the campaigns against ethnic data gathering, including the census, were organised.

It was also an argument against ethnic absolutism that Paul Gilroy had in mind when he spoke against proposals for a continuous national narrative proposed as the centralized national history curriculum that was introduced in schools under the terms of the 1988 Education Reform Act. The necessity for a national curriculum stimulated a sustained debate on the purposes and pedagogies of teaching history that divided along political lines. The political left may have welcomed proposals to make history a compulsory subject but generally remained suspicious of national history teaching, opposed to its use as a form of socialisation into a national heritage, and argued for an internationalist and skills-based approach to learning. For the political right, it was the increasing ethnic and religious diversity of Britain that justified and explained the need for a fact-driven national narrative that might encourage identification with the nation.[129] Gilroy's intervention was important because he rejected these terms of debate. He was neither for nor against national history and objected to the dualistic thinking that located people in a series of divided camps; as blacks and against whites or as victims against perpetrators. Instead, his concern was with ethnic absolutism and the 'reductive, essentialist understanding of ethnic and national difference which operates through an absolute sense of culture so powerful that it is capable of separating people off from each other and diverting them into social and historical locations that are understood to be mutually impermeable and incommensurable'. Adding to national history, by promoting histories of Empire to a pre-existing syllabus or 'tacking on the supposedly discrete and distinct histories of minority groups whose silenced and invisible presences can be shown to be dictating the hidden pattern of British national identity in the modern world' did little or nothing to challenge the assumptions or the circulation of ethnic absolutism.[130]

In fact, the idea that society consisted of discrete ethnic or cultural groups, with their own particular histories and experiences, prospered in cultural and educational policy generally, and in the production of public history, specifically, from the middle of the 1980s. An important reason for this was that the idea of bounded ethnic or cultural communities proved attractive to policymakers and civil servants who were grappling with the dilemmas imposed not only by the long transition to post-Fordist societies but also with an increasingly powerful neo-liberalism that monopolised a language of freedom and choice. The retrenchment of government, and the shedding of jobs in state-managed industries and public administration, was presented as necessary on both economic and ideological grounds. It was not only the alleged inefficiencies of state bureaucracies that justified programmes of closure and privatization but also their supposed inability to meet the needs and aspirations of a public living through a period of rapid social change. Centrally planned services provided through local authorities, or institutions like trade unions that embodied collectivist values and knowledge, were accused of denying opportunity and choice. The resulting attempt to 'hollow out the state', to reconfigure state activities from government towards governance, and to make 'investing, enabling and empowering' individuals and communities deliver better outcomes for social policy necessarily required a shift in the political imaginary.[131] A key part of this shift was the decline in thinking about the needs of economically defined classes towards addressing the concerns of particularised groups. Such groups were most often defined in terms of their culture and ethnicity and were encouraged to resist cultural domination, to defend their identity and to win recognition of their particular needs.[132]

The recognition and response to particularised ethnic needs was slowly becoming a defining feature of the multi-ethnic state. It can sometimes be difficult to identify the tangible consequences of this development for the ways in which people imagined themselves and others in relationship to the past. However, where policy declarations are explained in detail, as with the City of Birmingham District Council's *Equal Opportunities Policy Part One: Education for a Multicultural Society* (n.d) it is possible to begin to identify some of the consequences of the official adoption of what had previously been outsider histories. This is because, unusually, the policy document moves beyond a statement of general aims to a detailed rationale and to suggestions for action that ran to some thirty three pages in all. In those pages, whilst an attempt was made to identify and rectify the causes of social injustice for particular groups in Birmingham, it rendered history ineffective as an explanation of those injustices.

The second aim of Birmingham District Council's Equal Opportunities policy required all schools and colleges to 'be aware of and to provide for the particular needs of pupils having regard for their "racial" ethnic, cultural, historical, linguistic and religious backgrounds'. Somewhat confusingly, the accompanying rationale for this aim immediately recognised 'all children have backgrounds from which they arrive at school daily', that these backgrounds 'can be analysed under such headings as culture, history or language' and that the aim did not intend 'to suggest that only children from minority ethnic groups have needs or that they alone are specially in need of consideration; rather that if children of whatever origin to obtain the greatest benefit from their education, teaching must start from where they are'. This can be taken as an axiomatic principle of educational teaching practice. In so far as it related to previous learning experiences, to the accurate and sensitive judgement of the cognitive or linguistic capacities of individual pupils, it is unexceptional.

Yet, notwithstanding statements that seemed to indicate young people from immigrant backgrounds were no different to other young people, the policy advice issued to those in Birmingham's educational institutions was to 'be aware of and provide for the particular needs of students of particular "racial", ethnic, cultural, historical, linguistic' backgrounds. Quite what these needs were, or who they applied to, was, however, far from clear. One section of the rationale pointed out that 'though in common talk in Britain today, race and ethnicity are concepts which immediately call to mind black immigrants and their children', the policy included 'children from white minority ethnic groups, most notably in this city, the Irish community'. These groups were not racial because '"race" was a "false belief"' and 'there was only one race and that is the human race'. However, there were ethnic groups 'whose members have a common culture' and 'this concept of ethnicity subsumes not only the historical and linguistic background of people but also their geographical location, both before and after settlement in Britain'.[133]

This incorporation of diverse historical processes and linguistic and geographical specificities into the single category of ethnicity clearly signalled the continued difficulty with ethnic absolutism. Ethnic groups were assumed to be constituted by cultures that were historically defined and which bestowed identity on individuals whose educational well-being, and their wider incorporation into society, depended on the recognition of these ethnic cultures. Yet any assessment of the unity of ethnic cultures, even in the 1980s, would have encountered some obvious weaknesses. One of these weaknesses, as has been seen, was that the communities now designated as minority ethnic groups, by virtue of a shared ethnicity that subsumed history, were, in fact, very different. They came from different areas of the world, they migrated at different times and for a wide variety of reasons and they could have different religious beliefs. The assertion that they shared a common culture dictated by a common past was demonstrably false. As the debates in 'immigrant communities' around the 1960s and 1970s illustrated, there were multiple and competing histories that helped explain why Liverpool-born blacks might object to perceived West Indian leadership, why prominent black women's groups were organised in the 1970s and 1980s and why the Federation of Irish Societies (FIS) might have been dismissed by some working-class Irish for its middle-class values and concern for respectability. In other words, there are valid reasons to challenge the assumption that ethnic groups were organised and cohesive, with shared customs and values that came from the past.[134]

The primacy of ethnic absolutism over historical understanding became clearer when the document spelled out what exactly constituted 'their history'.

> Teachers and pupils, whether black or white, have this much in common – that much of their recent history has been within the British Empire and latterly the Commonwealth. White people have been conquerors, missionaries and administrators in the former colonies and dependencies from which mainly black people have come. The traditional English interpretation of history has accordingly favoured and justified, conquest, evangelism and exploitation. The view from the other side is quite otherwise. Their heroes and heroines are people who resisted, even though enslaved, conquered, exploited or ill-treated.

> Although some children may have migrated to Britain, the vast majority who were born here have also experienced prejudice and discrimination because their colour, ethnicity, food, clothes, customs or religious

practices are seen as being different and in some way unacceptable. A knowledge and understanding of the historical experience of people who make up our multicultural society is a necessary element in any effort to counter such prejudice and discrimination. For this to be effective, recognition has to be given to views of history from the perspective of black people and people from other minority ethnic communities.

All children need to understand the historical forces which have shaped the present multi-cultural society. School history should provide an account of the past with which black and minority ethnic children can identify in a positive way and which also relates to their experiences in Britain today. School history should enable children to examine critically interpretations of past events and should include African and Asian and Irish contributions to world development and some account of the processes of migration.

Among sound empirical observations, about the history of the British Empire and Commonwealth and its consequences for national history writing, the extract reveals a characteristic tendency to view history in binary terms in order to make sense of contemporary claims around ethnic cohesion and identity. The history of the British Empire and Commonwealth, and implicitly the political economy of the Atlantic slave trade, is reduced to a Manichean conflict between white and black people. But it is not necessary to deny the catastrophic consequences of slavery or imperialism in order to point out that neither was based on a single binary division between white oppressors and black victims. Similarly, 'a knowledge and understanding of the historical experience of people who make up our multicultural society' certainly has the potential to 'counter prejudice and discrimination' but this potential is immediately circumscribed by the assumption that there was a specific black or minority ethnic perspective that required 'recognition'. The content of this minority ethnic perspective remained largely implicit, but its express purpose, echoing the identity studies paradigm, was to 'provide an account of the past with which black and minority ethnic children can identify in a positive way' and which would include 'African, Asian and Irish contributions to world development'.

Although it has become axiomatic to imagine that a common point of geographical origin, sometimes located in a distant past, results in a single shared history that creates collective identities and requires recognition, this is a very particular act of historical imagination.

Its roots lay in European humanism and the Reformation, but it was only with modernity, and the emergence of modern nationalism, that historical identities became the dominant mode of understanding both individual and collective selves. It was this form of understanding that provided the original motivation for post-war scholar activists. Identified by the post-war state as alien elements in the national body, they felt the power of race and ethnic ideas. Their discussion and study groups, their political campaigns and their schools and cultural activities all explored, in some way or another, what it meant to be designated as a distinct racial or ethnic group. There was no uniformity among these groups but some projects and some activists pursued the study of race as a set of ideas, distributed and deployed by historical actors in specific historical conditions. Typically, such projects were concerned with inequalities in both material wealth and cultural resources and they deployed a vocabulary of power, the state, class relations and economic exploitation. Yet, and as the extract above clearly demonstrates, these critical analyses of race as ideology were marginalised as they became more mainstream. Instead, the a priori ascription of people into ethnic categories reduced the historical study to describing ethnic groups with whom people can identify proudly because of their contribution to 'world development'.[135]

The Birmingham Equal Opportunities policy document was unusual only in the detailed rationale it gave for promoting and recognising ethnic minority histories. Left-wing councils began to roll out policies in the education and cultural sectors that required the identification of diverse ethnic needs. These were hard-won, important and always precarious gains, but their endurance through recurrent political and educational controversies in the late 1980s and 1990s goes some way to explaining the process of multicultural drift. Unplanned, geographically uneven and far from popular, the validation of ethnic minority histories became a key part of the slow development of British multiculturalism.[136] According recognition and respect to ethnic minority communities, identifying their distinctive heritage and narrating their history, became a routine task for local government.

These are best understood as interim or short-run achievements. In Stella Dadzie's phrase they are 'tactical necessities'.[137] The national narrative was becoming plural, more groups could belong, but the form of belonging remained unchanged. Multicultural policies did not manage to disrupt or go beyond the idea that historical identities, based on race or ethnicity, were the proper basis of government and social policy. With the election of the New Labour in 1997 central government began a sustained effort to promote more plural versions of the national past. Among a raft of social policy innovations, the identification of different cultural traditions and histories, often invoked by that vague and elusive term ethnicity, became a consistent theme in the pursuit of a liberal multiculturalism.

Inclusion in the 'national script'

A defining feature of the New Labour government was its espousal of a third way in pursuit of social justice. Allied to the pursuit of economic efficiency through the promotion of ethical capitalism, New Labour's concept of social justice was premised on identifying and ensuring minimum standards and on promoting equality of opportunity. Commitment to economic redistribution was scaled back and governmental responsibility focused on creating the market conditions in which individuals could fulfil their potential and strong communities could flourish.[138]

Central to this version of social justice was the identification of, and response to, social exclusion.[139] The concept of social exclusion continued to refer to material poverty but also attempted to identify the psychological aspects of social alienation. Benefit payments to the poor might, for example, secure a minimal standard of living but had no mechanism for addressing the psychological and emotional states so often associated with poverty, unemployment and a wider climate of urban decay. This was, argued Prime Minister Tony Blair, a 'very modern problem, and one that is more harmful to the individual, more damaging to self-esteem, more corrosive for society as a whole'.[140] At a lecture to the Royal Society of Arts in 1999, Chris Smith, MP, then Secretary of State for Culture, argued that

> Of course in the battle for social regeneration bricks and mortar and safe roofs and good schools and the chance of a job are vital. But the starting point for all this has to be a sense that you achieve something as an individual, that there is something to aspire to in life, that you are worth something as a human being.[141]

For some critics the identification of the emotional needs of citizens, and the claim that these were justly the concerns of the state, were part of a new therapeutic ethos in society.[142] The starting point for social policy had to be ontological security and the feelings and emotions, or the subjective experiences, which underpinned secure identity, self-esteem and self-confidence. Alongside a huge increase in formal psychological diagnoses and interventions, therapeutic ideas, assumptions and practices began to permeate everyday life, popular culture and social policy.

History education, in both formal and informal settings, was not immune from this wider tendency to frame policies and practices in an emotional register. It became increasingly common to discuss historical processes and events in primarily emotional and experiential terms. Some historians, like Peter Mandler, even saw the opportunity to fix one's individual identity as one of the 'new social purposes of history'.[143] These claims to novelty are exaggerated but there was, by the end of the century, increasing interest in the ways in which historical research and education could ameliorate a widely reported sense of social dislocation. In the pace of social change, and in the decline of the stable employment and bounded communities, the past was increasingly identified as a place of respite and of certainty 'offering answers to questions as to who we are' and 'how we are produced as modern subjects'.[144]

In fact, and especially in the work of the influential Social Exclusion Unit (SEU), a social policy think tank located in the Cabinet Office between 1997 and 2010, historical narratives and resources were identified as a critical resource in establishing and maintaining individual and community identities. Arts education and cultural activities more broadly, were valued because they helped 'communities to express their identity, develop their own, self-reliant organisations' and related 'directly to individual and community identity'. 'Recognising and developing the culture of marginalised people and groups directly tackles their sense of being written out of the script.'[145] It followed that 'inclusion in the script' would promote a range of desirable outcomes including improved mental health for individuals, the regeneration of communities, increased social networking, better educational attainment for children and improved employment prospects.

However, 'inclusion in the script' was recognised as particularly difficult for individuals and groups who continued to feel the effects of discrimination. The extent of this discrimination against black people in Britain was set out in some detail by the work of the Stephen Lawrence Inquiry which was belatedly established after a long campaign in 1997, some four years after the brutal murder of the black teenager by white youths on the streets of London. Disturbed by continuing evidence of racist attitudes of even very young children, the Inquiry found a plethora of anti-racist policy documents and rhetoric but little in the way of implementation. The Inquiry's recommendations, therefore, went far beyond the circumstances of the murder to encompass general questions around social policy, ethnic diversity and race equality. In the 2000 Race Relations Amendment Act a new statutory duty was placed on public authorities to promote race equality and historical education was seen as a necessary precondition for inclusion in the national script.

One result of the Lawrence Inquiry and the amended race relations legislation that followed it was an increasing emphasis on the histories that had been championed by municipal multiculturalism. Migration, the histories of migrants and stories of empire and racism, should, it was frequently asserted, be better known. This conviction peppered government policy proposals such as *Excellence in Schools* (1997), where a good education was defined as providing access to this 'country's rich and diverse culture, to its history and to an understanding of its place in the world'.[146] Similarly, in 1998–1999 a government-initiated review of the National Curriculum, conducted by the Qualifications and Curriculum Authority, stressed that the school curriculum should contribute to the:

> development of pupils' sense of identity through knowledge and understanding of their spiritual, moral, social and cultural heritages and of the local, national, European and international dimensions … It should pass on the enduring values of society … It should develop [pupils'] knowledge and understanding of different beliefs and cultures.[147]

And a Home Office consultation paper on promoting race equality in public authorities began by affirming modern Britain as 'a diverse society … whose history has seen successive ways of migration both in and out of the country'. There followed statements on the 'the significant contribution made by black and Asian people fighting for Great Britain in the two great wars', the involvement of labour from the Caribbean, India and Pakistan in the post-war 'reconstruction effort', photographs that showed black and Asian men on active war service and further details and images of Britain's multicultural history included in a three-page appendix.[148] Yet it was in the Parekh report, *The Future of Multi-Ethnic Britain* (2000), that the argument for a more pluralistic, or ethnicised, version of the past was most clearly set out. Initially welcomed by New Labour, the report argued that the dominant version of the British national story, as a unified polity based on values of toleration, moderation and fair play, was both inaccurate and complacent. A more global history, and one which identified a long history of migration both to and from Britain, as well as the existence and legacies of empire, was a necessary element of any attempt to build more inclusive forms of social belonging. Historical practices, from the collection, conservation and archiving of materials to their use in academic and public history narratives, needed to change to reflect cultural diversity. Funding from local councils, the New Opportunities Fund and the Heritage Lottery Fund was designed to make the marginalised histories of selected ethnic communities permanent and tangible.[149]

This was, by now, a familiar argument. Scholar activists had, after all, been making much the same demand for more than twenty years but now there was a new condition, 'postcolonial melancholia', that described a national inability to identify and openly discuss the historical episodes and events that explained contemporary England. The basic procedures of historical research, the identification and close reading of historical documents contained in archive repositories, still excluded many people.[150] The teaching of history in schools might have had a multicultural element in theory but in practice it was rare, and usually reserved for schools that taught immigrants and their children.[151] In wider culture, there were still obvious limits to the national master narrative. When the Parekh Report suggested, unremarkably, that the idea of Britishness was usually imagined as white, a vociferous media response included an editorial in the *Daily Telegraph* that condemned the 'outrageous lie' that 'the history, identity and character of the British people is racist'.[152] But both the Parekh Report, and the media reaction to it, indicated how discussions about history and historical identities remained constrained by ideas about race.

The Parekh Report was a detailed and welcome argument for rethinking the British national master narrative but its analysis and recommendations were limited by the very strong notions of community and culture that it employed. Despite their fragmentation, fluidity and complexity, 'community traditions', it argued, 'will remain a strong source of identity and solidarity'.[153] Such formulations, and the assumption that traditional cultures are primary sources of identity and solidarity, attest to the influence of political scientist, lead author and former vice-chair of the Community Relations Commission, Bikhu Parekh. Culture, argued Parekh, 'has no essence', is 'a historically created system of meaning and significance', 'constantly contested, subject to change' and 'not a passive inheritance but an active process of creating meaning'.[154] But if this seemed to open up the possibility for critically studying the formation of cultures, that opportunity is immediately closed down by the insistence that the principal community attachments were 'historic', 'rooted', 'authentic' and 'traditional' ethnicities. Elsewhere, Parekh insisted that 'we are human beings but also cultural beings, born and raised within and shaped by a thick culture, which we can no doubt revise and even reject but only by embracing some other culture'.[155] In other words, culture, a term virtually synonymous with ethnicity, is thick and reaches all the way down into the individual through processes of socialisation. This formulation provides a plausible explanation for the emotional and symbolic power of ethnic identities, and one very much in keeping with the assumptions of race relations work, but it did not leave much room either for critique or for historical analysis.

If cultures are ethnic and ethnicities are historical, traditional and rooted, all that is required from the past are descriptive accounts of ethnic communities. Towards the end of the century there were clear signs that, as academic discipline, curriculum subject or cultural activity, historical practices were influenced by a therapeutic ethos in society and by the idea that everybody belonged to an ethnic culture in which they could find solace, esteem and identity. In turn, these ideas became one part of cultural and educational policies, especially in self-proclaimed multicultural cities like Birmingham, where these there were employed in the quest for social cohesion. Yet, and as historians David Parker and Paul Long have argued, the incorporation of subordinated histories into the official narratives might have helped to recast the city's 'identity as modern and progressive and cosmopolitan' but much state-sponsored historical practice was too 'steeped in nostalgia to encompass serious critical analysis of the local economy and social structure'.[156]

A new history of the city's Irish population was indicative of the ways in which the demands of multiculturalism shaped the production of local histories. Written by Professor of Community History, Carl Chinn, and published in 2003 by the Birmingham Library Services,

Birmingham Irish: Making Our Mark consists of solid empirical data and fascinating oral history on Irish migration to Birmingham over two centuries.[157] Yet it is a particularly sanitised account of Irish migrants and their ancestors. There is no consistent discussion of the significant differences of class and culture among Irish migrants; very little exploration of gendered histories of migration and settlement; nothing on the violence, alcoholism or mental health difficulties experienced by a disproportionate number of Irish migrants and their children; no recognition of any racism within it and a curiously benign view of the process of settlement that comes, in the second half of the book, directly from the testimonies of the migrants themselves. 'I've never experienced prejudice at any time' declares one interviewee, another is 'grateful to Birmingham and its friendly people' and a third declares 'how tolerant and kind hearted the Birmingham people were to the Irish and other immigrants who came to the city in great numbers'.[158] In fact, and apart from some very brief references to racism in the 1950s and 1960s, the only exception to this happy history are some temporary difficulties in the aftermath of the IRA bombings in 1974 from which the Irish community is now recovering. Chinn concludes, in a manner that was typical for this type of liberal multiculturalism: 'Irish people have played a leading part in the building of a successful multi-cultural city in which people can be proud of their distinct communities but can also be proud of what we share in common; our humanity and our belonging to Britain.'[159]

Migration to Birmingham, once discussed solely as a problem, was now part of the city's official histories and image. In both central and local government a more liberal version of the heritage industry was promoted for both therapeutic and economic reasons. Therapeutically, liberal histories of model minorities were widely claimed to make people proud, boost their self-esteem and promote positive messages about the ways in which people could live together with their differences. But the differences that really mattered were, of course, ethnic. Ethnic populations were increasingly identified as a key source of economic growth. Migrant communities had a kind of pioneering spirit, a determination to succeed and valuable local knowledge that would drive future prosperity in service-based cultural economies.[160]

'Ethnographic' rather than 'historiographic' was the verdict of sociologist Barnor Hesse on this liberal multiculturalism.[161] Positive histories of diversity were a welcome sign of change, agreed Gargi

Bhattacharyya, but they were accompanied by 'exotic tendencies' that failed to explain everyday racism.[162] Descriptive histories of ethnic cultures that contributed to England did nothing to challenge the assumptions of the national master narrative. Immigrants and their children were required to belong to identifiable and racialised cultures or communities, to conform to national values and to contribute to national prosperity. The role of history was genealogical and celebratory and its storytelling capacities promoted at the expense of its explanatory and critical potential. This was neatly illustrated when Liverpool was named as the European Capital of Culture for 2008 and Liverpool City Council Chief Executive, David Henshaw, was widely quoted as proclaiming that

> Liverpool was turning its back on its past. The city is growing up. We've got history and we should be proud of our history, but in the past we've been prisoners of our history. It's a momentous day for Liverpool because it's about looking forward.[163]

This amounted to a claim that that liberal multiculturalism, even where it arrived very late on the local scene, had successfully worked through some difficult legacies of the past. In Liverpool, the city councils' 'unreserved apology for its involvement in the slave trade and the continual effects of slavery on Liverpool's Black community', had been initiated by Councillor Myrna Juarez, a former student at the Charles Wootton College renamed in memory of the black civilian murdered by a racist mob in 1919. This went further than Prime Minister Tony Blair's 1997 'statement of remorse' for the Irish Famine that was caused 'by those who governed at the time'.[164] These apologies were, of course, a further characteristic feature of late twentieth-century multiculturalism. Their purpose was to confer recognition on minority groups, to identify what were understood as distinctive historical experiences and to show empathy for historical injustices involving government institutions. They may have been symbolically important for some individuals but, as David Henshaw's statement indicated, apologies were too often conflated by policymakers, politicians and some scholars with a process of historical education. Far from facilitating a working through or moving forward from the past, liberal multiculturalism sponsored a politically expedient form of forgetting. At the end of the twentieth century, historical ignorance around the lives of immigrants in England, and about empire, was profound. Contextualised and sensitive analysis of historical events and processes, and their legacies, was rare in the public sphere. Instead, and regardless of which particular culture they attached themselves to, individuals were understood to be bounded by cultures that were historically defined and given. History, therefore, offered ontological security to individuals. It was through the recognition and celebration of ethnic histories that the regeneration of selves and communities was to be achieved.

Conclusion: historical sensibilities

By the end of the twentieth century, declarations of cultural diversity were commonplace in social policy. But the meaning of cultural diversity, and its connection to wider debates around social justice, was much changed since the advent of municipal multiculturalism in the early 1980s. This was not simply because diversity had been identified as a key mechanism for combating social exclusion by central government. Instead, scholar activists, and the communities of interpretation that had helped to develop, distribute and sustain alternative historical narratives, ones that sought to explain racism and to uncover the legacies of British imperialism, had fractured and dispersed. Radical politics of class, feminism or ethnicity were deeply affected by the ending of the Cold War, by structural changes to the economy and by a widely reported sense that social relations were more fleeting and fragile, and people apparently more selfish and individualistic, by the century's end, compared with even twenty years previously.

The ways in which multiculturalism was affected by economic, political and social change was hinted at in a perceptive 2002 study sponsored by the charity and campaigning organisation, Birmingham Race Action Partnership. Conducted in the aftermath of the 9/11 bombings, the study was surprised to find that there appeared to have been a change in the meaning of ethnicity to a new generation of black and minority ethnic adults. 'Using the lens of ethnicity to identify the main differences and similarities between people may', the report argued, 'lead us to miss the myriad other very important aspects which go to make up an individual's identity'. Individual character traits and behavioural tendencies were seen as more significant than ethnicity for explaining behaviour and the 'apparent need of society to categorise them [young people] by ethnicity, not once or twice, but over and over again, was an obvious problem for them'.[165] Similarly, argued Fanshawe and Sriskandarajah in 2010, the time had come to review the accuracy and utility of orthodox accounts of cultural and ethnic diversity.[166] These were perceptive observations.

Ethnic categorisation, as has been shown, experienced a spectacular boom in the twenty years between 1980 and 2000. Collected in piecemeal and inconsistent fashion in the 1980s, championed by politicians who saw ethnic data as the key to 'doing something' for black groups in Britain, the collection and reporting of ethnicity only began in the United Kingdom census of 1990.[167] That first data sweep was based on a clear and unambiguous distinction between white and non-white populations. Whilst this was not without controversy, the distinction immediately began to break down. In the 2001 census, and as the result of vigorous lobbying, an Irish category was included, under the previously generic white heading, and a mixed origin category was added. These amendments may have been welcomed by some of the scholar activists who had campaigned against discrimi-nation in the 1980s but the proliferation of ethnic identities was not necessarily a sign of progress.

In the frequent injunctions to celebrate diversity, and in the policies designed to cultivate ethnic identities, there was little recognition of how these identities had been constructed in a society characterised by racism and inequality. The assumed therapeutic benefits of historical education were couched in terms of improving levels of esteem, of developing self-concepts and winning recognition for histories and cultures previously ignored, denigrated and marginalised. In this, the era of the cultural turn in the humanities and social sciences, it was subjectivities, identities and discourses that provided the language of analysis. Representation and respect, identity and community had become primary sites of political contestation, of academic analysis and a whole range of formal and informal educational activities at the end of the century. In these activities, and in a manner barely imaginable fifty years earlier, the histories of immigrants were increasingly visible in England.[168]

Yet in the practice of cultural difference, and in the associated elevation of ethnic histories as the source of strong identities, history was at risk of simply becoming a celebration of those differences and identities partly imposed by a racist society. An instrumental, descriptive and celebratory heritage, characterised by conceptual confusion and divorced from any adequate understanding of historical processes, too often replaced the more critical narratives once championed by scholar activists. Those narratives had been decisively shaped by the political convictions of the post-1968 generation and embraced an eclectic kind of materialism that was, at the end of the century, in hasty retreat. In addition, the sites and spaces of radical education and the ways in which they defined, published, distributed and discussed important bodies of knowledge, were becoming harder to find. This was important not so much for the demise of the particular political ambitions of scholar activists but because their materialism was profoundly historical. In their shared insistence that historical processes explained the shape of the world and the struggles of those in it scholar activists necessarily engaged with large-scale historical processes. They decisively rejected the terms of the dominant national master narrative, of the slow and patient development of freedoms for all in a tolerant and free society, and instead investigated capitalist expansion and accumulation, the development of global empires, slavery and famine, racism and exploitation. They did so, moreover, by coming together to read texts, to listen to music and to produce pamphlets and newspapers. In doing so they established a critical historical consciousness, one that rejected dominant historical narratives, and embarked upon a search for, and mobilisation of, 'a specific kind of experience of the past' and one that not only rendered problematic present value systems but also afforded individuals and groups the opportunity to define themselves in a manner 'unentangled by role determinations and prescribed, predefined patterns of self-understanding'. This opportunity pointed those groups simultaneously towards the past and the present because historical identity was imbued with an 'essential temporalisation' and understood as 'an interface of time and events, permanently in transition'.[169] Progress, change, development were written into these stories and, in their stress on human agency, they offered hope for those involved in struggles for social justice.

By the end of the century, by contrast, it was the emotional capacity of history that was most easily identifiable in the public sphere. History was valued because it was assumed capable of delivery strong ethnic identities that offered consolation to individuals, respect and recognition to groups and stability to society. The historical heritage that could help transform individuals and groups had decisively changed.[170] It was now primarily imagined as an ethnic history that conferred difference on groups and was likely to be consumed in new forms of media that facilitated the emergence of plural histories but also led to the 'excessive protecting of certain tribal or ethnic histories and the fetishisation of, for instance, working class white culture'.[171] In addition, the plurality of histories was not necessarily accompanied by critical dialogue and debate and so it did not encourage the kind of critical historical consciousness that a radical generation had dreamed of. Their struggles for a past, for a properly historical consciousness, would have to be renewed by a new generation of activists working in different circumstances whose first target would be the fog of ethnicity.

Notes

1 B. Thompson (ed.), *Before the Fire!* (Liverpool: Liverpool Teachers Association, 1981).

2 Garnett, *From Anger to Apathy*, p. 97.

3 Michael Keith, *Race, Riots and Policing: Lore and Disorder in a Multi-racist Society* (London: UCL Press 1993).

4 John Benyon and John Solomos, 'The simmering cities: urban unrest during the Thatcher years', *Parliamentary Affairs*, 41:3 (1988), 403.

5 Birmingham Heritage and Archives Services, MS 1611/C/1/3/6/2/10, Birmingham Community Relations Council Minutes, 14 October 1981, p. 1; Sheila Wright in Hansard (HC) vol. 8, col. 1444 (16 July 1981).

6 Stuart Hall, 'Conclusion: The Multi-Cultural Question', in Barnor Hesse (ed.), *Unsettled Multiculturalisms: Diasporas, Entanglements, 'Disruptions'* (London: Zed Books, 2000); Anthony Giddens, *Modernity and Self-Identity: Self and Society in the Late Modern Age* (Cambridge: Polity, 1991).

7 Roger Middleton, *The British Economy since 1945: Engaging with the Debate* (London: Macmillan, 2000), p. 25.

8 *Ibid.*, p. 25; Eric Hobsbawm, *Age of Extremes*, pp. 403–418; Garnett, *From Anger to Apathy*, pp. 69–70 .

9 Cabinet Office, *Ethnic Minorities and the Labour Market. Final Report* (London: Strategy Unit, 2003); Colin Brown, *Black and White Britain: The Third PSI Survey* (London: Gower, 1985 [1984]), pp. 315–323; Political and Economic Planning, *The Facts of Racial Disadvantage* (London: Political and Economic Planning, 1976).

10 Organisation for Economic and Co-operation and Development, *Historical Statistics 1970–2000* (Paris: OECD, 2002), p. 41 (table 2.11); Brian Jacobs, *Black Politics and Urban Crisis* (Cambridge: Cambridge University Press, 1986), pp. 9–10; R. Ward and F. Reeves, *Racial Disadvantage: West Indians in Businesses in Britain* (London: HMSO, 1980); Home Affairs Committee Sub-Committee on Race Relations

and Immigration, *Racial Disadvantage* (London: HMSO, 1981), pp. 8–9, tables 3.1 and 3.2.

11 See, for example, Christian Dustmann and Nikolaos Theodoropoulos, 'Ethnic minority immigrants and their children in Britain', *Oxford Economic Papers*, 62: 2 (2010), whose analysis finds 'no systematic pattern' between employment probabilities and discrimination (p. 230), a claim made easier by the claim that 'ethnic minority to immigration started not earlier than the 1950s' (p. 210), and, alongside this neglect of a long history of migrant settlement, a reluctance to acknowledge the real methodological limitations of self-report measures in survey data.

12 Bronwen Walter, *Outsiders Inside: Whiteness, Place and Irish Women* (London: Routledge, 2002), pp. 150–161.

13 Jon Murden, '"City of change and challenge": Liverpool since 1945', in Belchem (ed.), *Liverpool 800*, pp. 428, 440.

14 Ambalavaner Sivanandan, 'Britain's Gulags', in A. Sivanandan (ed.) *Communities of Resistance* (London: Verso, 1990), pp. 131–132.

15 Benyon and Solomos, 'Simmering cities', 404.

16 Home Office, *The Brixton Disorders 10–12 April 1981. Report of an Inquiry by Rt. Hon. Lord Scarman* (Cmnd 8427, London: HMSO, 1981), para. 2.20.

17 Cadbury Research Library, University of Birmingham, DA 6, Archives of the Birmingham Black Oral History Project, Box 2, Carlton Duncan transcript, p. 6; British Library, Sound and Moving Image Archive, C927/686, 'Our memories of the uprisings', witness seminar, 25 October 2010.

18 J. Stokes in Hansard (HC) vol. 3, col., 29 (13 April 1981); E. Powell in Hansard (HC) vol. 14, cols 1018–1020 (10 December 1981); Gilroy, *There Ain't No Black*, pp. 51–59.

19 W. Whitelaw in *Hansard* (HC) vol. 3, col. 30 (13 April 1981).

20 W. Whitelaw in *Hansard* (HC) vol. 8, col. 1404 (16 July 1981). For broader explanation and analysis on the problems allegedly posed by 'alien communities', see Gilroy, *There Ain't No Black*, ch. 3.

21 Thatcher Archive, 'THCR 5/1/5/128, 'Speech to the Board of Deputies of British Jews', M. Thatcher, 15 December 1981.

22 R. Boyson in *Hansard* (HC) vol. 982, col. 699 (3 April 1980).

23 Emily Robinson, *History, Heritage and Tradition in Contemporary Politics* (Manchester: Manchester University Press, 2012), p. 43.

24 For astute summary and analysis of the heritage debates, see Stuart Hall, 'Whose heritage? Un-settling "the heritage", re-imagining the post-nation', in Jo Littler and Roshi Naidoo (eds), *The Politics of Heritage: The Legacies of 'Race'* (Abingdon, Oxon.: Routledge, 2005).

25 Keith Joseph, 'Why teach history in school?', *Historian*, 2 (1984), 10–12; Phillips, *History Teaching*, p. 19.

26 Joseph, 'Why teach history?', 11. Clyde Chitty, *Eugenics, Race and Intelligence in Education* (London: Continuum, 2009), p. 105.

27 Chitty, *Eugenics*, pp. 104–106.

28 Raphael Samuel, 'Introduction: the little platoons', in Samuel (ed.), *The Making and Unmaking of British National Identity Volume II*, pp. xxxiii–xxxv.

29 Carolyn Steedman, *Dust* (Manchester: Manchester University Press, 2001), pp. 76–77.

30 On the 'undisciplined spaces of universities', see Eley, *Crooked Line*, p. 125; Warmington, *Black British Intellectuals*, ch. 6; Maguire, 'Working-class women of Irish descent', in Mahoney and Zmroczek (eds), *Class Matters*.

31 Gilroy, *There Ain't No Black*, ch. 2; John M. MacKenzie (ed.), *Imperialism and Popular Culture* (Manchester: Manchester University Press, 1986).

32 Centre for Contemporary Cultural Studies, *The Empire Strikes Back: Race and Racism in 70s Britain* (London: Hutchinson, 1982), p. 11.

33 In so far as work on race and immigration has been produced by historians, either empirically or as a tool of analysis, it emerged both significantly later, there is far less of it and, arguably, it has had a much more modest impact on either academic or popular understandings of the past. See, for example, the judgements of Eley, *Crooked Line*, pp. 126–127; Burrell and Panayi, 'Immigration, history and memory in Britain', p. 8; Paul Gilroy, *Postcolonial Melancholia* (New York: Colombia University Press, 2004) for the alienating consequences of this failure to understand British history.

34 Tony Kushner, *The Battle of Britishness: Migrant Journeys, 1685 to the present* (Manchester: Manchester University Press, 2012), chs 1 and 2; Jeremy Black, *Contesting History: Narratives of Public History* (London: Bloomsbury, 2014); Tony Taylor and Robert Guyver (eds), *History Wars and the Classroom: Global Perspectives* (Charlotte, NC: Information Age, 2012).

35 Roy Hattersley, Hansard (HC) vol. 8, cols 1397–1503 (16 July 1981).

36 See, for example, Trevor Jones's advice to local community groups in Liverpool that it was unwise 'to bite the hands that feeds you', *Liverpool Daily Echo* (13 March 1981).

37 Martin Loney, *Community against Government: The British Community Development Project 1968–1978* (London: Heinemann, 1983). NA, HO 389/2 Review of CD Project 1974.

38 Lord Swann, in Hansard (HL) vol. 426, cols 237–270 (16 December 1977); Chitty, *Eugenics, Race and Intelligence*, pp. 97–112.

39 David Alton in Hansard (HC), vol. 8, col. 1465 (16 July 1981).

40 Silverman, *Handsworth/Lozells Riots*, p. 48 (my emphasis).

41 Jed Fazakarley, 'Racisms "old" and "new" at Handsworth, 1985', *University of Sussex Journal of Contemporary History*, 13 (2009–10), 9.

42 Nathan Glazer and Ken Young, 'Ethnic pluralism and public policy', *Bulletin of the American Academy of Arts and Sciences*, 36:5 (1983), 19–20.

43 Murden, 'City of change and challenge', pp. 458–461.

44 Laurence Westgaph 'Don't disregard our city's black history', *Liverpool Echo* (12 May 2008).

45 John Carvel, *Turn Again Livingstone* (London: Profile, 1999), p. 4.

46 Stuart Lansley, Sue Goss and Christian Wolmar, *Councils in Conflict* (Basingstoke: Macmillan, 1989); Les Back and John Solomos, *Race, Politics and Social Change* (London: Routledge, 1995), pp. 177–179; Birmingham City Council Race Relations Unit, *Brumdata: Key Facts about Birmingham's Black and Ethnic Minority Population* (Birmingham: Birmingham City Council, n.d.); Birmingham City Council Race Relations Unit, *Aims and Objectives* (Birmingham, Birmingham City Council, n.d.).

47 Ian Hacking, *Historical Ontology* (Harvard, MA: Harvard University Press, 2002), p. 70 for the importance of history and contingency in the process of 'making up people'. For relevant discussion in the context of theories of ethnicity, see Bob Carter and Steve Fenton, 'Not thinking ethnicity: a critique of the ethnicity paradigm in an over-ethnicised sociology', *Journal for the Theory of Social Behaviour*, 40:1 (2009), 1–18.

48 1982/83 HC 33, vol. 9 House of Commons. Home Affairs Committee. Race Relations and Immigration Sub-Committee. Session 1982–1983. Ethnic and racial questions in the census. Minutes of evidence Monday 31 January 1983. Birmingham, appendix 2, pp. 297–299; Monday 7 February 1983, pp. 391–392.

49 On second class citizens see BEM 4/2/1/2, pamphlet by Haringey Black Pressure Group on Education, 'Ethnic record keeping in education: a recipe for disaster'.

50 Ghazala Faizi, *History of the Black Presence in London* (London: GLC, 1986); Sue Baxter, *The Chinese and Vietnamese in Birmingham* (Birmingham: BCC, 1986)

51 Faizi, *History of the Black Presence*, p. 4.

52 London Metropolitan Archives, LPSU/REPG/1/3, letter from Sylvia Collicott to Ethnic Minorities Unit, GLC, 20 December 1985.

53 London Metropolitan Archives, LPSU/REPG/2/31, paper for the GLC, Cultural Industries and Cultural Policy in London conference, 12 December 1983 by Parminder Vir and Alan Tomkins, 'The state and public cultural policies', pp. 5, 7.

54 Eley, *Crooked Line*, p. 125. One of the most important academic texts of the period intentionally mirrored and transferred some of the radical pedagogical practices already discussed. See Centre for Contemporary Cultural Studies (ed.), *Empire Strikes Back*, p. 11. For some biographical reflections, see Carby, 'Lost (and found?) in translation', 34–39; in respect of Black Studies, see M. Christian, 'Black Studies in the UK and US: a comparative analysis', in J.R. Davidson (ed.), *African American Studies* (Edinburgh: Edinburgh University Press, 2010), ch. 8.

55 Jagdish S. Gundara and Ian Duffield (eds), *Essays on the History of Blacks in Britain: From Roman Times to the Mid-Twentieth Century* (Aldershot: Avebury, 1992).

56 See, for example, N.P.K. Torkington (ed.), *The Social Construction of Knowledge: A Case for Black Studies* (Liverpool: Liverpool Hope Press, 1994). William Ackah and Mark Christian (eds), *Black Organisation and Identity in Liverpool: A Local, National and Global Perspective* (Liverpool: Charles Wootton College Press, 1997).

57 Gundara, and Duffield (eds), *Essays on the History of Blacks in Britain*, p. 2.

58 Greater London Council, *Policy Report on the Irish Community* (London: GLC, 1984), p. 11; Gray, 'From "ethnicity" to "diaspora"', p. 71; for an anthropological account of these processes, see John Nagle, *Multiculturalism's Double Bind: Creating Inclusivity, Cosmopolitanism and Difference* (Farnham: Ashgate, 2009).

59 Bernard Canavan, 'Irish in Britain History Workshop', *History Workshop Journal*, 12 (1981), 196–198.

60 The monthly seminars on the history of the Irish in Britain were held at the Irish Centre in Camden (London) where some of the subjects featured were included in *The De La Salle Brothers 1855–1975* (Charles McCarthy, 1986) and *Growing Up Irish in Liverpool* (Moy McCrory). The bibliography was published by Irish in Britain History Group, *A History of the Irish in Britain* (London, 1986).

61 Irish in Britain History Centre, undated publicity pamphlet; Irish in Britain History Group, Statement of Policy, undated typescript; Frank. Dolan, 'The reviving of MacSwiney', *Irish Post* (19 October 1985), p. 4.

62 Ivan Gibbons, 'Editorial', *Irish Studies in Britain*, 2 (1981), 3–4.

63 M. Sheehan, 'Changing the face of the Irish in Britain', *Irish Post* (26 December 1981), 6.

64 London Metropolitan University, Archives of the Irish in Britain, Irish in Britain Representation Group Box 1: 'Minutes of the second National Conference of the Irish in Britain representation', 26 March 1983, p. 4.

65 *Ibid.*, p. 2.

66 On language classes, see 'News', *Irish Studies in Britain*, 11 (1987), 5;

on theatre, see London Metropolitan University, Archives of the Irish in Britain, Irish in Britain Representation Group Box 1: *An Pobal Eirithe* [The Risen People], 3 [n.d.], 15; Mick Wallis, 'Present consciousness of a practical kind: structure of feeling higher education drama', in W. John Morgan and Peter Preston (ed.), *Raymond Williams: Politics, Education, Letters* (London: Palgrave Macmillan, 1993), pp. 129–162.

67 London Metropolitan Archives, LRB/FN/C4/02/09–10, Irish in Britain Representation Group (Camden), funding application to GLC Ethnic Minorities Unit for 1983–1984 (25 March 1983).

68 *Ibid.*, IBRG (Harrow), funding applications and reports 1983–1986.

69 London Metropolitan Archives, LRB/FN/C4/02/56, Irish in Britain Representation Group (Camden), funding applications and reports, 1985–1986.

70 Dipesh Chakrabarty, *Provincializing Europe: Postcolonial Thought and Historical Difference* (Princeton, NJ: Princeton University Press, 2007); Schwarz, 'Conquerors of truth'.

71 Stefan Berger, 'The power of national pasts: writing national history in nineteenth and twentieth century Europe', in Stefan Berger (ed.), *Writing the Nation: A Global Perspective* (Basingstoke: Palgrave Macmillan, 2007), p. 55.

72 London Metropolitan Archives, LPSU/REPG/3/1, typescript constitution of the London Irish Commission for Culture and Education, August 1984, p. 1.

73 See the contrasting views of correspondents R. Doherty ('Anti-racism not multi-culturalism') and C. O'Sullivan ('Irish not an ethnic minority'), *Irish Studies in Britain*, 7 (1985), 5; Bernadette Hyland, 'Searching for the young Irish rebels', *An Pobal Eirithe* [The Risen People], 2 (1988), 4.

74 London Metropolitan Archives, LRB/FN/C4/02/56, Irish in Britain Representation Group (Camden), funding applications and reports, 1985–1986.

75 Greater London Council, *Policy Report on the Irish Community* (London: GLC, 1984), pp. 7–8, for the ways in which the vision of England as the historical oppressor resulted in 'partial assimilation and cultural alienation' that imposed great psychological pressure on the Irish.

76 Henri Tajfel, *The Social Psychology of Minorities* (London: Minority Rights Group, 1978)

77 Phillip Ullah, 'Second generation Irish youth: identity and ethnicity', *New Community*, 12: 2 (1985), 315, 319.

78 Joshua A. Fishman, 'Language and ethnicity', in Howard Giles (ed.), *Language, Ethnicity and Intergroup Relations* (London: Academic Press, 1977). For a conceptual analysis of the distinction between

instrumental (or circumstantial) and primordial accounts of ethnicity see Verkuyten, *Social Psychology*, ch. 3.

79 Fitzpatrick, 'Irish in Britain', 4–5.

80 Joan Inglis, 'The Irish in Britain: a question of identity', *Irish Studies*, 3 (1982), 12, 14.

81 Liam Greenslade, 'White skin, white masks: psychological distress among the Irish in Britain', in Patrick O' Sullivan (ed.), *The Irish World Wide: History, Heritage, Identity vol. 2* (Leicester: Leicester University Press, 2002), pp. 220–221.

82 Trouillot, *Silencing the Past*, p. 24.

83 Alan Clinton, 'One step forward for Irish studies', *Irish Studies in Britain*, 11 (1987), 18 reports the foundation of the Irish Studies Centre at the Polytechnic of North London in 1986. The Institute of Irish Studies at the University of Liverpool followed in 1988.

84 Said, *Culture and Imperialism*, p. 276.

85 Paul Bracey, 'Perceptions of the contribution of an Irish dimension in the English History Curriculum', *Educational Review*, 62:2 (2010), 203–213.

86 London Metropolitan University, Irish in Britain Representation Group, Box 1: Reports on 1 (February 1984) and 2nd (1990) National Conferences on Irish Dimensions in British Education; letter and typescript document entitled 'Racism, education and the Irish in Britain', Mary Hickman (IBRG, Islington) to Frances Morrell (leader Inner London Education Authority), 5 August 1983.

87 Raymond Cochrane, 'Mental illness in immigrants to England and Wales: an analysis of mental hospital admission, 1971', *Social Psychiatry*, 12 (1977), 25–35; R. Cochrane, *The Social Creation of Mental Illness* (London: Longman, 1983).

88 Patrick Baert, *Time, Self and Social Being: Outline of a Temporalised Sociology* (Aldershot: Ashgate, 1992).

89 Liam Greenslade, 'V.N. Volosinov and social psychology: towards a semiotics of social practice', in Ian Parker and Russell Spears (eds), *Psychology and Society: Radical Theory and Practice* (London: Pluto, 1996), p. 125.

90 Gorge Padmore Library, BPM 4/3/1/1: Report of Training Working Party, 26 October 1981.

91 Author interview with Ian Law; transcript in possession of author.

92 See, for example, Ziggi Alexander and Audrey Dewjee, *Roots in Britain* (London: Brent, 1981); Ian Grosvenor and R.L. Chapman, *West Africa, West Indies, West Midlands* (Oldbury: Sandwell LEA, 1982); Madge Dresser, *Black and White on the Buses: The 1963 Colour Bar Dispute in Bristol* (Bristol: Bristol Broadsides, 1986); Sylvia Collicott, *Local–National–World Links: A Case Study of Haringey History*

(Haringey: Haringey Borough Council, 1986); Bradford Heritage Recording Unit *Destination Bradford* (Bradford: Bradford Heritage Recording Unit, 1987); Stephen Small, *The Politics of Black British History* (Wellingborough: Wellingborough District Racial Equality Council, 1991); *The Black Presence in Nottingham* (Nottingham: Nottingham County Council, 1993).

93 Myers and Grosvenor, 'Birmingham stories', 151–153.

94 Satnam Virdee, *Racism, Class and the Racialized Outsider* (Basingstoke: Palgrave Macmillan, 2014).

95 Len Garrison, 'The black historical past in British education', in Peter G. Stone and Robert MacKenzie (eds), *The Excluded Past: Archaeology and Education* (London: Routledge, 1994); Andrew Flinn and Mary Stevens, '"It is noh mistri, wi mekin histri". Telling our own story: independent and Community Archives in the United Kingdom, challenging and subverting the mainstream', in Jeannette Bastian and Ben Alexander (eds), *Community Archives: The Shaping of Memory* (London: Facet Publishing, 2009), pp. 12–15; Mike Phillips, 'Obituary: Lenford (Kwesi) Garrison (1943–2003)', *History Workshop*, 56 (2003), 295–297.

96 Len Garrison cited in Zhana, *Black Success Stories Volume I* (London: Zhana, 2006), p. 80.

97 Martin Jay, *Songs of Experience: Modern American and European Variations on a Universal Theme* (Berkeley, CA: University of California Press, 2005), pp. 199–215.

98 'Responses to roots', *Race and Class*, 19: 1 (1977), 84; Romain, *Connecting Histories*, pp. 92–93.

99 See, for example, the novelistic rendering of black British history by Remi Kapo, *A Savage Culture: Racism – A Black British View* (London: Quartet Books, 1981) and reviews that focus on historical method and accuracy by E. Lawrence, *Race and Class*, 24:1 (1982), 104–106 and by F. Dhondy, *New Society* (1 October 1981), 31.

100 Pamela Kirk, 'Black people can't be racist', *Guardian* (7 November 1979), p. 10. For a more measured account, see Joanna Bornat, 'Oral history and black history: conference report', *Oral History*, 8:1 (1980), 21–22. See also British Library, Sisterhood and After Collection, C1420/19, Amrit Wilson interviewed by Margaretta Jolly.

101 Carolyn Steedman, 'Who owns history? Nowhere else to be: the everyday life of history in the English eighteenth century', paper given to the International Congress on the Historical Sciences, Amsterdam, August 2010.

102 Bill Schwarz, 'The Communist Party Historians' Group 1945–1956', in Centre for Contemporary Cultural Studies, *Making Histories: Studies in History-Writing and Politics* (London: Hutchinson, 1982), p. 95.

More generally Stefan Berger and Chris Lorenz (eds), *Historians as Nation Builders in Modern Europe* (London: Palgrave Macmillan, 2010).

103 British Library, Sisterhood and After Collection C1420/20/5, Stella Dadzie interviewed by Rachel Cohen.

104 Jay Winter, *Dreams of Peace and Freedom: Utopian Movements in the 20th Century* (New Haven, CT: Yale University Press, 2006), ch. 5.

105 Gerrard, *Emancipation*, p. 233.

106 For description and apt critique, see Errol Lawrence, 'In the abundance of water the fool is thirsty', in CCCS, *Empire Strikes Back*. For similar contemporary approaches to migration and constructions of cultural identity, see Dinesh Bhugra, 'Migration, distress and cultural identity', *British Medical Bulletin*, 69:1 (2004), pp. 129–141.

107 Stafford Scott, 'White Britain, black truth', *Guardian* (30 March, 1987), p. 14.

108 Farrukh Dhondy, 'Review: a savage culture: racism – a black British view by R. Kapo', *New Society*, 1 October 1981, p. 31. N.A., 'Case for black history in mainstream agenda', *Charles Wootton News*, 25 (June 1991), 24.

109 Delroy Constantine Simms, 'Black history in Britain: the African British experience', *Black Heritage Today*, October/November 2005, 12–14.

110 Akyaaba Addai-Sebo interview at www.everygeneration.co.uk/index. php/black-british-history/bhm-black-history-month/24–akyaaba-addai-sebo (last accessed 20/11/13).

111 Simms, 'Black history in Britain'; for an alternative view, and one which invokes James's Marxism, see Hassan Mahamdallie, 'There is a place for all at the rendezvous of victory', at www.actsofachievement. org.uk/2006/opening.php (last accessed 24/08/07). For astute comment on the limitations of Black History Month, see Yasmin Alibhai-Brown, 'Black history should never be safe', in Yasmin Alibhai-Brown, *Some of My Best Friends Are: Collected Journalism 1989–2004* (London: Politicos, 2004), pp. 208–211.

112 BL, Sisterhood and After Collection C1420/20/6; Stella Dadzie interviewed by Rachel Cohen; Second Chance to Learn Women's History Group, *No-One Ever Mentions Love: An Inside View of Black and White Relationships* (Liverpool: Liverpool Community College), pp. 1–3.

113 British Library, Sisterhood and After Collection, C1420/19, Amrit Wilson interviewed by Margaretta Jolly, transcript, p. 93.

114 Black Cultural Archives, Oral/31, Oral Histories of the Black Women's Movement, Beverley Bryant transcript, p. 24.

115 Pratibha Parmar, 'Black feminism: the politics of articulation', in

Jonathan Rutherford (ed.), *Identity, Community, Culture, Differences* (London: Lawrence & Wishart, 1990), p. 107; Kalbir Shukra, *The Changing Pattern of Black Politics in Britain* (London: Pluto, 1998), chs 3 and 4.

116 Paul Gilroy, 'Nationalism, history and ethnic absolutism', *History Workshop Journal*, 30:1 (1990), 114–120.

117 Mary Fulbrook, *Historical Theory* (London: Routledge, 2002), p. 175.

118 Jill Liddington, 'What is public history? Publics and their pasts, meanings and practices', *Oral History*, 30:1 (2002), 84.

119 Brian Graham, 'Heritage as knowledge: capital or culture', *Urban Studies*, 39:5–6 (2002), 1008.

120 David Lowenthal, *The Heritage Crusade and the Spoils of History* (Cambridge: Cambridge University Press, 1998); Sara McDowell, 'Heritage, memory and identity', in Brian Graham and Peter Howard (eds), *The Ashgate Companion to Heritage and Identity* (Ashgate, 2008).

121 Bradford Heritage Recording Unit, *Destination Bradford: A Century of Immigration* (Bradford: Bradford Libraries and Information Service, 1987); Hammersmith and Fulham Ethnic Communities Oral History Project, *The Motherland Calls: African Caribbean Experiences* (Hammersmith and Fulham Ethnic Communities Oral History Project, 1989); Hammersmith and Fulham Archives and Local History Centre, GB/NNAF/C58264, Ethnic Communities Oral History Project, 1987–2002, miscellaneous materials.

122 Karamat Iqbal, *Dear Birmingham: A Conversation with My Hometown* (n.p., XLibris, 2013), pp. 34–38.

123 Curran *et al.*, *Culture Wars*.

124 Malcolm Dick, 'Travelling through time: migration and the black experience', in I. Grosvenor, R. McLean and S. Roberts, *Making Connections: Birmingham Black International History* (Birmingham: BPBFG, 2002), pp. 275–289.

125 Richard Hatcher, 'Social justice in education after the Conservatives: the relevance of Barry Troyna's Work', in Patricia J. Sikes and Fazal Rizvi (eds), *Researching Race and Social Justice in Education: Essays in Honour of Barry Troyna* (Stoke-on-Trent: Trentham Books, 1997), 131–136.

126 See, for example, John Solomos and Les Beck, *Race, Politics and Social Change* (London: Routledge, 1995).

127 British Library, Sisterhood and After Collection C1420/20/5, Stella Dadzie interviewed by Rachel Cohen.

128 Small, *Black British History*, pp. 3–5; Roshi Naidoo 'Never mind the buzzwords: "race", heritage and the liberal agenda', in Littler and Naidoo (eds), *Politics of Heritage*, pp. 37, 45.

129 Robert Phillips, *History Teaching, Nationhood and State: A Study in Educational Politics* (London: Cassell, 1998).

130 Gilroy, 'Nationalism', 115, 118.

131 John Clarke and Janet Newman, *The Managerial State: Power, Politics and Ideology in the Making of Social Welfare* (London: Sage, 1997), p. 134.

132 Nancy Fraser, *Justice Interruptus: Critical Reflections on the Postsocialist Condition* (London: Routledge, 1997), p. 4.

133 City of Birmingham District Council, *Equal Opportunities Policy Part One: Education for a Multicultural Society* (Birmingham, n.d.), pp. 4, 22.

134 For researching stressing the ambiguities of identification, see G. Gaskell and P. Smith, 'Are young blacks really alienated?', *New Society* 14 May 1981, pp. 260–261; Barry Troyna, 'Differential commitment to ethnic identity by black youths in Britain', *New Community*, 7:3 (1981), 406–414.

135 City of Birmingham District Council, *Equal Opportunities Policy Part One*, pp. 23–24.

136 S. Hall, 'From Scarman to Stephen Lawrence', *History Workshop Journal*, 48 (1999), 187–197.

137 British Library, Sisterhood and After Collection C1420/20/5, Stella Dadzie interviewed by Rachel Cohen; Small, *Black British History*, p. 4.

138 Eric Shaw, *Losing Labour's Soul? New Labour and the Blair Government 1997–2007* (London: Routledge), ch. 2.

139 *Ibid.* See also, John Welshman, *From Transmitted Deprivation to Social Exclusion: Policy, Poverty and Parenting* (Bristol: Policy Press, 2007), chs 7 and 8.

140 T. Blair, 'Bringing Britain together' speech given at Stockwell Park School, south London, 8 December 1997, at www.webarchive. nationalarchives.gov.uk/20090114000528/http://cabinetoffice.gov.uk/ media/cabinetoffice/social_exclusion_task_force/assets/publications_ 1997_to_2006/pm_speech_seu.pdf (last accessed 21/07/14).

141 Chris Smith, 'Government and the arts', in M. Wallinger and M. Warnock (eds), *Art for All? Their Policies and Our Culture* (London: Peer, 2000), p. 15.

142 Frank Furedi, *Therapy Culture: Cultivating Vulnerability in an Uncertain Age* (London: Routledge 2004).

143 Peter Mandler, *History and National Life* (London: Profile, 2002), p. 148; Steedman, *Dust*.

144 Catherine Hall, 'Histories, empires and the postcolonial moment', in Iain Chambers and Lidia Curti (eds), *The Post-Colonial Question: Common Skies, Divided Horizons* (London: Routledge, 1996), p. 66.

145 Policy Action Team 10, *Report to the Social Exclusion Unit*, pp. 8, 30, at http://webarchive.nationalarchives.gov.uk/20090114000528/http:// cabinetoffice.gov.uk/social_exclusion_task_force/publications.aspx (last accessed 21/07/14).

146 Department for Education and Employment, *Excellence in Schools* Cmnd, 3681 (London: HMSO, 1997), p. 9.

147 Qualifications and Curriculum Authority, *The Review of the National Curriculum in England: The Secretary of State's Proposals* (London: Qualifications and Curriculum Authority, 1998), pp. 4–5.

148 *Race Relations (Amendment) Act 2000. New Laws for a Successful Multi-Racial Britain* (London: Home Office, 2001), pp. 1, 7, 36–38.

149 Flinn and Stevens, 'Telling our own story', p. 18.

150 Tony Kushner, 'Social inclusion: a historian's perspective', *Immigrants and Minorities*, 20:2 (2001), 75–83.

151 Julia Bush, 'Moving on – and looking back', *History Workshop Journal*, 36 (1993), 183–194.

152 Ian Grosvenor and Kevin Myers, 'Engaging with history after Macpherson', *Curriculum Journal*, 12:3 (2001), 288–289.

153 Parekh Report, *The Future of Multi-Ethnic Britain: Report of the Commission on the Future of Multi-Ethnic Britain* (London: Profile, 2000), para. 3.42.

154 Bhikhu Parekh, *Rethinking Multiculturalism: Cultural Diversity and Political Theory* (Basingstoke: Macmillan, 2000), pp. 143, 148, 175. For analysis, see Ralph Grillo, 'Cultural essentialism and cultural anxiety', *Anthropological Theory*, 3:2 (2003), 157–173.

155 Bhikhu Parekh, 'Barry and the dangers of liberalism', in P. Kelly (ed.) *Multiculturalism Reconsidered: 'Culture and Equality' and Its Critics* (Cambridge: Polity, 2002), p. 141.

156 David Parker and Paul Long, 'Reimaging Birmingham: public history, selective memory and the narration of urban change', *European Journal of Cultural Studies*, 6 (2003), 160, 169.

157 Birmingham City Council, *Library and Information Services Divisional Plan 2003–04* (Birmingham: Birmingham City Council, 2004), pp. 3–4.

158 Carl Chinn, *Birmingham Irish: Making Our Mark* (Birmingham: Birmingham City Council, 2003), pp. 118–119, 122, 131.

159 Chinn, *Birmingham Irish*, p. 180.

160 Birmingham City Council, *Highbury 3: Report of the Proceedings* (Birmingham: Birmingham City Council, 2001).

161 Barnor Hesse, 'Unsettled multiculturalisms', in Barnor Hesse (ed.), *Unsettled Multiculturalisms*, p. 10.

162 Bhattacharyya, *Riding Multiculturalism*, pp. 263–364.

163 'Liverpool named Capital of Culture', at http://news.bbc.co.uk/1/hi/ entertainment/2959944.stm (last accessed 15/12/11).

164 Richard Benjamin, 'Museums and sensitive histories: the International Slavery Museum', in A. L. Araujo (ed.), *Politics of Memory: Making Slavery Visible in the Public Space* (New York: Routledge, 2012); Jason A. Edwards and Amber Luckie, 'British Prime Minister Tony Blair's Irish potato famine apology', *Journal of Conflictology*, 5:1 (2014), 42–51. For a critical and astute reading of these apologies, see Michel Rolph-Trouillot, 'Abortive rituals: historical apologies in the global era', *Interventions: International Journal of Postcolonial Studies*, 2:2 (2000), 171–186.

165 Jackie Beavan, *Beyond Racial Identity* (Birmingham: Birmingham Race Action Partnership, 2002), p. 6.

166 Simon Fanshawe and Dhananyanan Sriskandarajah, *'You Can't Put Me in a Box': Superdiversity and the End of Identity Politics in Britain* (London: Institute for Public Policy Research, 2010).

167 See, for example, the revealing exchange in Home Affairs Committee, *Race Relations and Immigration Select Committee* (HC, 1982–1983, 33, vol. VIII), pp. 257–262.

168 Philip Gleason, 'Identifying identity: A semantic history', *Journal of American History*, 69:4 (1983), 910–931.

169 Rusen, *History*, pp. 32–34.

170 See, for example, debates on the uses of heritage reported in Sean Creighton, 'The Black British History Experience Diversity Matters Conference', *Black and Asian Studies Association Newsletter*, 39 (April 2004), 13–18.

171 Jerome De Groot, 'Empathy and enfranchisement: popular histories', *Rethinking Histories: The Journal of Theory and Practice of History*, 10:3 (2006), 411; Jerome De Groot, *Consuming History: Historians and Heritage in Contemporary Popular Culture* (London: Taylor & Francis, 2008); Christopher R. Hughes, 'ICTs and remembering the 200th anniversary of the abolition of the slave trade in Britain: an occasion for celebration or remorse?', *Journal of Historical Sociology*, 25:2 (2012), 240 for the finding that the 'bicentenary campaign had little resonance for a population in which slavery is not already a part of social memory'.

Conclusion

In every era an attempt must be made anew to wrest tradition away from the conformism that is about to overpower it. (Walter Benjamin, *Theses on the Philosophy of History*)

Racism rests on the ability to contain blacks in the present, to repress and to deny the past. (Paul Gilroy, *There Ain't No Black in the Union Jack*)

In October 2010 the newly appointed Minister for Education in the coalition government, Michael Gove, told the Conservative party conference that

One of the under-appreciated tragedies of our time has been the sundering of our society from its past. Children are growing up ignorant of one of the most inspiring stories I know – the history of our United Kingdom. Our history has moments of pride, and shame, but unless we fully understand the struggles of the past we will not properly value the liberties of the present. The current approach we have to history denies children the opportunity to hear our island story.[1]

The comments stimulated a fresh bout of the history wars that that have periodically erupted in former colonising and colonised states over the last fifty years. Historians, educationalists, politicians and commentators debated once again the content, interpretation and teaching of national history in schools. One persistent feature in these debates, and a key reason for their longevity, has been the concern that national identity, and most often a specifically British national identity, is in decline. Even if survey data does not conclusively bear out these concerns, and suggest fairly stable emotional attachments to dual national identities in the United Kingdom, a new emphasis on national history has been promoted as a response to some of the political, social and economic changes of the last six decades.² The demise of the British Empire, entry into the European Union, the re-emergence of Celtic nationalisms, the pace and scale of immigration, the development of multiculturalism and an alleged decline in levels of historical knowledge among the general population have all been offered as reasons for returning to a single and coherent national history. Michael Gove's is only the most recent in a long line of commentators whose wish is for a return to a Whig interpretation of history that would not have looked out of place at the 1951 Festival of Britain.³ Proceeding chronologically, and devised specifically to reveal a 'special tradition of liberty' it would, according to Dominic Sandbrook, consist of stories 'shot through with a deep sense of national pride' that were 'capable of making up a nation's collective memory'; a 'history of vivid characters and bloody battles' that would 'fire the imagination and bind the generations'.⁴

Despite the long struggles of scholar activists in the post-war period, the allure of a dominant national master narrative appeared to remain just as strong in the new century. Ignoring or marginalising centuries of immigration, blaming a 'liberal elite' for allowing the excessive immigration that became a source of legitimate (rather than racist) concern and national discord, this kind of national master narrative has little of relevance to say about migration and national identity in a new era of super-diversity. Against rapid social change it retains historical concepts that were relevant in a period of high nationalism and, as far as migrants are concerned, a restrictive vocabulary of integration and adaptation to English values. There are, of course, methodological difficulties in decisively identifying the causal power of a national master narrative but the resilience of Whig history, and of the banal nationalism endorsed in all kinds of state administration, at least begins to help explain why, among all the countries of the European Union, the British continue to be among the most anxious about immigration.⁵ Convinced of an ethnic unity guaranteed by their shared history, persuaded of their decency and tolerance, immigration is routinely viewed as a threat and immigrants as problems requiring close scrutiny and management.⁶

The resilience and power of Whig history as the basis of a popular but somewhat defensive patriotism was challenged by the arrival of migrants from decolonising states. Black and Irish immigrants had been in Britain for centuries, were part of the migrations of the wider British world and while they certainly faced discrimination they were free not only to settle to life in the metropolitan centre of the British Empire but also to lay claim to, and feel affinity for, an inclusive British identity that was global and monarchical, black and white.[7] However, in the post-war rebuilding of the world order a more defensive ethnic nationalism became prominent. In fact, and despite the tendency to dispense with a Nazi language of blood, descent and race and an imperial language of tribes, forced population movements on the continent of Europe and anti-colonial struggles around the globe encouraged the idea that nations were the proper expression of ethnic identities. While the work of the United Nations Educational, Scientific and Cultural Organization (UNESCO) established that race was a biological fiction, its anthropologists and psychologists ended up promoting ethnicity instead. In theory at least, and in contrast to the biology of race, ethnicity was socially constructed and performed but it continued to be employed to describe and analyse differences between nations, cultures and, in some contexts and somewhat confusingly, races. All that changed was that ethnicity was dependent not on biology but on social and cultural activities and, specifically and importantly, on shared ancestry, historical memories, a common culture forged over time, a homeland and a sense of solidarity. In the post-war world, ethnic historicism, and its vocabulary of natives and strangers, insiders and outsiders, black and white gained a new lease of life from the social sciences.

Imperial networks of the British world, recently the subject of renewed investigation by historians, were forgotten and marginalised in this period partly because they did not fit well with ethnic historicism. Just as the critical and academic study of the British Empire began in the 1950s, it was sidelined in popular national narratives. The chaotic and restless movement of capital, goods, people and ideas in the British world were silenced by the development and influence of race relations as an applied science. It became customary to think of the working class as spatially entrenched and ethnically homogeneous and, especially over the past decade, to prefix the description and explanation of working-class attitudes and behaviours with the adjective white. White people, it is now frequently argued in both the humanities and the social sciences have a racial identity too.[8] However, and as geographer Ben Rogaly and historian Becky Taylor have recently made clear, such descriptions woefully underestimate the extent to which narratives of movement and migration underpin contemporary working-class identities.[9] In addition, of course, the retention of the concept of race, even in the form of a social construction rather than biological reality, has made it more difficult to develop critical accounts of the contemporary racism that so blighted the lives of many immigrants and their descendants.

Drawing on static concepts of national, cultural and ethnic difference, race relations analyses were utilised in official circles to assess the desirability of potential immigrants to Britain, in academic life to investigate immigrant behaviour and relationships and, politically, informed the popularity of anti-immigration campaigns usually associated with Enoch Powell. Ethnic historicism also structured the study of immigrants in the field of social psychology. Identity studies that sought to explore the actual operation of ingroup–outgroup distinctions tended to focus resolutely on the minds and behaviour of young black people. In projects dedicated to raising educational achievement, the provision of positive role models and mentoring, it was levels of self-esteem and self-concepts that became the overriding educational concern at the expense of structural inequalities. As Heidi Mirza has argued, whilst such programmes have been a 'lifeline to many young Black and Asian people who have been damaged by the effects of racism, we still need to acknowledge its roots in the cultural deficit model and understand its limitations'.[10]

Ethnic historicism was, in other words, a critical part of the wider processes of racialisation and ethnicisation, in which static race and ethnic identities were ascribed to immigrants that placed them decisively outside of a much narrower English national identity. The perceived possession or absence of whiteness was certainly a crucial element in these ascriptions. Skin colour (along with gender and a racialised reading of history) was employed to mark a boundary of belonging. Yet it is important to insist that white skin or the imagined qualities of whiteness did not exhaust, and cannot convincingly be conflated with, processes of racialisation. Despite their apparent whiteness, for example, the Irish in England remained a marginal and suspect population, their right to citizenship was 'continually questioned' and their difference was reinforced by a 'pervasive stream of jokes embedded in the culture'.[11] Indeed, recent work on British attitudes to race ideas has stressed complexity, pointing, for example, to the positive evaluation and encouragement of white-Maori marriages in New Zealand and to ways in which conceptions of Britishness, far from being bounded by skin colour, were open for selective embrace by 'anti-colonial nationalists as well as empire loyalists, by black South Africans and Trinidadians as well as by descendents of English or Scots settlers'.[12] Similarly, studies on England in the 1950s has stressed the complexity of responses to immigrants that ranged from hostility, rejection and denial at one end, to hospitality, solidarity, identification and desire at the other; elements which sometimes coexisted in contradictory and unconscious ways'.[13] Yet, and as historian Tony Kushner has argued, the fact that we know so little about pro-immigration and anti-racist campaigns is an indication of how a black–white binary has served to structure historical research but also the configuration of the social sciences more generally.[14]

Despite some of the insistent claims of whiteness scholars, the post-war world did not divide simply along black–white lines. Being white, argues Bill Schwarz, by far the most persuasive historian of whiteness as a 'structure of feeling' or 'symbolic world', was not always the same old story. 'Ethnic identity, as much as any other identity, generally entails a degree of choice' and Schwarz's considerable achievement is to show how and why Enoch Powell's vision of a *White Man's World* appealed so widely to post-war Britons.[15] Real, emotional and thinking subjects populate his pages, not simply the products of discourse, dupes acting under the dictates of false consciousness or people performing their assumed racial or ethnic identity. Schwarz's story is of actors, conditioned by historical processes, that were often hidden or opaque and which they struggled to identify, name and understand.

Struggles for a Past has tried to tell a story about the attribution of race and ethnic characteristics, and responses to it, in the period after 1951. It has deliberately chosen to focus on both black and white immigrants because its primary interest has been in the ways in which some of those people have attempted to respond to their identification as an alien other. Excluded by the dominant master narrative, that was championed by the state, immigrants and their children often turned to the past in the attempt to establish personal and social identities in England. They did so because they found in the past resources to enable them to critique their ethnicisation and, ultimately, to develop new modes of identification.

Of course, these modes of identification could vary widely. Not every immigrant, and not all of their children, consciously turned to the past in order to understand how they were seen in wider society. Most post-war immigrants and their children had to deal with discrimination, with feelings of not belonging, or being different, but could do so as entirely a private matter. 'Keeping your head down' and 'trying to get on' are not easily identifiable as strategies but, and especially for first generation immigrants, it was probably the most common response to their reception in England. Religious faith, belief in hard work and in the power of education to improve the life chances of their children, enabled many in this first generation to postpone questions about how they fitted in to wider society.[16]

However, and for a second generation of immigrants, a secure place in society and a satisfactory social identity became a priority. Securing those roles required challenging the dictates of race relations research and elaborating discontent in educational, cultural and political campaigns. As second generation immigrants protested against racism, discrimination and police brutality, they reflected on their place in history. As they researched and reflected on their place in history, they drew on, or created, alternative narratives of the past in which ancestors became central actors, Britain featured as an imperial antagonist and new regimes of time, new events, dates and processes, were offered as the foundation of new social identities. *Struggles for a Past* has identified some of the spaces and places where this happened. It makes no claim to be comprehensive but has outlined some of the activities that helped to codify and make concrete black and Irish identities in England. Scholar activists were critical in developing a culture of history and historical thinking in the struggles of immigrant and minority communities in post-war England. They helped to make those communities history minded. In newspapers, pamphlets, calendars, posters, radio and television programmes, oral testimonies and written histories, scholar activists set out the events, ideas and processes that they saw as making their distinctive identities in England. These were the artefacts of memory that enabled second generation immigrants to picture and imagine themselves, and their place in society, anew.

These artefacts are best understood as an appeal to memory rather than history. They are important because they succeeded not just in expanding public knowledge of British imperialism but also in stimulating emotional and empathetic responses. Memories of the

Middle Passage and slavery, or of Cromwellian conquest and the Irish famine, spoke powerfully to individuals who, often for the first time, saw themselves reflected as actors in historical processes. This reflection was, of course, the result of a specific historical imagination in which individuals were primarily constituted by ethnic ancestors. As the changes to the census in 1991 clearly demonstrated, this was a powerful form of imagination that helped to create new social identities.[17]

However, embracing ethnic ancestors as the primary source of social identity, and then demanding recognition of historical traumas endured by the group, rests on a therapeutic ethos in which remembrance and recognition provides a form of emotional closure.[18] Social psychologists of identity working in the 1970s began to explore just these issues. Yet, the model of explanation offered here, of identification, guilt and reparation, closes down the possibilities of truly historical thinking. For historical explanation cannot rest on accounts of winners and losers but requires an analysis of politics, economics, ideology and culture. Many of the scholar activists who campaigned in the 1970s realised this. They were part of a post-1968 culture in which historical materialism remained an important intellectual resource, even if they were often involved in critiquing its limitations. For less important than the politics it supported was a historical mode of explanation that included, as a key theme, the creation and maintenance of inequality. Indeed, for some radical scholar activists black was a political colour, that could include the Irish, and which referred to all those individuals and groups adversely affected by discrimination.[19]

Processes of social change create their own dynamics. Scholar activists managed to mainstream questions of recognition and diversity through long and bitter struggles of the 1980s and 1990s. Although in their analyses ethnicity was often tied to historical processes that had produced inequalities, a softer and more therapeutic model of understanding was increasingly apparent. The celebration of ethnic or cultural diversity became commonplace because, it was claimed, it could ensure individual well-being, community cohesion and boost the economy. Under the conditions of political pluralism history was no longer a resource for critically understanding contemporary identities but a celebration of tradition, an affirmation of identity and the definition of who we are. As Paul Gilroy has acutely argued, the promotion of both 'state-sponsored patriotism and ethnic-absolutism' made the 'work involved in knowing oneself and understanding the traditional, defining norms of one's own official culture is not as easy as it might have been in the past'.[20] Long-term historical processes, deindustrialisation, consumerism and the advent of new technologies, help explain these difficulties. But so too, and more specifically, do the profound changes wrought by these processes to cultures of history. For as critical communities of interpretation fractured, historical imaginations receded. The result is that the national master narrative continues to be profoundly ignorant of the realities of British imperialism and, instead, remains anchored to a populist memory of good against evil in the Second World War. If this memory has acquired the status of an ethnic myth, it is only the most powerful example of how the mobilisation of ethnic memories has clouded history.[21] Simple stories of ethnic difference, of the arrival, settlement, struggle and contribution of distinct ethnic groups to English society, have become a characteristic feature of liberal multiculturalism. It is possible, though far from certain, that these stories may have promoted tolerance and respect for some collective identities. Yet, and especially as a result of the demographic and social patterns that constitute a new era of 'super-diversity', it will become necessary to write histories of social change that are not organised around fixed ethnic identities, around the boundaries of black and white and around contributions to an ill-defined national good. For the purpose of historical study is neither celebration nor denunciation. Perhaps it is time to reclaim a radical education in which history does not affirm identities but seeks to understand the causes of inequality in the modern world.

Notes

1 Michael Gove, speech to the Conservative Party conference, 5 October 2010, at http://centrallobby.politicshome.com/latestnews/article-detail/newsarticle/speech-in-full-michael-gove (last accessed 21/07/14).
2 See, for example, Eurobarometer 80, *Public Opinion in the European Union. Tables of Results* (Brussels: European Commission, 2013), table 142; Anthony Heath and Jane Roberts, *British Identity: Its Sources and Possible Implications for Civic Attitudes and Behaviour* (London: Ministry of Justice, 2008), pp. 5–11; Alison Park, Caroline Bryson and John Curtice (eds), *British Social Attitudes: the 31st Report* (London: NatCen Social Research, 2014), p. 66; Vron Ware, *Who Cares about*

Britishness? A Global View of the National Identity Debate (London: Arcadia, 2007).

3 Terry Haydn, 'History in schools and the problem of the "nation"', *Education Sciences*, 2 (2012), 277–280.

4 Dominic Sandbrook, 'Who needs washerwomen when you've got spitfires and drake?', 9 September 2010, at www.historyextra.com/blog/who-needs-washerwomen-when-you%E2%80%99ve-got-spitfires-and-drake (last accessed 08/04/12).

5 Eurobarometer 80, *Public Opinion in the European Union. First Results* (Brussels: European Commission, 2013), p. 11. Only citizens of Malta were more concerned about immigration.

6 See Park *et al.* (eds), *British Social Attitudes*, pp. 61, 64–67, for the finding that the 'threshold of Britishness' has got higher over time and their somewhat optimistic analysis that ethnic and exclusive notions of national identity will decline because younger generations are less dependent on exclusive ethnic ideas.

7 Spry Rush, *Bonds of Empire*, pp. 235–240.

8 Burkett, *Constructing Post-Imperial Britain: Britishness, 'Race' and the Radical Left in the 1960s* (Basingstoke: Palgrave Macmillan, 2013), p. 8.

9 Ben Rogaly and Becky Taylor, *Moving Histories of Class and Community: Identity, Place and Belonging in Contemporary England* (Basingstoke: Palgrave Macmillan, 2009).

10 Heidi Mirza, '"Race", gender and educational desire', *Race, Ethnicity and Education*, 9:2 (2006), 148.

11 Corbally, 'Jarring Irish', 112; Delaney, *Irish in Post-War Britain*, pp, 177–179, 205–209.

12 Stephen Howe, 'Review essay: British worlds, settler worlds, world systems, and killing fields', *Journal of Imperial and Commonwealth History*, 40:4 (2012), 693. On New Zealand, see Damon Ieremia Salesa, *Racial Crossings: Race, Intermarriage and the Victorian British Empire* (Oxford: Oxford University Press, 2012).

13 Nava, 'Sometimes antagonistic', 17–18.

14 Kushner, *We Europeans*, pp. 3–5; for similar comment, see Nava, 'Sometimes, antagonistic', 459; Brian Alleyne, 'An idea of community and its discontents: towards a more reflexive sense of belonging in multicultural Britain', *Ethnic and Racial Studies*, 25:4 (2002), 607–627; Mary J. Hickman and Bronwen Walter, 'Deconstructing whiteness: Irish women in Britain', *Feminist Review*, 50 (1995), 6–12.

15 Schwarz, *White Man's World*, p. 189.

16 Delaney, *Irish in Post-War Britain*, pp. 195–207.

17 David I. Kertzer and Dominique Arel, 'Censuses, identity formation and the struggle for political power', in David I. Kertzer and Dominique

Arel (eds), *Census and Identity: The Politics of Race, Ethnicity and Language in National Censuses* (Cambridge: Cambridge University Press, 2002); K. Leech, *A Question in Dispute: The Debate about an Ethnic Question in the Census* (London: Runnymede Trust, 1989).

18 K. Hodgkin and S. Radstone, 'Introduction', in Katharine Hodgkin and Susannah Radstone (eds), *Memory, History, Nation: Contested Pasts* (Brunswick, NJ: Transaction, 2007), pp. 8–9.

19 Gerrard, *Radical Childhoods*, pp. 134–136.

20 Gilroy, *Postcolonial Melancholia*, p. 25.

21 *Ibid.*, p. 89.

Bibliography

Primary sources

BBC Written Archives Centre
Black Power radio programme (1968) papers

Birmingham Heritage and Archive Services
All Faiths for One Race archive
Banner Theatre archive
Indian Workers Association papers
Dr Molly Barrow papers
Charles Parker archive
Vanley Burke collection

Black Cultural Archives
Stella Dadzie papers
Heart of the Race Project: Oral Histories of the Black Women's Movement
Ansel Wong papers

British Library, London
Sisterhood and After Oral History Collection

Cadbury Research Library
Archives of the Birmingham Black Oral History Project

George Padmore Library
John La Rose papers

Hammersmith and Fulham Archives and Local History Centre
Archives of the Ethnic Minorities Oral History Project

Liverpool Record Office
Liverpool/Merseyside Community Relations Commission papers

London Metropolitan Archives, London
Greater London Council archives
London Council of Social Services papers
London Strategic Policy Unit archives

London Metropolitan University
Archives of the Irish in Britain

National Archives, Kew
Community Relations Commission papers
Metropolitan Police records

Thatcher Archive, Churchill College, Cambridge
Thatcher MSS (digital collection),

Wellcome Library, London
Henri Tajfel papers

Working Class Movement Library, Manchester
Irish in Britain Representation Group papers

Primary printed materials

Alexander, Ziggi and Audrey Dewjee, *Roots in Britain* (London: Brent Library Service, 1981).
Arnott, Hilary, 'School of the streets', *Race Today* (March 1971).
Banton, Michael, *The Coloured Quarter: Negro Immigrants in an English City* (London: Jonathan Cape, 1955).
Baxter, Sue, *The Chinese and Vietnamese in Birmingham* (Birmingham: Birmingham City Council, 1986).
Bergman, J. and B. Coard, 'Trials and tribulations of a self-help group', *Race Today* (April 1972).
Bhatnagar, J. 'Teaching racial tolerance', *Race Today* (June 1970).
Birmingham City Council Race Relations Unit, *Brumdata: Key Facts about Birmingham's Black and Ethnic Minority Population* (Birmingham: Birmingham City Council, n.d.).
Birmingham City Council Race Relations Unit, *Aims and Objectives* (Birmingham: Birmingham City Council, n.d.).
Birmingham City Council, *Highbury 3: Report of the Proceedings* (Birmingham: Birmingham City Council, 2001).
Bishton, Derek and Brian Homer, *Talking Blues: The Black Community Speaks About its Relationship with the Police* (Birmingham: AFFOR, 1978).

Bornat, Joanna, 'Oral history and black history: conference report', *Oral History*, 8:1 (1980).

Bradford Heritage Recording Unit, *Destination Bradford* (Bradford: Bradford Heritage Recording Unit, 1987).

British Council of Churches' Working Party on Britain as a Multi-Racial Society, *The New Black Presence in Britain: A Christian Scrutiny* (London: Community and Race Relations Unit of the British Council of Churches, 1976).

Calley, Malcolm, *God's People: West Indian Pentecostal Sects in England* (Oxford: Oxford University Press, 1965).

Chase, Louis, 'Some of my grouses', *New Community*, 3:1–2 (1974).

City of Birmingham District Council, *Equal Opportunities Policy Part One: Education for our Multicultural Society* (Birmingham: Birmingham City Council, n.d.).

Clark, N., 'Dachwyng Saturday School', in A. Ohri, B. Manning and P. Curno (eds), *Community Work and Racism* (London: Routledge, 1982).

Clarke, Sebastien, *Jah Music: The Evolution of the Popular Jamaican Song* (London: Heinemann, 1980).

Clinton, Alan 'One step forward for Irish studies', *Irish Studies in Britain*, 11 (1987).

Cochrane, R., 'Mental illness in immigrants to England and Wales: an analysis of mental hospital admission 1971', *Social Psychiatry*, 12:1 (1977).

Cochrane, R., *The Social Creation of Mental Illness* (London: Longman, 1983).

Collicott, Sylvia, *Local–National–World Links: A Case Study of Haringey History* (Haringey: Haringey Borough Council, 1986).

Committee for Black Studies, *The Case and the Course: A Treatise on Black Studies* (n.p.: Committee for Black Studies, 1973).

Community Relations Commission Great Britain, *Towards a Multi-Racial Society* (London: Community Relations Commission, 1970).

Community Relations Commission, *Educational Needs of Children from Minority Groups* (London: Community Relations Commission, 1974).

Community Relations Commission, *Review of the Race Relations Act* (London: Community Relations Commission, 1975).

Community Relations Commission, *Urban Deprivation, Racial Inequality and Social Policy* (London: HMSO, 1977).

Dooley, P., *The Irish in Britain* (Watford: Connolly Association, 1943).

Dhondy, Farukh, 'Teaching young blacks', *Race Today* (May/June, 1978).

Dresser, Madge, *Black and White on the Buses: The 1963 Colour Bar Dispute in Bristol* (Bristol: Bristol Broadsides, 1986).

Dummett, Ann, *A Portrait of English Racism* (Harmondsworth: Penguin, 1973).

Dummett, Ann, *Who Is My Neighbour? The Race Question in the United Kingdom* (Liverpool: Institute of Socio-Religious Studies, 1977).

Ealing Community Relations Council, *Race Relations and the Secondary School Curriculum: A Statement of Minimum Requirements* (London: Community Relations Commission, 1970).

Egbuna, Obi, *Destroy this Temple: The Voice of Black Power in England* (London: MacGibbon & Kee, 1971).

Garrison, Len, *Black Youth, Rastafarianism and the Identity Crisis in Britain* (London: ACER, 1979).

Gaskell, G. and P. Smith, 'Are young blacks really alienated?', *New Society*, 14 May 1981.

Ghazala, Faizi, *History of the Black Presence in London* (London: Greater London Council, 1986).

Gibbons, Ivan, 'Editorial', *Irish Studies in Britain*, 2 (1981).

Gifford, Antony, Wally Brown and Ruth Bundy, *Loosen the Shackles: First Report of the Liverpool 8 Inquiry into Race Relations in Liverpool* (London: Karia Press, 1988).

Grosvenor, Ian and R.L. Chapman, *West Africa, West Indies, West Midlands* (Oldbury: Sandwell LEA, 1982).

Harrison, Paul, 'The Irish English', in Paul Barker (ed.), *The Other Britain* (London: Routledge & Kegan Paul, 1982).

Hashmi, F., *The Psychology of Racial Prejudice* (London: Community Relations Commission, 1968).

Hill, Clifford, *Black Churches: West Indian and African Sects in Britain* (London: Community and Race Relations Unit of the British Council of Churches, 1971).

Hiro, Dillip, *Black British, White British* (London: Eyre & Spottiswoode, 1971).

Holden, Tony, *Black Consciousness and White Liberation* (n.p., Zebra Project, 1981).

Holden, Tony, *People, Churches and Multi-Racial Projects: An Account of English Methodism's Response to Plural Britain* (London: Methodist Church Division of Social Responsibility, 1984).

Inglis, Joan, 'The Irish in Britain: a question of identity', *Irish Studies*, 3 (1982).

Irish in Britain History Group, *A History of the Irish in Britain* (London: Irish in Britain History Centre, 1986).

Jackson, John Archer, 'The Irish in Britain', *Sociological Review*, 10:1 (1962).

Jackson, John Archer, *The Irish in Britain* (London: Routledge & Kegan Paul, 1963).

Jahoda, Marie, 'The roots of prejudice', *New Community*, 4:2 (1975).

John, Gus, 'La Rose, John Anthony (1927–2006), *Oxford Dictionary of National Biography* (Oxford: Oxford University Press, January 2010; online edn January 2011).

Joseph, Keith, 'Why teach history in school?', *Historian*, 2 (1984).

Kapo, Remi, *A Savage Culture: Racism – A Black British View* (London: Quartet Books, 1981).

Kenny, Mary, 'Being Irish in England', *New Society*, 34:68 (30 October 1975).

Kirby, Sandy, 'Black studies', *New Society*, 27:59 (28 March 1974).

Lambeth City Council, *Forty Winters on: Memories of Britain's Post-war Caribbean Immigrants* (Lambeth: Lambeth City Council, 1988).

Leech, Kenneth, *A Question in Dispute: The Debate about an Ethnic Question in the Census* (London: Runnymede Trust, 1989).

Lennon, S., '"Off the boat": Irish women talk about their experiences of living in England', *Spare Rib*, 94 (May 1980).

Liverpool Youth Organisations Committee, *Special But Not Separate: A Report on the Situation of Young Coloured People in Liverpool* (n.p., Liverpool, 1968).

Loney, Martin, *Community against Government: The British Community Development Project 1968–1978* (London: Heinemann, 1983).

Louden, Delroy, 'Self-esteem and locus of control in minority group adolescents', *Ethnic and Racial Studies*, 1:2 (1978).

Louden, Delroy, 'A comparative study of self-concepts among minority and majority group adolescents in English multi-racial schools', *Ethnic and Racial Studies*, 4:2 (1981).

MacAmhlaigh, Dónal, *An Irish Navy: The Diary of an Exile* (Cork: Collins Press, 2008).

MacStíofáin, Seán, *Memoirs of a Revolutionary* (London: Gordon Cremonesi, 1975).

Marsh, Alan, 'Reports from correspondents: education', *New Community*, 1:5 (1972).

Marsh, Alan, 'Tolerance and pluralism in Britain: perspectives in social psychology', *New Community*, 1:4 (1972).

Miles, Robert, 'Between two cultures? The case of Rastafarianism', *Social Science Research Council Working Papers on Ethnic Relations*, 10:1 (1978).

Milner, David, *Children and Race* (Harmondsworth: Penguin, 1975).

Moody, Harold, 'The Wilberforce centenary celebrations, Hull, July 23–29', *The Keys*, 1:2 (1933).

Moody, Harold, 'The president's message', *The Keys*, 2:3 (1934).

Morris, Sam, 'Black Studies in Britain', *New Community*, 11:3 (1973).

Morrish, Ivor, *The Background of Immigrant Children* (London: George Allen & Unwin, 1971).

Mullard, Chris, *Black Britain* (London: George Allen & Unwin, 1973).

[no author] *The Black Presence in Nottingham* (Nottingham: Nottingham County Council, 1993).

[no author] 'A case for black history in mainstream agenda', *Charles Wootton News*, 25 (June 1991).

[no author] 'Responses to *Roots*', *Race and Class*, 19:1 (1977).

[no author] *What is the Connolly Association? Constitution and Explanation* (Ripley, n.d. *c*.1965).

Ó Briain, Art, 'Some notes on the history of the Gaelic League of London', *Capuchin Annual 1944* (Dublin: n.p., 1944).

Parekh, Bhikhu (ed.), *Colour, Culture and Consciousness: Immigrant Intellectuals in Britain* (London: George Allen & Unwin, 1974).

Pemberton, P., E. Pemberton and J.R. Maxwell-Hughes (eds), *Pilgrims Progress: A History of the Wesleyan Holiness Church, 1958–1983* (Handsworth: Wesleyan Holiness Church District Office, 1983).

Peppard, Nadine, 'Into the third decade', *New Community*, 1:1 (1972).

Political and Economic Planning, *The Facts of Racial Disadvantage* (London: Political and Economic Planning, 1976).

Ray, P., 'The majority of the problem', *New Community*, 1:3 (1972).

Rex, John, 'Race relations research in an academic setting: a personal note', *Home Office Research Bulletin*, 8 (1979).

Rex, John and Robert Moore, *Race, Community and Conflict: A Study of Sparkbrook* (Oxford: Oxford University Press/Institute of Race Relations, 1967).

Richmond, A.H., *The Colour Problem: A Study of Racial Relations* (Harmondsworth: Penguin, 1955).

Richmond, A.H., 'Theoretical orientations in studies of ethnic group relations in Britain', *Man*, 57 (1957).

Richmond, A.H., 'Applied social and public policy concerning racial relations in Britain', *Race*, 1:2 (1959).

Richmond, A.H., 'Social and psychological explanations of racial prejudice: some light on the controversy from recent researches in Britain', *Pacific Sociological Review*, 4:2 (1961).

Rodney, Walter, *The Groundings with My Brother Brothers* (London: Bogle L'Ouverture, 1969).

Rodney, Walter, *How Europe Underdeveloped Africa* (London: Bogle L'Ouverture, 1972).

Sanmuganathan, S., 'The ancient civilisation of Africa', *The Keys*, 1:4 (1934) and 1:5 (1934).

Second Chance to Learn Women's History Group, *No-One Ever Mentions Love: An Inside View of Black and White Relationships* (Liverpool: Liverpool Community College, n.d.).

Sharpe, Nancie, 'Cardiff's coloured population', *The Keys*, 1:3 (1934).

Small, Stephen, *The Politics of Black British History* (Wellingborough: Wellingborough District Racial Equality Council, 1991).

Thompson, B. (ed.), *Before the Fire!* (Liverpool: Liverpool Teachers Association, 1981).

Troyna, Barry, 'Differential commitment to ethnic identity by black youths in Britain', *New Community*, 7:3 (1981).

Ullah, Phillip, 'Second generation Irish youth: identity and ethnicity', *New Community*, 12:2 (1985).

Ward, R. and F. Reeves, *Racial Disadvantage: West Indians in Businesses in Britain* (London: HMSO, 1980).

Watson, J.L., *Between Two Cultures: Migrants and Minorities in Britain* (Oxford: Blackwell, 1977).

Newspapers and journals
Birmingham Post
Gaelic League of London Half-Yearly Magazine
Irish Post
The Keys
New Society
Race Today
The Times
West Indian Gazette

Official publications
Central Advisory Council for Education (England), *Children and Their Primary Schools* ('the Plowden Report') (London: HMSO, 1967).

Committee of Inquiry into the Education of Children from Ethnic Minority Groups, *West Indian Children in Our Schools: Interim Report of the Committee of Inquiry into the Education of Children from Ethnic Minority Groups* ('the Rampton Report') (London: HMSO, 1981).

Committee of Inquiry into the Education of Children from Ethnic Minority Groups, *Education for All: Report of the Committee of Inquiry into the Education of Children from Ethnic Minority Groups* ('the Swann Report') (Cmnd 9453, London: HMSO, 1985).

Department for Education and Employment, Excellence in Schools (Cmnd 3681, London: HMSO, 1997).

Hansard
Home Affairs Committee, Sub Committee on Race Relations and Immigration Select Committee, *Education Volume 1, Report* (HC, 1972–1973, 405–I).

Home Affairs Committee, Sub Committee Race Relations and Immigration Select Committee, *Education Volume 2, Evidence* (HC, 1972–1973, 405–II).

Home Affairs Committee, Sub-Committee on Race Relations and Immigration, *Racial Disadvantage* (London: HMSO, 1981).

Home Affairs Committee, Sub-Committee on Race Relations and Immigration Select Committee, *Minutes of Evidence, Monday 24 January 1983, Haringey* (HC, 1982–83, 33–VIII).

Home Affairs Committee, Sub-Committee on Race Relations and Immigration Select Committee, *Ethnic and Racial Questions in the Census: Minutes of Evidence. Monday 31 January 1983* (HC, 1982–1983, 33–ix).

Home Office, *Organisation of Race Relations Administration: Observations on the Report of the Select Committee on Race Relations and Immigration* (Cmnd 6603, London: HMSO, 1976).

Home Office, *The Brixton Disorders, 10–12 April 1981: Report of an Inquiry* ('The Scarman Report') (Cmnd 8247, London: HMSO, 1982).

Home Office Race Relations (Amendment) Act 2000. *New Laws for a Successful Multi-Racial Britain.* (London: Home Office, 2001).

Films and documentaries
The Colony (1964)
Family Portrait (1950)
Festival in London (1951)
The Irishmen (1965)
Pressure (1975)
Remembering Roots, BBC Radio 4 (27 March 2007)

Secondary sources

Ackah, William and Mark Christian (eds), *Black Organisation and Identity in Liverpool: A Local, National and Global* (Liverpool: Charles Wootton College Press, 1997).

Addai-Sebo, Akyaaba, 'Interview', *Every Generation*, at www.everygeneration. co.uk/index.php/black-british-history/bhm-black-history-month/24-akyaaba-addai-sebo (last accessed 20/11/13).

Adi, Hakim, *West Africans in Britain 1900–1960: Nationalism, Pan-Africanism and Communism* (London: Lawrence & Wishart, 1998).

Akeson, D.H., with S. Farren and J. Coolahan, 'Pre-university education, 1921–84', in J. R. Hill (ed.), *A New History of Ireland Volume VII* (Oxford: Oxford University Press, 2003).

Alexander, V., 'A mouse in a jungle: the black Christian woman's experiences in the church and society in Britain', in D. Jarrett-Macauley (ed.), *Reconstructing Womanhood, Reconstructing Feminism: Writings on Black Women* (London: Routledge, 1996).

Alibhai-Brown, Yasmin, *After Multiculturalism* (London: Foreign Policy Centre, 2000).

Alibhai-Brown, Yasmin, *Some of My Best Friends Are: Collected Journalism 1989–2004* (London: Politicos, 2004).

Alleyne, Brian, 'An idea of community and its discontents: towards a more reflexive sense of belonging in multicultural Britain', *Ethnic and Racial Studies*, 25:4 (2002).

Alleyne, Brian, *Radicals against Race: Black Activism and Cultural Politics* (Oxford: Berg, 2002).

Alleyne, Brian, 'Anti-racist cultural politics in post-imperial Britain: the New Beacon Circle', in M. Cote, R.J.F. Day and G. de Peuter (eds), *Utopian Pedagogy: Radical Experiments Against Neoliberal Globalization* (Toronto: University of Toronto Press, 2007).

Alleyne, Brian, 'John La Rose', *History Workshop Journal*, 64 (2007).

Anderson, Benedict, *Imagined Communities: Reflections on the Origin and Spread of Nationalism* (London: Verso, 1983).

Angelo, A.M., 'The Black Panthers in London, 1967–1972', *Radical History Review*, 103 (2009).

Archer, Margaret, *Being Human: The Problem of Agency* (Cambridge: Cambridge University Press, 2000).

Aspden, Kester, *The Hounding of David Oluwale* (London: Vintage, 2008).

Austin, David, 'Introduction to Walter Rodney', *Small Axe*, 10 (2001).

Back, Les and John Solomos, *Race, Politics and Social Change* (London: Routledge, 1995).

Baert, Patrick, *Time, Self and Social Being: Outline of a Temporalised Sociology* (Aldershot: Ashgate, 1992).

Bailkin, Jordanna, *The Afterlife of Empire* (Berkeley, CA: University of California Press, 2012).

Banton, Michael, 'The colour line and the colour scale in the twentieth century', *Ethnic and Racial Studies*, 35: 7 (2012).

Barber, Paul, *Foster Kid: A Liverpudlian Childhood* (London: Sphere, 2007).

Barkan, Elazar, *The Retreat of Scientific Racism: Changing Concepts of Race in Britain and the United States between the World Wars* (Cambridge: Cambridge University Press, 1992).

Beavan, Jackie, *Beyond Racial Identity* (Birmingham: Birmingham Race Action Partnership, 2002).

Beckford, Robert, *Jesus Dub: Theology, Music and Social Change* (London: Routledge, 2006).

Beiner, Guy, *Remembering the Year of the French: Irish Folk History and Social Memory* (Madison, WI: University of Wisconsin Press, 2009).

Belchem, John, 'Priests, publicans and the poor: ethnic enterprise and migrant networks in mid-nineteenth century Liverpool', *Immigrants and Minorities*, 23:2–3 (2005).

Belchem, John, 'Whiteness and the Liverpool-Irish', *Journal of British Studies*, 44:1 (2005).

Belchem, John, *Irish, Catholic and Scouse: The History of the Liverpool-Irish, 1800–1939* (Liverpool: Liverpool University Press, 2007).

Belchem, John, *Before the Windrush: Race Relations in 20th century Liverpool* (Liverpool: Liverpool University Press, 2014).

Belchem, John and Donald M. MacRaild, 'Cosmopolitan Liverpool', in John Belchem (ed.), *Liverpool 800: Culture, Character and History* (Liverpool: Liverpool University Press, 2006).

Bell, Duncan, *The Idea of Greater Britain: Empire and the Future of World Order, 1860–1900* (Princeton, NJ: Princeton University Press, 2007).

Benjamin, Richard, 'Museums and sensitive histories: the International Slavery Museum', in A.L. Araujo (ed.), *Politics of Memory: Making Slavery Visible in the Public Space* (New York: Routledge, 2012).

Bentley, Michael, *Modernising England's Past: English Historiography in the Age of Modernism, 1870–1970* (Cambridge: Cambridge University Press, 2005).

Benyon, John and John Solomos, 'The simmering cities: urban unrest during the Thatcher years', *Parliamentary Affairs*, 41:3 (1988).

Berger, Stefan, 'The power of national pasts: writing national history in nineteenth and twentieth Century Europe', in S. Berger (ed.), *Writing the Nation: A Global Perspective* (Basingstoke: Palgrave Macmillan, 2007).

Berger, Stefan (ed.), *Writing the Nation: A Global Perspective* (Basingstoke: Palgrave Macmillan, 2007).

Berger, Stefan and Chris Lorenz (eds), *Historians as Nation Builders in Modern Europe* (Basingstoke: Palgrave Macmillan, 2010).

Black, Jeremy, *Contesting History: Narratives of Public History* (London: Bloomsbury, 2014).

Blackburn, Robin, *The American Crucible: Slavery, Emancipation and Human Rights* (London: Verso, 2011).

Bland, Lucy, 'White women and men of colour: miscegenation fears in Britain after the Great War', *Gender and History*, 17:1 (2005).

Boyce, Frank, 'From Victorian "little Ireland" to heritage trail: Catholicism, community and change in Liverpool's docklands', in Roger Swift and Sheridan Gilley (eds), *The Irish in Victorian Britain* (Dublin: Four Courts Press, 1999).

Boyle, M., 'Edifying the rebellious Gael', in D. Harvey (ed.), *Celtic Geographies: Old Culture, New Times* (London: Routledge, 2002).

Bracey, Paul, 'Perceptions of the contribution of an Irish dimension in the English History Curriculum', *Educational Review*, 62:2 (2010).

Breuilly, John, 'The historical conditions for multiculturalism', in J. Eade, M. Barrett, C. Flood and R. Race (eds), *Advancing Multiculturalism Post 7/7* (Newcastle: Cambridge Scholars).

Bulmer, Martin, *The Chicago School of Sociology* (Chicago, IL: University of Chicago Press, 1984).

Bunce, Robin and Paul Field, 'Obi B. Egbuna, C.L.R. James and the birth of Black Power in Britain: black radicalism in Britain 1967–72', *Twentieth Century British History*, 22:3 (2011).

Bunce, Robin and Paul Field, *Darcus Howe: A Political Biography* (London: Bloomsbury, 2013).

Bunyan, Tony, *The History and Practice of the Political Police in Britain* (London: Friedman, 1976).

Burkett, Jodi, *Constructing Post-Imperial Britain: Britishness, 'Race' and the Radical Left in the 1960s* (Basingstoke: Palgrave Macmillan, 2013).

Burrow, John, *A Liberal Descent: Victorian Historians and the English Past* (Cambridge: Cambridge University Press, 1983).

Bush, Barbara, *Imperialism, Race and Resistance: Africa and Britain 1919–1945* (London: Routledge, 1999).

Bush, Julia, 'Moving on – and looking back', *History Workshop Journal*, 36 (1993).

Busteed, Melvyn, 'I shall never return to Hibernia's bowers: Irish migrant identities in early Victorian Manchester', *North West Geography*, 1:1 (2001).

Cabinet Office, *Ethnic Minorities and the Labour Market. Final Report* (London: Strategy Unit, 2003).

Canavan, Bernard, 'Irish in Britain History Workshop', *History Workshop Journal*, 12 (1981).

Canavan, Bernard, 'Story-tellers and writers: Irish identity in emigrant labourers' autobiographies, 1870–1970', in P. O' Sullivan (ed.), *The Irish World Wide. History, Heritage, Identity Volume III: The Creative Migrant* (Leicester: Leicester University Press, 1994).

Carby, Hazel, 'Lost (and found?) in translation', *Small Axe*, 13:1 (2008).

Carter, Bob, *Realism and Racism: Concepts of Race in Sociological Research* (London: Routledge, 2000).

Carter, Bob and Steve Fenton, 'Not thinking ethnicity: a critique of the ethnicity paradigm in an over-ethnicised sociology', *Journal for the Theory of Social Behaviour*, 40:1 (2009).

Carter, Bob, Clive Harris and Shirley Joshi, 'The racialisation of black immigration: the Conservative government 1951–55', in W. James and C. Harris (eds), *Inside Babylon: The Caribbean Diaspora in Britain* (London: Verso, 1993).

Carter, Trevor and J. Coussins, 'Back to school? The police, the education system and the black community', in E. Cashmore and E. McLaughlin, *Out of Order? Policing Black People* (London: Routledge, 1991).

Carvel, John, *Turn Again Livingstone* (London: Profile, 1999).

Centre for Contemporary Cultural Studies, *The Empire Strikes Back: Race and Racism in 70s Britain* (London: Hutchinson, 1982).

Cesarani, David, *Justice Delayed: How Britain Became a Refuge for Nazi War Criminals* (London: Heinemann, 1992).

Chakrabarty, Dipesh, *Provincializing Europe: Postcolonial Thought and Historical Difference* (Princeton, NJ: Princeton University Press, 2007).

Chamberlain, Mary and Selma Leydesdorff, 'Transnational families: memories and narratives', *Global Networks*, 4:3 (2004).

Chew, S. and A. Rutherford (eds), *Unbecoming Daughters of the Empire* (Hebden Bridge: Dangeroo Press, 1993).

Chinn, Carl, 'The Irish in early Victorian Birmingham', in Roger Swift and Sheridan Gilley (eds), *The Irish in Victorian Britain: The Local Dimension* (Dublin: Four Courts Press, 1999).

Chinn, Carl, *Birmingham Irish: Making Our Mark* (Birmingham: Birmingham City Council, 2003).

Chitty, Clyde, *Eugenics, Race and Intelligence in Education* (London: Continuum 2009).

Christian, Mark, 'Black Studies in the UK and US: a comparative analysis', in J.R. Davidson (ed.), *African American Studies* (Edinburgh: Edinburgh University Press, 2010).

Clapson, Mark, 'The American contribution to the urban sociology of race relations in Britain from the 1940s to the early 1970s', *Urban History*, 33:2 (2006).

Clarke, John and Janet Newman, *The Managerial State: Power, Politics and Ideology in the Making of Social Welfare* (London: Sage, 1997).

Clarke, Sister Sarah, *No Faith in the System* (Cork: Mercier, 1995).

Clay, Dave, 'The changing face of community participation: the Liverpool black experience', *Participatory Action and Learning*, 58 (June 2008).

Clay, Steven and Rodney Phillips, *A Secret Location on the Lower East Side: Adventures in Writing, 1960–1980* (New York: Granary, 1998).

Collini, Stefan, *Absent Minds: Intellectuals in Britain* (Oxford: Oxford University Press, 2006).

Conekin, Becky, *'The Autobiography of a Nation': The 1951 Festival of Britain* (Manchester: Manchester University Press, 2003).

Conekin, Becky, Frank Mort and Chris Waters, 'Introduction', in Becky Conekin, Frank Mort and Chris Waters (eds), *Moments of Modernity: Reconstructing Britain 1945–1964* (London: Rivers Oram Press, 1999).

Constantine Simms, Delroy, 'Black history in Britain: the African British experience', *Black Heritage Today*, October/November 2005.

Corbally, John, 'The jarring Irish: postwar immigration to the heart of empire', *Radical History Review*, 104 (2009).

Corrigan, Phillip and Derek Sayer, *The Great Arch: English State Formation as Cultural Revolution* (Oxford: Blackwell, 1985).

Cosgrave, R.A., 'A usable past: history and the politics of the national past in late Victorian England', *Parliamentary History*, 27:1 (2008).

Creighton, Sean, 'The Black British History Experience Diversity Matters conference', *Black and Asian Studies Association Newsletter*, 39 (April 2004).

Cremin, Lawrence, *Traditions of American Education* (New York: Basic Books, 1977).

Curtis, L.P., *Anglo-Saxons and Celts* (Bridgeport, CT: University of Bridgeport, 1968).

Curtis, L.P., *Apes and Angels: the Irishman in Victorian Caricature* (Washington, DC: Smithsonian Institute Press, 1971).

Curtis, Liz, *Nothing But the Same Old Story: The Roots of Anti-Irish Racism* (London: Information on Ireland, 1984).

Dabydeen, David and Nana Wilson-Tagoe, *A Reader's Guide to West Indian and Black British Literature* (Hatfield: Hansib, 1988).

Davis, Patsy, 'Birmingham's Irish community and the Murphy riots of 1867', *Midland History*, 31 (2006).

Delaney, Enda, *The Irish in Post-war Britain* (Oxford: Oxford University Press, 2007).

Deneckere, Gita and Thomas Welskopp, 'The "nation" and "class": European national master-narratives and their social "other"', in Stefan Berger and Chris Lorenz (eds), *The Contested Nation: Ethnicity, Class, Religion and Gender in National Histories* (Basingstoke: Palgrave Macmillan, 2008).

Dick, Malcolm, 'Travelling through time: migration and the black experience', in Ian Grosvenor, Rita McLean and Sian Roberts (eds), *Making Connections: Birmingham Black International History* (Birmingham: Black Pasts, Birmingham Futures Group, 2002).

Dodd, Phillip, *The Battle Over Britain* (London: Demos, 1995).

Doyle, M. (ed.), *A History of the Irish Post* (Dublin: Smurfit Media, 2000).

Dustmann C. and N. Theodoropoulos, 'Ethnic minority immigrants and their children in Britain', *Oxford Economic Papers*, 62 (2010).

Edwards, Jason A. and Amber Luckie, 'British Prime Minister Tony Blair's Irish potato famine apology', *Journal of Conflictology*, 5:1 (2014).

Elkins, Caroline, *Britain's Gulag: The Brutal End of Empire in Kenya* (London: Jonathan Cape, 2005).

Eltis, David, 'Europeans and the rise and fall of African slavery in the Americas: an interpretation', *American Historical Review*, 98:5 (1993).

English, Jim, 'Empire day in Britain, 1904–1958', *Historical Journal*, 49:1 (2006).

Esty, Jed, *A Shrinking Island: Modernism and National Culture in England* (Princeton, NJ: Princeton University Press, 2003).

Eurobarometer 80, *Public Opinion in the European Union. Tables of Results* (Brussels: European Commission, 2013).

Fanshawe, Simon and Dhananyanan Sriskandarajah, '*You Can't Put Me in a Box*': *Superdiversity and the End of Identity Politics in Britain* (London: Institute for Public Policy Research, 2010).

Fay, Brian, *Critical Social Science: Liberation and its Limits* (Oxford: Polity, 1987).

Fazakarley, Jed, 'Racisms "old" and "new" at Handsworth, 1985', *University of Sussex Journal of Contemporary History*, 13 (2009–10).

Feldman, David, 'Why the English like turbans: multicultural politics in British history', in David Feldman and Jon Lawrence (eds), *Structures and Transformations in Modern British History* (Cambridge: Cambridge University Press, 2011).

Fenderson, Jonathan, James Stewart and Kabria Baumgartner, 'Expanding the history of the Black Studies movement: some prefatory notes', *Journal of African American Studies*, 16 (2012).

Fields, Karen E. and Barbara J. Fields, *Racecraft: The Soul of Inequality in American Life* (London: Verso, 2012).

Fishman, Joshua A., 'Language and ethnicity', in H. Giles (ed.), *Language, Ethnicity and Intergroup Relations* (London: Academic Press, 1977).

Fitzpatrick, David, 'The Irish in Britain: settlers or transients?', *Labour History Review* 57:3 (1992).

Fitzpatrick, David, 'A curious middle place: the Irish in Britain', in Roger Swift and Sheridan Gilley (eds), *The Irish in Britain: The Local Dimension* (Dublin, Four Courts Press, 1999).

Fitzpatrick, Ellen, *Endless Crusade: Women Social Scientists and Progressive Reform* (Oxford: Oxford University Press, 1990).

Flick, Uwe (ed.), *The Psychology of the Social* (Cambridge: Cambridge University Press, 1998).

Flinn, Andrew and Mary Stevens, '"It is noh mistri, wi mekin histri". Telling our own story: independent and community archives in the United Kingdom: challenging and subverting the mainstream', in J. Bastian and B. Alexander (eds), *Community Archives: The Shaping of Memory* (London: Facet Publishing, 2009).

Foot, Paul, *Immigration and Race in British Politics* (Harmondsworth: Penguin, 1965).

Fraser, Nancy, *Justice Interruptus: Critical Reflections on the Postsocialist Condition* (London: Routledge, 1997).

Freire, Paulo, *Pedagogy of the Oppressed* (London: Penguin, 1996 [1970]).

Fritzsche, Peter 'The case of modern memory', *Journal of Modern History*, 73:1 (2001).

Fritzsche, Peter, *Stranded in the Present: Modern Time and the Melancholy of History* (Cambridge, MA: Harvard University Press, 2004).

Fryer, Peter, *Staying Power: the History of Black People in Britain* (London: Pluto, 1984).

Fulbrook, Mary, *Historical Theory* (London: Routledge, 2002).

Furedi, Frank, *The Silent War: Imperialism and the Changing Perception of Race* (London: Pluto, 1998).

Furedi, Frank, *Therapy Culture: Cultivating Vulnerability in an Uncertain Age* (London: Routledge 2004).

Gannon, Darragh, 'Celticism in exile: the London Gaelic League, 1917–1921', *Proceedings of the Harvard Celtic Colloquium*, 30 (2010).

Garnett, Mark, *From Anger to Apathy: The British Experience since 1975* (London: Jonathan Cape, 2007).

Garrison, Len, 'The black historical past in British education', in P.G. Stone and R. MacKenzie (eds), *The Excluded Past: Archaeology and Education* (London: Routledge, 1994).

Gerloff, Roswith, *A Plea for Black British Theologies: The Black Church Movement in Britain and its Transatlantic Cultural and Theological Interaction* (New York: Peter Lang, 1992).

Gerrard, Jessica, 'Self-help and protests: the emergence of black supplementary schooling in England', *Race, Ethnicity and Education*, 16:1 (2013).

Gerrard, Jessica, *Radical Childhoods: Schooling and the Struggle for Social Change* (Manchester: Manchester University Press, 2014).

Gibbon, Peter, 'Colonialism and the Great Starvation in Ireland 1845–9', *Race and Class*, 17:2 (1975).

Gifford, Antony, Wally Brown and Ruth Bundey, *Loosen the Shackles: First Report of the Liverpool 8 Inquiry into Race Relations in Liverpool* (London: Karia Press, 1989).

Gilroy, Paul, 'Nationalism, history and ethnic absolutism', *History Workshop Journal*, 30 (1990).

Gilroy, Paul, *There Ain't No Black in the Union Jack: The Cultural Politics of Race and Nation* (London: Routledge, 1998 [1987]).

Gilroy, Paul, *Postcolonial Melancholia* (New York: Colombia University Press, 2004).

Gilroy, Paul, 'Could you be loved? Bob Marley, anti-politics and universal sufferation', *Critical Quarterly*, 47: 1–2 (2005).

Glazer, Nathan and Ken Young, 'Ethnic pluralism and public policy', *Bulletin of the American Academy of Arts and Sciences*, 36:5 (1983).

Gleason, Philipp, 'Identifying identity: A semantic history', *Journal of American History*, 69 (1983).

Golbourne, Harry, 'Africa and the Caribbean in Caribbean consciousness and action in Britain', *David Nicholls Memorial Lectures, no. 2* (David Nicholls Memorial Trust, Oxford: University of Oxford, 2000).

Goldberg, Chad A., 'Robert Park's marginal man: the career of a concept in American sociology', *Laboratorium*, 4:2 (2012).

Goodhart, David, *The British Dream: Successes and Failures of Post-War Immigration* (London: Atlantic, 2013).

Graham, Brian, 'Heritage as knowledge: capital or culture?', *Urban Studies*, 39:5–6 (2002).

Grant, Colin, *Negro with a Hat: The Rise and Fall of Marcus Garvey and His Dream of Mother Africa* (London: Jonathan Cape, 2008).

Gray, Breda, 'From "ethnicity" to "diaspora": 1980s emigration and "multicultural" London', in A. Bielenberg (ed.), *The Irish Diaspora* (London: Longman, 2000).

Gray, Peter, 'The making of mid-Victorian Ireland? Political economy and the memory of the Great Famine', in Peter Gray (ed.), *Victoria's Ireland? Irishness and Britishness, 1837–1901* (Dublin: Four Courts Press, 2004).

Greater London Council, *Policy Report on the Irish Community* (London: GLC, 1984).

Green, Marci and Ian Grosvenor, 'Making subjects: history writing, education and race categories', *Paedagogica Historica*, 33:3 (1997).

Greenslade, Liam, 'V.N. Volosinov and social psychology: towards a semiotics of social practice', in Ian Parker and Russell Spears (eds), *Psychology and Society: Radical Theory and Practice* (London: Pluto Press, 1996).

Greenslade, Liam, 'White skin, white masks: psychological distress among the Irish in Britain', in Patrick O' Sullivan (ed.), *The Irish World Wide: History, Heritage, Identity vol. 2* (Leicester: Leicester University Press, 2002).

Greenslade, Liam, Maggie Madden and Moss Pearson, 'The "problem" of the health of Irish people in Britain', in Lara Marks and Michael Worboys (eds), *Migrants, Minorities and Health: Historical and Contemporary Studies* (London: Routledge, 1997).

Grillo, R.D., 'Cultural essentialism and cultural anxiety', *Anthropological Theory*, 3:2 (2003).

Grosvenor, Ian, *Assimilating Identities; Racism and Educational Policy in Post 1945 Britain* (London: Lawrence & Wishart, 1997).

Grosvenor, Ian, 'There's no place like home: education and the making of national identity', *History of Education*, 28:3 (1999).

Gundara, Jagdish S. and Ian Duffield (eds), *Essays on the History of Blacks in Britain: From Roman Times to the Mid-Twentieth Century* (Aldershot: Avebury, 1992).

Hacking, Ian, *Historical Ontology* (Harvard, MA: Harvard University Press, 2002).

Hall, Catherine, 'Histories, Empires and the Postcolonial Moment', in Iain Chambers and Lidia Curti (eds), *The Post-Colonial Question: Common Skies, Divided Horizons* (London, 1996).

Hall, Catherine, 'What is a West Indian?', in Bill Schwarz (ed.), *West Indian Intellectuals in Britain* (Manchester: Manchester University Press, 2003).

Hall, Catherine, *Macaulay and Son: Architects of Imperial Britain* (Yale, CT: Yale University Press, 2012).

Hall, Catherine and Sonya O. Rose, 'Introduction: being at home with the empire', in Catherine Hall and Sonya O. Rose (eds), *At Home with the Empire: Metropolitan Culture and the Imperial World* (Cambridge: Cambridge University Press, 2006).

Hall, Stuart (interviewed by Bill Schwarz), 'Breaking bread with history: C.L.R. James and the Black Jacobins', *History Workshop Journal*, 46:2 (1998).

Hall, Stuart, 'From Scarman to Stephen Lawrence', *History Workshop Journal*, 48 (1999).

Hall, Stuart, 'Conclusion: the multi-cultural question', in B. Hesse (ed.), *Unsettled Multiculturalisms: Diasporas, Entanglements, Transruptions* (London: Zed Books, 2000).

Hall, Stuart, 'Whose heritage? Un-settling "the heritage", re-imagining the post-nation', in Jo Littler and Roshi Naidoo (eds), *The Politics of Heritage: The Legacies of 'Race'* (Abingdon, Oxon.: Routledge, 2005).

Halsey, A.H., *A History of Sociology in Britain* (Oxford: Oxford University Press, 2004).

Hammersmith and Fulham Ethnic Communities Oral History Project, *The Motherland Calls: African Caribbean Experiences* (Hammersmith and Fulham Ethnic Communities Oral History Project, 1989).

Harris, Roxy and Sarah White (eds), *Changing Britannia: Life Experience with Britain* (London: New Beacon, 1999).

Harte, Liam, 'You want to be a British paddy? The anxiety of identity in post-war Irish writing', in D. Keogh, F. O'Shea and C. Quinlan (eds), *The Lost Decade: Ireland in the 1950s* (Cork: Mercier, 2004).

Hatcher, Richard 'Social justice in education after the Conservatives: the relevance of Barry Troyna's work', in Patricia J. Sikes and Fazal Rizvi (eds), *Researching Race and Social Justice in Education: Essays in Honour of Barry Troyna* (Stoke-on-Trent: Trentham, 1997).

Haydn, Terry, 'History in schools and the problem of the "nation"', *Education Sciences*, 2 (2012).

Heath, A. and J. Roberts, *British Identity: Its Sources and Possible Implications for Civic Attitudes and Behaviour* (London: Ministry of Justice, 2008).

Heathorn, Stephen, *For Home, Country and Race: Constructing Gender, Class and Englishness in the Elementary School, 1880–1914* (Toronto: University of Toronto Press, 2000).

Henry, W. 'Lez', 'Reggae, Rasta and the role of the deejay in the black British experience', *Contemporary British History*, 26:3 (2012).

Herman, Ellen, *The Romance of American Psychology: Political Culture in Age of Experts* (Berkeley, CA: University of California Press, 1995).

Hesse, Barnor, 'Unsettled multiculturalisms', in B. Hesse (ed.), *Unsettled Multiculturalisms: Diasporas, Entanglements, Transruptions* (London: Zed Books, 2000).

Hickman, Mary J., *Religion, Class and Identity: The State, the Catholic Church and the Education of the Irish in Britain* (Aldershot: Avebury, 1995).

Hickman, Mary J., 'Alternative historiographies of the Irish in Britain: a critique of the segregation/assimilation model', in Roger Swift and Sheridan Gilley (eds), *The Irish in Victorian Britain: The Local Dimension* (Dublin, Four Courts Press, 1999).

Hickman, Mary J., 'The religio-ethnic identities of teenagers of Irish descent', in M. Hornsby-Smith (ed.), *Catholics in England: Historical and Sociological Perspectives* (London: Geoffrey Chapman, 1999).

Hickman, Mary J., 'Difference, boundaries, community: the Irish in Britain', in Malcolm Miles (ed.), *City Cultures Reader* (London: Routledge, 2003).

Hickman, Mary, Lyn Nickels Thomas and Sara Henri Silvestri, 'Social cohesion and the notion of "suspect communities": a study of the experiences and impacts of being "suspect" for Irish communities and Muslim communities in Britain', *Critical Terrorism Studies*, 5:1 (2012).

Hickman, Mary J. and B. Walter, 'Deconstructing whiteness: Irish women in Britain', *Feminist Review*, 50 (1995).

Hillyard, Paddy, *Suspect Community: People's Experience of the Prevention of Terrorism Acts in Britain* (London: Pluto Press, 1992).

Hobsbawm, Eric, *Age of Extremes: The Short Twentieth Century, 1914–1991* (London: Penguin, 1994).

Holmes, Colin, *John Bull's Island: Immigration and British Society 1871–1971* (Basingstoke: Macmillan, 1988).

Honeyford, Ray, *The Commission for Racial Equality: British Bureaucracy Confronts the Multiethnic Society* (Brunswick, NJ: Transaction, 1999).

Howe, Stephen, *Ireland and Empire: Colonial Legacies in Irish History and Culture* (Oxford: Oxford University Press, 2000).

Howe, Stephen, 'Review essay: British worlds, settler worlds, world systems, and killing fields', *Journal of Imperial and Commonwealth History*, 40:4 (2012).

Hughes, C.R., 'ICTs and remembering the 200th anniversary of the abolition of the slave trade in Britain: an occasion for celebration or remorse?', *Journal of Historical Sociology*, 25:2 (2012).

Humphreys, Paul and John Gus, *Because They're Black: Police Power and Black People* (Hardmonsworth: Penguin, 1972).

Hyland, Bernadette, 'My '70s: west of Ireland, east of Manchester', *North West Labour History*, 27 (2002).

Iqbal, Karamat, *Dear Birmingham: A Conversation with My Hometown* (n.p., XLibris, 2013).

Jackson, John Archer, 'The Irish in Britain', *Sociological Review*, 10:1 (1962).

Jackson, John Archer, *The Irish in Britain* (London: Routledge & Kegan Paul, 1963).

Jacobs, Brian, *Black Politics and Urban Crisis* (Cambridge: Cambridge University Press, 1986).

James, C.L.R., *At the Rendezvous of Victory: Selected Writings* (London: Allison & Busby, 1984).

James, C.L.R., *The Black Jacobins: Toussaint L'Overture and the San Domingo Revolution* (London: Penguin, 1991 [1938]).

Jay, Martin, *Songs of Experience: Modern American and European Variations on a Universal Theme* (Berkeley, CA: University of California Press, 2005).

Jenkinson, Jacqueline, *Black 1919: Riots, Racism and Resistance in Imperial Britain* (Liverpool: Liverpool University Press, 2008).

John, Gus, *The Black Working-Class Movement in Education and Schooling and the 1985–86 Teachers Dispute* (London: Black Parents' Movement, 1986).

John, Gus, 'La Rose, John Anthony (1927–2006)', *Oxford Dictionary of National Biography* (Oxford: Oxford University Press, Jan 2010; online edn Jan 2011).

Johnson, Richard 'Historical returns: transdisciplinarity, cultural studies and history', *European Journal of Cultural Studies*, 4:3 (2001).

Joyce, Patrick, 'More secondary modern than postmodern', *Rethinking History*, 5:3 (2001).

Kansteiner, Wulf, 'Finding meaning in memory: a methodological critique of collective memory studies', *History and Theory*, 41:2 (2002).

Katz, Judith, *White Awareness Handbook for Anti-Racism Training* (Duncan, OK: University of Oklahoma Press, 1978).

Katznelson, Ira, *Black Men and White Cities* (London: Institute for Race Relations and Oxford University Press, 1973).

Kenyon, John, *The History Men: The Historical Profession in England Since the Renaissance* (London: Weidenfeld & Nicolson, 1983).

Kershaw, Baz, 'Alternative theatres, 1946–2000', in Baz Kershaw (ed.), *The Cambridge History of British Theatre Volume III: Since 1895* (Cambridge: Cambridge University Press, 2004).

Kertzer, David I. and Dominique Arel, 'Censuses, identity formation and the struggle for political power', in David I. Kertzer and Dominique Arel (eds), *Census and Identity: The Politics of Race, Ethnicity and Language in National Censuses* (Cambridge: Cambridge University Press, 2002).

Killian, Lewis M., *Black and White: Reflections of a White Southern Sociologist* (Oxford: General Hall, 1994).

Killingray, David (ed.), *Africans in Britain* (London: Frank Cass, 1994).

Killingray, David, '"To do something for the race": Harold Moody and the League of Coloured Peoples', in Bill Schwarz (ed.), *West Indian Intellectuals in Britain* (Manchester: Manchester University Press, 2003).

Killingray, David, '"A good West Indian, a good African, and, in short, a good Britisher": black and British in a colour-conscious empire, 1760–1950', *Journal of Imperial and Commonwealth History*, 36:3 (2008).

Killingray, David, *Fighting for Britain: African Soldiers in the Second World War* (Woodbridge: James Currey, 2010).

Koditschek, T., *Liberalism, Imperialism and the Historical Imagination: Nineteenth Century Visions of a Greater Britain* (Cambridge: Cambridge University Press, 2011).

Kramer, Paul, 'Empires, exceptions and Anglo-Saxons: race and rule between the British and the United States Empires, 1880–1910', *Journal of American History*, 88:4 (2008).

Kuklik, Henrika, *The Savage within: The Social History of British Anthropology, 1885–1945* (Cambridge: Cambridge University Press, 1991).

Kushner, Tony, 'Social inclusion: a historian's perspective', *Immigrants and Minorities*, 20:2 (2001).

Kushner, Tony, *We Europeans? Mass Observation, 'Race' and British Identity in the Twentieth Century* (Aldershot: Ashgate, 2004).

Kushner, Tony, *Remembering refugees: Then and Now* (Manchester: Manchester University Press, 2006).

Kushner, Tony, *The Battle of Britishness: Migrant Journeys, 1685 to the Present* (Manchester: Manchester University Press, 2012).

Kushner, Tony and Kenneth Lunn (eds), *Traditions of Intolerance: Historical Perspectives on Fascism and Race Discourse in Britain* (Manchester: Manchester University Press, 1989).

Kynaston, David, *Family Britain, 1951–57* (London: Bloomsbury, 2010).

Lawrence, Errol, 'In the abundance of water, the fool is thirsty', in Centre for Contemporary Cultural Studies (eds), *The Empire Strikes Back: Race and Racism in 70s Britain* (London: Hutchinson, 1982).

Lebow, Richard Ned, *White Britain and Black Ireland: The Influence of Stereotypes on Colonial Policy* (Philadelphia, PA: Institute for the Study of Human Issues, 1976).

Lees, Lynn Hollen, *Exiles of Erin: Irish Migrants in Victorian London* (Manchester: Manchester University Press, 1979).

Lewis, Rupert, *Walter Rodney's Intellectual and Political Thought* (Detroit, MI: Wayne State University Press, 1998).

Liddington, Jill, 'What is public history? Publics and their pasts, meanings and practices', *Oral History*, 30:1 (2002).

Logan, Phillip C. *Humphrey Jennings and British Documentary Film: A Reassessment* (Farnham: Ashgate, 2011).

Long, Paul, *The Aesthetics of Class in Postwar Britain* (Newcastle: Cambridge Scholars Publishing, 2008).

Long, Paul, 'Representing race and place: black Midlanders on television in the 1960s and 1970s', *Midland History*, 36:2 (2011).

Lorenz, C., 'Representations of Identity: ethnicity, race, class, gender and religion. An introduction to conceptual history', in Stefan Berger and Chris Lorenz (eds), *The Contested Nation: Ethnicity, Class Religion and Gender in National Histories* (Basingstoke: Palgrave Macmillan, 2008).

Lovell, Steven (ed.), *Generations in Twentieth-Century Europe* (Palgrave Macmillan, 2007).

Lowenthal, David, *The Heritage Crusade and the Spoils of History* (Cambridge: Cambridge University Press, 1998).

Lucassen, Leo, *The Immigrant Threat: The Integration of Old and New Migrants in Western Europe since 1850* (Urbana, IL: University of Illinois Press, 2005).

Lunn, Kenneth, 'Immigration and reaction in Britain, 1880–1950: rethinking the "legacy of empire"', in Jan Lucassen and Leo Lucassen (eds), *Migration, Migration History, History: Old Paradigms and New Perspectives* (New York: Peter Lang, 1999).

Luthra, M. and R. Oakley, *Combating Racism Through Training: A Review of Approaches to Race Training in Organisations* (Coventry: Centre for Research in Ethnic Relations, 1991).

McDowell, Sara, 'Heritage, Memory and Identity', in Brian Graham and Peter Howard (eds), *The Ashgate Companion to Heritage and Identity* (Farnham: Ashgate, 2008).

MacKenzie, John M. (ed.), *Imperialism and Popular Culture* (Manchester: Manchester University Press, 1986).

McLaughlin, Kenneth, *Surviving Identity: Vulnerability and the Psychology of Recognition* (London: Routledge, 2012).

MacPherson, D.A.J., *Women and the Irish Nation: Gender, Culture and Irish Identity* (Basingstoke: Palgrave Macmillan, 2012).

MacRaild, Donald M. (ed.), *Irish Migrants in Modern Britain* (Palgrave Macmillan, 1999).

MacRaild, Donald M., 'Irish immigration and the "condition of England question": the roots of an historiographical tradition', *Immigrants and Minorities*, 14:1 (1995).

MacRaild, Donald M. (ed.), *The Great Famine and Beyond: Irish Migrants in Britain in the Nineteenth and Twentieth Centuries* (Dublin: Irish Academic Press, 2000).

Maguire, Meg, 'Missing links: working class women of Irish Descent', in Pat Mahoney and Christine Zmroczek (eds), *Class Matters: Working Class Women's Perspectives on Social Class* (London: Verso, 1997).

Mahamdallie, H. 'There is a place for all at the rendezvous of victory', *Acts of Achievement*, October 2006, www.actsofachievement.org.uk/2006/opening.php) (last accessed 22/11/13).

Malik, Kenan, *The Meaning of Race* (London: Palgrave Macmillan, 1996).

Malik, Sarita, *Representing Black Britain: A History of Black and Asian Images on British Television* (London: Sage, 2002).

Mamdani, Mahood, *Define and Rule: Native as Political Identity* (Cambridge, MA: Harvard University Press, 2012).

Mandler, Peter, *History and National Life* (London: Profile, 2002).

Mandler, Peter, 'Margaret Mead amongst the natives of Great Britain', *Past & Present* 204:1 (2009).

Mangan, A.M., *Me and Mine: A Warm Hearted Memoir of a London Irish Family* (London: Virago, 2011).

Matera, M., 'An empire of development: Africa and the Caribbean in God's chillun', *Twentieth Century British History*, 23:1 (2012).

Matthews, Wade, *The New Left, National Identity and the Breakup of Britain* (Leiden: Brill, 2013).

Melman, Billie, *The Culture of History: English Uses of the Past, 1800–1953* (Oxford: Oxford University Press, 2006).

Meredith, Martin, *The State of Africa: A History of the Continent since Independence* (London: Free Press, 2005 [2006]).

Middleton, Roger, *The British Economy since 1945: Engaging with the Debate* (London: Macmillan, 2000).

Mills, David, *Difficult Folk? A Political History of Social Anthropology* (Oxford: Berghahn, 2008).

Mirza, Heidi Safia, '"Race", gender and educational desire', *Race, Ethnicity and Education*, 9:2 (2006)

Moore, Tony, *Policing Notting Hill: Fifty Years of Turbulence* (Hook, Hants.: Waterfield Press, 2013).

Moran, James, *Irish Birmingham: A History* (Liverpool: Liverpool University Press, 2010).

Morawska, Eva, 'Immigrants, transnationalism, and ethnicization: a comparison of this great wave and the last', in G. Gerstle and J.H. Mollenkopf (eds), *E Pluribus Unum? Contemporary and Historical Perspectives on Immigrant Political Incorporation* (New York: Russell Sage, 2001).

Morgan, Kenneth, 'The British identity, 1851–2008', *British Scholar*, 1:1 (2008).

Mullard, Chris, *Black Britain* (London: George Allen & Unwin, 1973).

Myers, Kevin, 'Faith in history: memory, multiculturalism and the legacies of Empire in postwar England', *History of Education*, 40:6 (2011).

Myers, Kevin, 'Cultures of history: minority histories and the politics of the past in post-war England', in Irial Glynn and J. Olaf Kleist (eds), *History,*

Memory and Migrant Incorporation (Basingstoke: Palgrave Macmillan, 2012).

Myers, Kevin and Ian Grosvenor, 'Birmingham stories: local histories of migration and settlement and the practice of history', *Midland History*, 36:2 (2011).

Nagle, John, *Multiculturalism's Double Bind: Creating Inclusivity, Cosmopolitanism and Difference* (Farnham: Ashgate, 2009).

Naidoo, Roshi, 'Never mind the buzzwords: "race", heritage and the liberal agenda', in Jo Littler and Roshi Naidoo (eds), *The Politics of Heritage, The Legacies of Race* (Abingdon, Oxon.: Routledge, 2005).

Nava, Mica, *Visceral Cosmopolitanism: Gender, Culture and the Normalisation of Difference* (Oxford: Berg, 2007).

Nava, Mica, 'Sometimes antagonistic, sometimes ardently sympathetic: contradictory responses to migrants in postwar Britain', *Ethnicities*, 14:3 (2014).

Ó Gráda, C., 'Making Irish famine history in 1995', *History Workshop Journal*, 42 (1996).

O'Day, Alan, 'Imagined Irish communities: networks of social communication of the Irish diaspora in the United States and Britain in the late nineteenth and early twentieth centuries', *Immigrants and Minorities*, 23:2–3 (2005).

O'Day, Alan, 'A conundrum of Irish diasporic identity: mutative ethnicity', *Immigrants and Minorities*, 27:2–3 (2009).

Obelkevich, Jim, 'New developments in history in the 1950s and 1960s', *Contemporary British History*, 14:4 (2000).

Orwell, George, 'The lion and the unicorn: socialism and the English genius', in S. Orwell and I. Angus (eds), *The Collected Essays, Journalism and Letters of George Orwell Volume II* (Harmondsworth: Penguin, 1970).

Panayi, Panikos, *An Immigration History of Modern Britain: Multicultural Racism since 1800* (Harlow: Pearson, 2010).

Parekh, Bhikhu, *Rethinking Multiculturalism. Cultural Diversity and Political Theory* (Basingstoke: Macmillan, 2000).

Parekh, Bhikhu, 'Barry and the dangers of liberalism', in P. Kelly (ed.), *Multiculturalism Reconsidered: 'Culture and Equality' and Its Critics* (Cambridge: Polity, 2002).

Park, Alison, Chris Bryson and John Curtice (eds), *British Social Attitudes: the 31st Report* (London: NatCen Social Research, 2014).

Parker, David and Paul Long, 'Reimagining Birmingham: public history, selective memory and the narration of urban change', *European Journal of Cultural Studies*, 6:2 (2003).

Parmar, Pratibha, 'Black feminism: the politics of articulation', in J. Rutherford (ed.), *Identity, Community, Culture, Differences* (London: Lawrence & Wishart, 1990).

Parsons, Gerald, 'Filling a void? Afro-Caribbean identity and religion', in Gerald Parsons (ed.), *The Growth of Religious Diversity: Britain from 1945* (London: Routledge, 1993).

Patterson, T.R. and R.D.G. Kelley, 'Unfinished migrations: reflections on the African diaspora and the making of the modern world', *African Studies Review*, 43:1 (2000).

Paul, Kathleen, *Whitewashing Britain: Race and Citizenship in the Postwar Era* (London: Cornell University Press, 1997).

Paul, Kathleen, 'From subjects to immigrants: black Britons and national identity, 1948–1962', in Richard Weight and Abigail Beach (eds), *The Right to Belong: Citizenship and National Identity in Britain, 1930–1960* (London: Tauris, 1998).

Paul, Kathleen, 'Communities of Britishness: migration in the last gasp of Empire', in Stuart Ward (ed.), *British Culture and the End of Empire* (Manchester: Manchester University Press, 2001).

Pettitt, Lance, 'Phillip Donnellan, Ireland and dissident documentary', *Historical Journal of Film, Radio and Television*, 20:3 (2000).

Phillips, Anne, *Multiculturalism without Culture* (Princeton, NJ: Princeton University Press, 2007).

Phillips, Mark Salber, 'History, memory and historical distance', in Peter Seixas (ed.), *Theorizing Historical Consciousness* (Toronto: University of Toronto Press, 2004).

Phillips, Mike, 'Obituary: Lenford (Kwesi) Garrison (1943–2003)', *History Workshop*, 56 (2003).

Phoenix, Ann, *Social Psychology Matters* (London: Open University Press, 2007).

Pilkington, Edward, 'The West Indian community and the Notting Hill Riots of 1958', in Panikos Panayi (ed.), *Racial Violence in Britain in the Nineteenth and Twentieth Centuries* (Leicester: Leicester University Press, 2003).

Polsgrove, Carol, *Writers in a Common Cause* (Manchester: Manchester University Press, 2009).

Pooley, Colin, 'Living in Liverpool: the modern city', in John Belchem (ed.), *Liverpool 800: Culture, Character and History* (Liverpool: Liverpool University Press, 2006).

Poovey, Mary, 'Curing the "social body": James Kay and the Irish in Manchester", *Gender and History*, 5:2 (1993).

Porter, Bernard, *The Absent-Minded Imperialists: Empire Society and Culture in Britain* (Oxford: Oxford University Press, 2004).

Prashad, Vijay, *The Darker Nations: A People's History of the Third World* (London: New Press, 2007).

Radstone, Susannah and Bill Schwarz (eds), *Memory: Histories, Theories, Debates* (New York: Fordham University Press, 2010).

Reay, Diane and Heidi Mirza, 'Uncovering genealogies of the margins: black supplementary schooling', *British Journal of Sociology of Education*, 18:4 (1997).

Rich, Paul, *Race and Empire in British Politics* (Cambridge: Cambridge University Press, 1990).

Richards, Graham, *'Race', Racism and Psychology: Towards a Reflexive History* (London: Routledge, 1997).

Robbins, Keith, 'Ethnicity, religion, class and gender and the "Island story/ ies": Great Britain and Ireland', in Stefan Berger and Chris Lorenz (eds), *The Contested Nation: Ethnicity, Class, Religion and Gender in National Histories* (Palgrave Macmillan, 2008).

Robinson, Cedric J., *Black Marxism: The Making of the Black Radical Tradition* (Chapel Hill, NC and London: University of North Carolina Press, 2000).

Robinson, Emily, *History, Heritage and Tradition in Contemporary Politics* (Manchester: Manchester University Press, 2012).

Rodgers, Daniel T., *Age of Fracture* (Cambridge, MA: Harvard University Press, 2012).

Rogaly, Ben and Becky Taylor, *Moving Histories of Class and Community: Identity, Place and Belonging in Contemporary England* (Basingstoke: Palgrave Macmillan, 2009).

Rolph-Trouillot, Michel, 'Abortive rituals: historical apologies in the global era', *Interventions: International Journal of Postcolonial Studies*, 2:2 (2000), 171–186.

Romain, Gemma, *Connecting Histories: A Comparative Exploration of African-Caribbean and Jewish History and Memory in Modern Britain* (London: Kegan Paul, 2006).

Rose, Sonya, *Which People's War? National Identity and Citizenship in Wartime Britain 1939–1945* (Oxford University Press, 2003).

Ross, Dorothy, 'Changing contours of the social science disciplines', in T.M. Porter and D. Ross (eds), *The Cambridge History of Science Volume VII: The Modern Social Sciences* (Cambridge: Cambridge University Press, 2003).

Rowe, Michael, 'Sex, "race" and riot in Liverpool, 1919', *Immigrants and Minorities*, 19:2 (2000).

Rusen, Jorn, *History: Narration, Interpretation, Orientation* (Oxford: Berghahn, 2005).

Said, E., *Culture and Imperialism* (2nd edn, London: Vintage, 1994).

Salesa, Damon Ieremia, *Racial Crossings: Race, Intermarriage and the Victorian British Empire* (Oxford: Oxford University Press, 2012).

Samuel, Raphael 'Introduction: the little platoons', in R. Samuel (ed.), *The Making and Unmaking of British National Identity Volume II: Minorities and Outsiders* (London: Routledge, 1989).

Samuel, Raphael, 'An Irish religion', in Raphael Samuel (ed.), *Patriotism: The Making and Unmaking of British National Identity Volume II: Minorities and Outsiders* (London: Routledge, 1989).

Samuel, Raphael, 'A case for national history', *International Journal of Historical Teaching, Learning and Research*, 3:1 (2003).

Samuel, Raphael, *The Lost World of British Communism* (London: Verso, 2006).

Sandbrook, Dominic, *Never Had It So Good: A History of Britain from Suez to the Beatles* (London: Abacus, 2006).

Sandbrook, Dominic, *White Heat: A History of Britain in the Swinging Sixties* (London: Little Brown, 2006).

Schaffer, Gavin, *Racial Science and British Society, 1930–62* (Basingstoke: Palgrave Macmillan, 2008).

Schwarz, Bill, 'The Communist Party Historians' Group 1945–1956', in Centre for Contemporary Cultural Studies (ed.), *Making Histories: Studies in History-Writing and Politics* (London: Hutchinson, 1982).

Schwarz, Bill 'Conquerors of truth: reflections on postcolonial theory', in Bill Schwarz (ed.), *The Expansion of England: Race, Ethnicity and Cultural History* (London: Routledge, 1996).

Schwarz, Bill, 'Introduction: the expansion and contraction of England', in B. Schwarz (ed.), *The Expansion of England: Race, Ethnicity and Cultural History* (London: Routledge, 1996).

Schwarz, Bill, 'Unspeakable histories: diasporic lives in Old England', in P. Osborne and S. Sandford (eds), *Philosophies of Race and Ethnicity* (London: Continuum, 2002).

Schwarz, Bill, 'Afterword: the predicament of history', in Bill Schwarz (ed.), *West Indian Intellectuals in Britain* (Manchester: Manchester University Press, 2003).

Schwarz, Bill 'Crossing the seas', in Bill Schwarz (ed.), *West Indian Intellectuals in Britain* (Manchester: Manchester University Press, 2003).

Schwarz, Bill, *The White Man's World: Memories of Empire* (Oxford: Oxford University Press, 2011).

Shaw, Eric, *Losing Labour's Soul? New Labour and the Blair Government 1997–2007* (London: Routledge, 2007).

Sherwood, Marika, *Pastor Ekarte and the African Churches Mission, Liverpool 1932–64* (London: Savannah Press, 1994).

Sherwood, Marika, *Origins of Pan-Africanism: Henry Sylvester Williams and the African Diaspora* (London: Routledge, 2011).

Shukra, K., *The Changing Pattern of Black Politics in Britain* (London: Pluto, 1998).

Singh, Gurharpal and Tatla Darshan Singh, *Sikhs in Britain: The Making of a Community* (London: Zed Books, 2006).

Sivanandan, Ambalavaner, 'RAT and the degradation of black struggle', *Race and Class*, 26:4 (1985).

Sivanandan, Ambalavaner, 'Britain's Gulags', in Ambalavaner Sivanandan (ed.), *Communities of Resistance* (London: Verso, 1990).

Small, Stephen and John Solomos, 'Race immigration and politics in Britain: changing policy agendas and conceptual paradigms 1940s–2000s', *International Journal of Comparative Sociology*, 47:3–4 (2006).

Smith, Chris, 'Government and the arts', in Mark Wallinger and Mary Warnock (eds), *Art for All? Their Policies and Our Culture* (London: Peer, 2000).

Solomos, John, *Race and Racism in Britain* (Basingstoke: Palgrave Macmillan, 2003).

Solomos, John and Les Beck, *Race, Politics and Social Change* (London: Routledge, 1995).

Sooben, Phillip N., *The Origins of the Race Relations Act* (Warwick: Centre for Research into Ethnic Relations, 1990).

Southgate, Beverley, 'Memories into something new: histories for the future', *Rethinking History*, 11: 2 (2007).

Spencer, Ian, *British Immigration Policy since 1939: The Making of Multi-Racial Britain* (London: Routledge, 1997).

Steedman, Carolyn, 'State sponsored autobiography', in Becky Conekin, Frank Mort and Chris Waters (eds), *Moments of Modernity: Reconstructing Britain 1945–1964* (London: Rivers Oram Press, 1999).

Steedman, Carolyn, *Dust* (Manchester: Manchester University Press, 2001).

Stenhouse, Lawrence *et al.*, *Teaching about Race Relations: Problems and Effects* (London: Routledge & Kegan Paul, 1982).

Stuchtey, Benedikt, 'Literature, liberty and the life of the nation: British historiography from Macaulay to Trevelyan', in Stefan Berger, Mark Donovan and Kevin Passmore (eds), *Writing National Histories: Western Europe Since 1800* (London: Routledge, 1999).

Swift, Roger, 'Identifying the Irish in Victorian Britain: recent trends in historiography', *Immigrants and Minorities*, 27:2–3 (2009).

Swift, Roger and Gilley, Sheridan (eds), *The Irish in Victorian Britain: The Local Dimension* (Dublin, Four Courts Press, 1999).

Tabili, Laura, 'Social networks and organization building in Britain's interwar black communities', in Gabriella Hauch (ed.), *Geschlecht, Klasses, Ethnizität: 28. Internationale Tagung der Historikerinnen und Historiker der Arbeiterbewegung* (Wien: Europaverlag, 1993).

Tabili, Laura, *'We Ask for British Justice': Workers and Racial Difference in Late Imperial Britain* (Ithaca, NY: Cornell University Press, 1994).

Tabili, Laura, 'A homogeneous society? Britain's internal "others", 1800–present', in Catherine Hall and Sonya O. Rose (eds), *At Home with the*

Empire: Metropolitan Culture and the Imperial World (Cambridge: Cambridge University Press, 2006).

Tajfel, Henri, *The Social Psychology of Minorities* (London: Minority Rights Group, 1978).

Tajfel, Henri (ed.), *European Developments in Social Psychology. The Social Dimension: European Developments in Social Psychology Volumes I and II* (Cambridge: Cambridge University Press, 1984).

Taylor T. and R. Guyver (eds), *History Wars and the Classroom: Global Perspectives* (Charlotte, NC: Information Age, 2012).

Taylor, A.J.P., *English History 1914–1945* (Oxford: Oxford University Press, 1965).

Taylor, Miles, 'The beginnings of modern British social history?', *History Workshop Journal*, 43 (1997).

Thompson, E.P., 'The peculiarities of the English', in E.P. Thompson, *The Poverty of Theory and Other Essays* (London: Merlin Press, 1978).

Thompson, K., *Under Siege! Racial Violence in Britain* (London: Penguin, 1988).

Thomson, Alistair, 'Moving stories: oral history and migration studies', *Oral History*, 27: 1 (1999).

Thomson, M., *Psychological Subjects: Identity Culture and Health in Twentieth Century Britain* (Oxford: Oxford University Press, 2006).

Torkington, N.P.K. (ed.), *The Social Construction of Knowledge: A Case for Black Studies* (Liverpool: Liverpool Hope Press, 1994).

Toynbee, Jason, *Bob Marley: Herald of a Postcolonial World* (Cambridge: Polity, 2007).

Trouillot, Michel-Rolph, *Silencing the Past: Power and the Production of History* (Boston, MA: Beacon, 1995).

Troyna, Barry, 'Race and racism: the limitations of research and policy', *British Journal of Educational Studies*, 39:4 (1991).

Troyna, Barry and Jenny Williams, *Racism, Education and the State* (London: Croom Helm, 1986).

Turner, J., 'Minority rights protection in the United Kingdom', in European Centre for Minority Issues (ed.), *European Yearbook of Minority Issues 2001/2* (The Hague: Kluwer, 2003).

Vallance, Edward, *A Radical History of Britain: Visionaries, Rebels and Revolutionaries – The Men and Women Who Fought for Our Freedoms* (London: Little Brown, 2009).

van Dijk, F.J., 'Chanting down Babylon outernational: the rise of Rastafari in Europe, the Caribbean, and the Pacific', in N.S. Murrell, W.D. Spencer and A.A. McFarlane (eds), *Chanting Down Babylon: The Rastafari Reader* (Philadelphia, PA: Temple University Press, 1998).

Verkuyten, Maykel, *The Social Psychology of Ethnic Identity* (Hove: Routledge, 2005).

Vertovec, Steven, 'Super-diversity and its implications', *Ethnic and Racial Studies*, 30:6 (2007).

Virdee, Satnam, 'Forward to the past: race, the colour scale and Michael Banton', *Ethnic and Racial Studies*, 35:7 (2012).

Virdee, Satnam, *Racism, Class and the Racialized Outsider* (Basingstoke: Palgrave Macmillan, 2014).

Voogd, Jan, *Race, Riots and Resistance: The Red Summer of 1919* (Oxford: Peter Lang, 2008).

Walker, Clive, *The Prevention of Terrorism in British Law* (Manchester: Manchester University Press, 1986).

Wallis, Mick, 'Present consciousness of a practical kind: structure of feeling higher education drama', in W.J. Morgan and P. Preston (eds), *Raymond Williams: Politics, Education, Letters* (London: Palgrave Macmillan, 1993).

Walsh, Patrick, '"Paltry abridgements": school texts and teaching history in nineteenth century India and Ireland', in D. Dickson, J. Pyz and C. Shepard (eds), *Irish Classrooms and British Empire: Imperial Contexts in the Origins of Modern Education* (Dublin: Four Courts Press, 2012).

Walter, Bronwen, *Outsiders Inside: Whiteness, Place and Irish Women* (London: Routledge, 2002).

Walter, Bronwen, 'Celebrations of Irishness in Britain: second-generation experiences of St Patrick's Day', in M.C. Considère-Charon, P. Laplace and M. Savaric (eds), *The Irish Celebrating: Festive and Tragic Overtones* (Newcastle: Cambridge Scholars Press, 2008).

Ward, Dave 'Putting down roots: an interview with Levi Tafari', in M. Murphy and D. Rees-Jones, *Writing Liverpool: Essays and Interviews* (Liverpool: Liverpool University Press, 2007).

Ward, Stuart (ed.), *British Culture and the End of Empire* (Manchester: Manchester University Press, 2001).

Ware, Vron, *Who Cares about Britishness? A Global View of the National Identity Debate* (London: Arcadia, 2007).

Warmington, Paul, *Black British Intellectuals and Education: Multiculturalism's Hidden History* (Abingdon: Routledge, 2014).

Waters, Chris, '"Dark strangers", in our midst: discourses of race and nation in Britain, 1947–1963', *Journal of British Studies*, 36:2 (1997).

Webster, Wendy, *Englishness and Empire 1939–1965* (Oxford: Oxford University Press, 2005).

Webster, Wendy, 'There'll always be an England: representations of colonial wars and immigration, 1948–1968', in Simon Faulkner and Anandi Ramamurphy (eds.), *Visual Culture and Decolonisation in Britain* (Aldershot: Ashgate, 2006).

Welshman, John, *From Transmitted Deprivation to Social Exclusion: Policy, Poverty and Parenting* (Bristol: Policy Press, 2007).

White, Jerry, *London in the Twentieth Century: A City and Its People* (London: Viking, 2001).

White, Sarah, Roxy Harris and Sharmilla Beezmohun (eds), *A Meeting of the Continents: The International Book Fair of Radical Black and Third World Books, 1982–1995* (London: New Beacon, 2005).

Winter, Jay, *Dreams of Peace and Freedom: Utopian Movements in the 20th Century* (New Haven, CT: Yale University Press, 2006).

Witt, Andrew, *The Black Panthers in the Midwest: The Community Programs and Services of the Black Panther Party in Milwaukee, 1966–1977* (New York: Routledge, 2007).

Woods, P., 'Newsreel coverage of Indian independence and partition', in C. Kaul (ed.), *Media and the British Empire* (Basingstoke: Palgrave, 2006).

Wright, Patrick, *On Living in an Old Country* (2nd edn, Oxford: Oxford University Press, 2009).

Zhana, *Black Success Stories: Celebrating People of African Heritage* (London: Zhana, 2006).

Unpublished

Connell, Kieran, 'A micro-history of "black Handsworth": towards a social history of race in Britain' (Ph.D. thesis, University of Birmingham, 2011).

Lowrance-Floyd, E., 'Losing an empire, losing a role? The commonwealth vision, British identity and African decolonization, 1959–1963' (Ph.D. dissertation, University of Kansas, 2012).

McLennan, N., 'Irish connections: London's county associations', unpublished paper given to the Irish in Britain seminar series, London Metropolitan University, 10 June 2009.

Peach, A., 'The Irish in Birmingham during the nineteenth century' (Ph.D. dissertation, De Montford University, 2000).

Steedman, Carolyn, 'Who owns history? Nowhere else to be: the everyday life of history in the English eighteenth century', paper given to the International Congress on the Historical Sciences, Amsterdam, August 2010.

Ziesler, K.I., 'The Irish in Birmingham, 1830–1970' (Ph.D. thesis, University of Birmingham, 1989).

Index